*Praise for the first edition*:

"Dan has really put a great tool into a lot of people's hands. Heshang Gong has been living in a cave as far as anyone interested in Laozi has been concerned. Now he's out. And the introduction as well as the textual aids for the non-Chinese reading reader at the back really make this a major contribution to the field, especially to those readers leery of the scholarly gauntlet."
- Red Pine (Bill Porter), translator of *Lao-Tzu's Taoteching: with Selected Commentaries of the Past 2000 Years*

"Reid has translated the beguiling verse of this ancient text within the framework of the 2,000-year-old Ho-Shang Kung Commentary, an obscure but authentic commentary that clarifies many points which have baffled both Chinese scholars and Western translators.

Translating the original words of the Tao Teh Ching line by line, he follows each line with his translation of the matching commentary from Ho-Shang Kung ("The Riverside Sage"). This format provides the reader with new perspectives on this multi-faceted classic, with The Riverside Sage serving as the reader's knowing guide.

Like the great English translator Arthur Waley, Dan G. Reid taught himself how to read classical Chinese, so he brings his own viewpoint to his work, not the views of a particular "school of thought" in Sinology. Translating the Tao Teh Ching has long been regarded as the ultimate litmus test for a translator of Chinese. Reid has passed the test with flying colors."
- Daniel P. Reid (no relation), translator of *My Journey in Mystic China* (Chinese memoirs of the late writer & translator John Blofeld), author of *The Tao of Health, Sex, & Longevity*, and *The Tao of Detox*

"Wonderful work and translation. I am growing spiritually from reading it!"
- Dr. Michael Saso, Professor Emeritus of Religion, University of Hawai'I, Ph.D Classical Chinese, Author of *Teachings of Taoist Master Chuang*

"Ho-Shang Kung lived in today's Langya area of Shandong Province (琅琊). He was an accomplished Taoist alchemy practitioner and it is said that he became an immortal on Tiantai mountain – nowadays Rhi-Zhao county, Shandong Province.

His commentary on the *Tao Te Ching* (河上公章句) naturally carries a deep understanding of Taoist meditation, and differs greatly from that of other commentators who tried to explain the Tao Te Ching only philosophically. Written at a time when there were almost no related commentaries, it has long been the most popular. To translate it by following the exact meaning is not an easy task, but Dan G. Reid is well capable of such a task. By reading this commentary, readers can gain additional perspective and understanding of this ancient classic."

- Master Hu Xuezhi, author of *Revealing the Tao Te Ching*, and *Discourse on Chuang Tzu*. Master Hu teaches Taoist meditation and philosophy on Wudang Mountain

"I found this book to be very helpful in bringing a deeper understanding of Lao Zi's work and of how it has been understood in ancient times… This volume provides a wonderful tool to delve into the text in a very deep way."

- Review by Solala Towler (author of *Practicing the Tao Te Ching*) in The Empty Vessel: The journal of Taoist philosophy and practice, Winter 2017 issue

"In my own use of the DDJ as a Daoist practice scripture it was very important to clearly see how this DDJ commentary is a guide for key Daoist concepts like emptiness, wuwei, stillness, speaking few words, yielding, the quiet dragon, and more.

As a Daoist priest and founder of a Daoist lineage, American Dragon Gate Lineage, I highly recommend this translation by Reid and have actually made it required study for my priests-in-training."

- Shifu Michael J. Rinaldini, Daoist Abbot and founder of the American Dragon Gate Lineage of Quanzhen Daoism. Author of *A Daoist Practice Journal: Come Laugh With Me*; and *A Daoist Practice Journal, Book 2: Circle Walking, Qigong & Daoist Cultivation*

# The Heshang Gong Commentary on Lao Zi's Dao De Jing

老子河上公章句

by Heshang Gong, and Lao Zi

Second Edition

Translations and additional commentary by Dan G. Reid

Center Ring Publishing
Montreal, QC, Canada
dan.g.reid@gmail.com
www.facebook.com/HoShangKung

Copyright © 2015, 2019 Dan G. Reid
All rights reserved.

Cover art: "Inquiring of the Dao," by Dai Jin (1388-1462 AD). A depiction of the Yellow Emperor going out to meet the Daoist Sage Guangcheng Zi in the Kongtong Mountains, the story of which appears in the *Zhuang Zi*, chapter 11.

All rights reserved. No part of this book may be reproduced in any form or by any means, electronic or mechanical, including photocopying, recording, or by any information storage and retrieval system, without permission in writing from the author.

The Heshang Gong Commentary on Lao Zi's Dao De Jing, Second Edition, translations and additional commentary by Dan G. Reid
Paperback
ISBN10: 0994978162
ISBN13: 978-0-9949781-6-5

The intention of this publication is for guidance and suggestion relevant to the subject matter presented. Readers should use their own discretion and consult their doctors before engaging in any of the physical or mental exercises contained therein. The author and publisher shall have neither liability nor responsibility to any person or entity with respect to any loss or damage caused, or alleged to be caused, directly or indirectly by reading or following the instructions in this book.

*Thank you to the many teachers, scholars, priests, monks, and practitioners who have shared insights into Daoism and Classical Chinese in online forums. Your consideration for nameless strangers has led to the development of this book. Were it not for your thoughtful input, correspondence, and fellowship, I would not have had the knowledge or inspiration to put this translation out into the world.*

Distant waves, each page
Riding winds of ancient words
Back to the ocean

# CONTENTS

**Translator's Introduction**
Heshang Gong, the Riverside Elder ................................................. i
Dao, De, and Oneness in Heshang Gong's Commentary (2nd edition) .......... iv
Dao, De, and Oneness in Heshang Gong's Commentary (1st edition) .......... vii
Ethics and Kindness in the Dao De Jing (2nd edition) ......................... ix
The Politics of Lao Zi (2nd edition) ............................................. xi
Dating the Heshang Gong Commentary ............................................. xii
Dating the Dao De Jing and its Authors ......................................... xiv
Translating the Dao De Jing ..................................................... xvi
Notes on the Translation and Translator's Commentary ......................... xvi

**The Heshang Gong Commentary on Lao Zi's Dao De Jing**
Volume One: Dao ................................................................. 2
Volume Two: De .................................................................. 101

**Appendix**
Reading Classical Chinese ....................................................... 218
Brief Pinyin Pronunciation Guide ................................................ 224
Straw-Dogs and Benevolence in Chapter Five of the Dao De Jing ............... 225
Dan G. Reid ..................................................................... 235

# Translator's Introduction

## Romanization and Pronuciation of Chinese Words

Please note that modern pinyin spelling of Chinese names and terms will be used throughout this book. While many English speakers have become accustomed to the earlier Wade-Giles romanization of Chinese words, few native Chinese speakers outside of Taiwan recognize words spelled in this system. Moreover, the linking of syllables in pinyin renders many names and terms unrecognizable to those familiar only with Wade-Giles. Thus, Tao Te Ching will appear as Dao De Jing, Lao Tzu as Lao Zi, Chuang Tzu as Zhuang Zi, hsing as xing, Ho-Shang Kung as Heshang Gong, and so forth. For a brief guide on pinyin pronunciation, please see the appendix.

## Heshang Gong, the Riverside Elder

Very little is known about the life of Heshang Gong. His reputation is that of a reclusive hermit, and his name is only known as the epithet Riverside Elder (河上公;[1] pinyin romanization: Heshang Gong; Wade-Giles romanization: Ho-Shang Kung).

Heshang Gong's insights into Daoist wisdom, history, cosmogony, and meditative practices, have been an essential aid to understanding the meaning, applicability, and cultural context of the *Dao De Jing* for approximately 2000 years. He was the first to explain, in written form, its many paradoxical idioms and place them in context of the time and culture in which they were written. Every subsequent commentary, re-editing, and translation of the *Dao De Jing* has absorbed some degree of influence from his work.

While Heshang Gong's contributions to linguistic preservation have been appreciated for millennia, his early articulation of the connections between Lao Zi's verses and the Daoist meditative practices later known as Nei Dan is not so well acknowledged.

Nei Dan, or Internal Alchemy, seeks to transcend the limits of physical existence through the cultivation of the "three treasures" of vital essence (ching/jing), energy-breath (chi/qi), and spirit (shen). This is done, in part, by merging one's pure nature (xing) with destiny-life-force (ming), said later by Ma Danyang (11 century AD) to be one of the many turns of phrase for the merging of energy-breath and spirit.[2] Such concepts can be found in earlier Chinese texts, including the *Zhuang Zi* (circa 350 BC), and later become a central focus in cryptic and detailed Nei Dan manuals, culminating in the teachings of the Quan Zhen (Complete Reality) patriarchs (circa 8th

---

[1] Shang 上 being an early form of "anshang, 岸上, bank/shore"
[2] Komjathy, Luis. *The Way of Complete Perfection: A Quanzhen Daoist Anthology.* Albany: State University of New York Press, 2013.

to 11th century AD), to whom over 80 religious Daoist sects are traced. While some of these manuals provide rather specific and detailed energetic maneuvers, they more commonly explain the processes of transformation which they say will naturally follow a prolonged clarity of the heart and mind. This is the same method described by Heshang Gong, for example, in his comments on chapter 16 ("... *peace and stillness are the correct way to return to pure nature (xing) and the destiny-life-force (ming).*") and chapter 38:

> (The rulers of antiquity) did not teach the people virtues, but caused them to follow their natural spontaneity, thereby supporting the development of their pure nature (xing), and destiny-life-force (ming).

Heshang Gong's place in the Daoist tradition is a subject meriting an entire book of its own, and so cannot be approached here in considerable depth. An overwhelming validation of Heshang Gong's import, however, can be found in the teachings of Ma Danyang. Ma Danyang, the second patriarch of the Quan Zhen Daoist Sect, was the closest student of Wang Chongyang who in the mid 11th century AD developed the Quan Zhen Sect of Daoism. The Quan Zhen Sect (Quan Zhen Pai) is one of the only two major lineage branches of Daoism, the other being Zheng Yi Pai, aka Tian Shi Dao, or "Way of the Celestial Masters" which began in 142 AD. In the *Discourse Record of Perfected Danyang*, Ma Danyang dissuades students from excessive textual study, warning that it will confuse the mind and obstruct actual training. He recommends, however, that if a student wants to study scriptures they should read only Heshang Gong's commentary on the *Dao De Jing*, and Master Jin Ling's commentary on the *Yin Fu Jing (Classic of Yin Talisman)*. Reading nothing but these two texts, and presumably following his personal guidance, Ma Danyang says will be enough for them to train in internal cultivation "without obstruction."[3]

Another area in which Heshang Gong's commentary is significant in the history of Chinese energy cultivation is his departure from some earlier manuals' "jing building" methods, which relied largely on diet and regimented sexual activity.[4] Though he briefly notes the importance of stretching in order to maintain a supple body,[5] provides general cautions against an indulgent diet, and provides much guidance for one's conduct in the world, Heshang Gong eschewed all "external" approaches to internal cultivation. This is to say that, beyond receiving a balance of nutrients from food, he makes no mention of ingesting, or absorbing, earthly substances in order to

---

[3] Komjathy, Luis. *The Way of Complete Perfection: A Quanzhen Daoist Anthology*. Albany: State University of New York Press, 2013. p. 88

[4] See Cleary's "Sex, Health, and Long Life," a translation of texts attributed to the Yellow Emperor, found in the Mawangdui tombs, the contents of which are dated to approximately 200 BC

[5] See chapter 22

Note: Stretching exercises from the Han Dynasty are preserved in the silk Daoyintu painting (c. 168 BC), the reconstruction of which provides illustrations of 44 stretching postures. These postures appear to have been dynamic movements synchronized with the breath, as some of them resemble movements common to many qigong (also spelled chi kung) styles. Similar exercises, called the Five Animal Frolics, were also developed near the end of the first century AD by the celebrated doctor, Hua Tuo. With an emphasis on toning internal organs, these exercises are also also qigong practices.

nourish jing, qi, and shen. Instead, Heshang Gong's commentary presents a path to nourishing the three treasures followed by connecting to Nature's Way and Virtue (Dao and De), returning to the simplicity of nature (zi ran), arriving at the tranquility of desirelessness, and reflecting the principles of Dao in our worldly interactions. Thereby, one roots themselves in the beneficence of Dao, Virtue, and Oneness, while becoming a conduit for the natural and harmonious order of all things.

In Heshang Gong's elucidations of Lao Zi's imagery, he refers to ancient Chinese medical concepts which figure prominently in later Nei Dan manuals. This suggests that Heshang Gong was familiar with some of the many influential texts available during the Han Dynasty (206BC-220AD), such as *"The Yellow Emperor's Treatise on Internal Medicine,"* and perhaps also the *Guan Zi*[6] which contained the *Nei Ye (Internal Cultivation)* and other texts on the "art of the heart-mind" (xin shu).

The *Guan Zi* was edited near the turn of the first century by a famous scholar and official named Liu Xiang (77-6BC), who also edited and catalogued much of the Han imperial library. Some of Heshang Gong's terminology shows the influence of Han literature, an example of which can be found in the term zhi pu 質樸. Literally "plain substance," zhi pu means "natural and simple," or "unsophisticated." The popular English rendering of pu, "simple," as "the uncarved block" in Daoist translations, likely stemmed from Heshang Gong's use of this term. It appears in several prominent Han texts, including the *Han Shu*, and *Shuo Yuan*, both of which were part of Liu Xiang's work.

Liu Xiang was a distant relative of Liu An,[7] who edited the *Huainan Zi*,[8] an important compilation of Daoist thought which Heshang Gong also appears to have read, given the breadth of his knowledge in areas of Daoist theory. If Heshang Gong did, in fact, have access to these texts, it seems likely that he would have also discovered and read the *Nei Ye (Internal Cultivation)*, *Xin Shu (Art of the Heart-Mind)*, and *Bai Xin (Purifying the Heart-Mind)*, early Daoist meditation texts with many similarities to the *Dao De Jing*. Those who have studied the *Nei Ye* (c. 350 BC) may perceive traces of its influence in Heshang Gong's commentary on the *Dao De Jing*, though it may be that these similarities stemmed from a common oral tradition in which Heshang Gong was immersed. The latter of these two theories is explored further in my second book, *The Thread of Dao: Unraveling Early Daoist Oral Traditions in Guan Zi's Purifying the Heart-Mind (Bai Xin), Art of the Heart-Mind (Xin Shu), and Internal Cultivation (Nei Ye)*.

It would be conjecture to suggest that Heshang Gong may have been a descendent of the Liu family, but less so to suggest that he knew of their contributions during the Han era, and that someone with Heshang Gong's level of study had access to

---

[6] The *Guan Zi* is a compilation of political and philosophical treatise, some of which are attributed to the 7th century BC Prime Minister Guan Zhong, while others have been attributed to the Jixia Academy. The Jixia Academy was a center of learning, and debates, between the 100 Schools of Thought around the 3rd century BC, during the lifetimes of Zhuang Zi (370-287BC) and Mencius (372-289BC).
[7] Liu An (d. 122 BC) was a grandson of the founding Emperor of the Han Dynasty, Liu Bang. At 16 years old, he became "Prince of Huainan."
[8] Lit. "The Masters of Huainan"

many of the texts made more readily accessible by the Liu family.[9]

This level of scholarship and literary access might also account for Heshang Gong's knowledge of ancient Chinese medical theory, and his employment of terms such as "the ethereal and bodily spirits (hun and po)," "the six emotions," and "the five natures," in his commentary.[10] The theories behind these terms explain the correlations between emotion and related organs, their various states of balance and imbalance, and their influences on bodily health, vitality, longevity, and personal virtues. That Heshang Gong was aware of these theories before they became a central part of the Daoist lexicon, suggests that he may have also been a practicing healer – a vocation to which many Daoist adepts are drawn, following years of interest in the interactions between body and spirit. This familiarity with Chinese medical theory would have likely influenced his equation of governing the nation with governing the body, as would a familiarity with Guan Zi's texts on the art of the heart-mind, all of which some 400-500 years earlier employed this paradigm of political metaphors when discussing matters of the body and spirit.

Though he managed to live and practice his guidance, remaining humble and inconspicuous, the legacy of Heshang Gong's work continues to bless untold millions as the Dao De Jing's principal commentary. He remains, still to this day, a bounteous example of Lao Zi's words: "When achievements are completed, their recognition should continue, but the individual should withdraw."

## Dao, De, and Oneness in Heshang Gong's Commentary
(added to 2nd edition)

One of the early terms used by Lao Zi to describe internal cultivation is "embracing Oneness" (抱一, bao yi), found also in the Guan Zi as "guarding Oneness" (守一) and "holding Oneness" (執一). The importance of this concept is shown further in the frequency of its appearance in Heshang Gong's commentary. I have explored early instructions on the practice of "embracing Oneness" in the introduction to *The Thread of Dao: Unraveling Early Daoist Oral Traditions*, relating especially to consolidating will (zhi) and intention (yi) as described in the *Guan Zi* and *Guigu Zi*. This consolidation of will and intention, however is more applicable to the *technique* of embracing Oneness, rather than a definition of Oneness itself. To understand what these Daoist masters meant by Oneness, we may find invaluable keys in Heshang Gong's commentary. For example, in his comments on Lao Zi's chapter 51, Heshang Gong appears to offer the meaning behind his frequent use of the term Oneness:

> 道生之，道生萬物。
> "Dao actuates them"
> Dao actuates the myriad things.

---

[9] Liu Xiang's son, Liu Xin, also followed in this tradition of scholarship, by starting the Old Texts school of Confucianism.
[10] See, especially, chapter six, and the footnote in chapter five.

德畜之，德，一也。一主布氣而蓄養物形之，一為萬物設形像也。
"Virtue takes care of them"
"Virtue," here, means "Oneness." Oneness is the host of all things. It surrounds them with energy-breath, and gathers and rears things into form. Oneness establishes the form and image of all things.
勢成之。一為萬物作寒暑之勢以成之。
"Power completes them"
Oneness uses the power of hot and cold to complete all things.

As he reveals here, when Heshang Gong refers to Oneness, or holding Oneness, he refers not so much to unity and wholeness as he does to the power which spontaneously harmonizes and balances all things – otherwise often referred to as De/Virtue. Similar to the name of the Zheng Yi Daoist sect (often translated as "Orthodox Unity"), Oneness is the zheng yi – the "aligning oneness" to which all things are subject. The movement of De is the movement toward wholeness. Not an assimilation into oneness (thought this literally translates " 一 "), but the cooperative diversity of wholeness. This is the nature of De/Oneness, and the expression of the all encompassing Dao. Chapters 51, 22, and 39, especially, reveal a force or *Virtue* that brings about this alignment, wholeness, balance and harmony. Lao Zi calls this force De, the Virtue (of Dao), while Heshang Gong tends to refer to it as Oneness. As chapter 51 explains:

> Dao actuates them
> Virtue takes care of them, extends their lifespans
> Teaches them, completes them
> Tests them, raises them
> And brings them back (to their pure natures)

Chapter 22 describes this process:

> That which is flexible is preserved
> That which is bent is straightened
> That which is empty is filled
> That which is broken is repaired
> That which is lacking acquires
> That which is excessive becomes confused
> Therefore, the Sage embraces Oneness
> So as to bring the world into alignment

Chapter 39 (which happens to follow the *Dao De Jing*'s defining chapter on Virtue – chapter 38) describes the effect of embracing Oneness, and provides ample support for Heshang Gong's equation of Oneness with Virtue, knowing from chapter 51 that Virtue is attributed the power of perfecting and completing life:

> In the beginning was the attainment of Oneness
>
> Heaven attained Oneness and became clear
> Earth attained Oneness and became serene
> Gods attained Oneness and became spiritually powerful
> Valleys attained Oneness and became full
> The myriad things attained Oneness and were born
> Lords and kings attained Oneness and all under Heaven became loyal

Another helpful example to understand this equation is Heshang Gong's reference to chapter 39 in his comments on chapter 10:

> "Embrace Oneness. Can you do this without letting (your coporeal spirits) flee?"
> People who can embrace Oneness, and not let it leave them, extend their lives. In Oneness, Dao began to situate life by the supreme harmony of the vital energy-breaths. Therefore it is said: "Oneness covered the world with names."
>
> Heaven attained Oneness and became clear. Earth attained Oneness and became serene. Lords and kings attained Oneness and became upright and peace-loving. Going within, it is mind; going outwards it is actions; in covering all with its blessing, it is Virtue. All the names together are One. Referring to Oneness, it is said: "In a unified consciousness, there is no division (or doubt)."

To further this equation of De, the force which fosters and perfects life, with Oneness, we can also look to the ancient text, *The Great One Gave Birth to Water (Tai Yi Sheng Shui)*, found alongside the earliest known fragments of the *Dao De Jing* at Guodian, and dated to around 350 BC. The *Tai Yi Sheng Shui* describes "the Great One":

> The Great One gave birth to water. Water then returned to meet the Great One and thereby fashioned Heaven. Heaven returned to meet the Great One and thereby fashioned Earth. Heaven and Earth joined together and thereby fashioned spirit (conscious essence) and illumination. Spirit and illumination joined together and thereby fashioned Yin and Yang. Yin and Yang joined together and thereby fashioned the Four Seasons. The Four Seasons joined together and thereby fashioned Cold and Hot. Cold and Hot joined together and thereby fashioned Moisture and Dryness. Moisture and Dryness joined together, thereby fashioning the year, and then stopped...
>
> Thus, the Great One is found in water. It moves through the seasons, completes a cycle, and then begins again. Thus, the Great One is the mother of the myriad things. At once diminishing, at once filling, it uses itself as the thread

(joining) all things. This is what Heaven cannot kill, what Earth cannot bury, and what Yin and Yang cannot fashion. Those of noble character who understand this, we call Sages.

With these descriptions of the Great One, both in the *Dao De Jing*, and *Tai Yi Sheng Shui*, we can see that Virtue is, as Heshang Gong points out in chapter 51, another title for Oneness. Thus, in finding Heshang Gong's mentions of "embracing Oneness," we can understand this as embracing the power of Dao – Virtue (De) – and allowing it to spontaneously harmonize, purify, and align – to spontaneously (zi ran) "govern" us internally and bring about the Great Peace (tai ping) that Dao brings to a nation.

As Heshang Gong demonstrates throughout his commentary, the Dao of governing the body and the Dao of governing the nation follow the same principles, revealing that Lao Zi's verses speak simultaneously of three dimensions: 1) governing oneself; 2) governing the nation; and 3) the principles of Dao governing all existence and non-existence as implemented through Oneness – Virtue.

## Dao, De, and Oneness in Heshang Gong's Commentary
(from 1st edition)

Given the multitude of interpretations regarding these mysteries, whether personal, religious, or scholarly, the following is perhaps best received as a working understanding, rather than as a definition of terms.

Though written, literally, as "德 virtue," De, in Daoism, is the nature of Dao. Dao is the ordering principles, "道 the Path, Way, or method," through which all things come into being, and reach the complete perfection of their intrinsic natures (性 xing). While considered an independent part of existence, De is also the nature, quality, or character, of Dao's principles. It is this character of Dao's principles which make Dao the mother of all things. As Lao Zi explains in chapter 51:

> Dao actuates them
> Virtue takes care of them, extends their lifespans
> Teaches them, completes them
> Tests them, raises them
> And brings them back (to their pure natures)
> Actuates them but does not possess them
> Sets them in motion but does not expect of them
> Extends their lives without ruling and controlling
> This is called Fathomless Virtue

All of existence is united by its shared origin in Dao, and reliance on Virtue for continuation. In this shared origin, and base of perpetuation, lies Oneness. While Oneness refers to the unification of all things, this unification also resides in each and every thing, and holds the key to realizing Dao. As Heshang Gong comments in chapter one: "People who maintain the absence of desire will be able to observe the key to Dao. 'The key' is Oneness." That Oneness can be found in all things is also apparent in Lao Zi's words from chapter one:

> Thus, always without desires
> Observing its inner subtlety
> Always with desires
> Observing its outer surface
> These two were born together, yet differ in name
> Together, they are called Fathomless Mystery
> This mystery, ever more mystifying
> Is a multitude of gates
> All leading to the subtlety within

Dao can be observed in the external world, and internal world, of all things. Everything is governed by its principles. To apprehend, not only the unification *of*, but the unification *within* all things, is also called Oneness. Heshang Gong explains that by "holding Oneness" it is possible to bring about harmony in ourselves and in the world. To hold Oneness is to embrace Dao, Virtue, and everything in existence, within, while knowing that these are not separate. They exist together in oneself and all other things. There is no separation, but merely our perception of it.

As Heshang Gong comments in chapter 10, "Referring to Oneness, it is said: 'In a unified consciousness, there is no division (or doubt)'." By seeing things as separate from the Oneness, we separate ourselves from Dao and Virtue, from Heaven and Earth, and from the path of returning to our intrinsic natures. By moving toward this separation, we cannot be perfected – we cannot be completed according to the intrinsic natures bestowed upon us before birth.

As a peach tree can only reach the complete perfection of its intrinsic nature as a peach tree, we can only reach the complete perfection of the intrinsic natures bestowed upon us; and we can only do this by not resisting Dao and Virtue, for it is Dao and Virtue which bring it about. All we can do, is to get our separate-minded and interfering desires out of their way. As Lao Zi says in chapter 37

> The Dao is always effortless yet without inaction
> When lords and kings can guard this within
> The myriad things eventually transform themselves
> Transforming, yet desiring to do so intentionally
> I pacify this desire with the simplicity of the nameless
>
> The simplicity of the nameless removes all desires
> When the tranquility of desirelessness is established
> The world stabilizes itself

"The simplicity of the nameless" refers to Dao; however, this phrase also alludes to an important lesson in the *Dao De Jing* which is that people effectively destroy themselves by seeking fame and renown. This, again, brings us back to separateness, desires, and veering from the clear path. Chapter 53 illustrates that people love to distinguish themselves, yet stray far from Dao by doing so. "The granaries are so empty, yet their clothes so full of colour," could be taken as a comment on the inner condition awaiting those who desire to be distinguished. Heshang Gong also makes this important point clear in his final comment, on chapter 81, "(Sages) do not follow lowly competitions for merit or fame, and as a result are able to retain their wisdom and merits."

## Ethics and Kindness in the Dao De Jing (added to 2nd edition)

A tendency to deny that the *Dao De Jing* has any ethical framework, or teachings of kindness toward others, has persisted in both the East and the West. This is likely due to longstanding competitions between Buddhists, Confucians, and Daoists, with the added influence of Christian missionaries – often unwitting participants in Western imperialism and cultural colonization – all of whom seized on their misunderstanding of a few chapters that appear to scoff at common ethics. A simple contextualization within the *Dao De Jing* itself shows that these chapters, in fact, warn of fabricated demonstrations of virtue which arises when individuals lose their inner harmony and groups lose their collective harmony, generally as a result of avarice and envy (see chapter 3).

Rather than simply offering a checklist of moral prescriptions, Lao Zi attempts to provide a guide to inner harmony, knowing that when people attain this harmony and contentment they will naturally seek to live out this inner harmony with others, in peace. Rather than list thousands of "correct" behaviours for every situation, Lao Zi sought to instill that from which all good behaviours arise, working from within the individual to extend out to society. Using external authority, law, praise and shame to coerce internally disharmonious people into harmonious behaviour does not solve the root of the problem, but only encourages people to act out of a desire for reward or a fear of punishment. This strategy is unreliable and unsustainable, as the behaviours it encourages will disappear with the rewards and punishments.

> If I were steadfast in understanding
> I would simply walk the Great Path
> Having only one rightful fear
> The Great Way is like cleared land
> Yet the people love narrow tracks
> (*Dao De Jing*, chapter 53)

The difficulty is not that people are unable to distinguish right from wrong, but that their desires, envy, and conceit cause them to lose contentment, to contend with one another, and to prove their superiority. Thus, Lao Zi demonstrated these tendencies while showing the path to contentment, to self-sufficiency, where such behaviours would dissolve as people return to their inborn virtues and their inborn desire to live in harmony with nature and other human beings.

To break down Lao Zi's teachings into a checklist of prescribed morals would be to miss his point entirely – that morality cannot be prescribed, that people should return to their inborn virtue, and that the virtuous should not try to force others by telling them what to do. Thus, writing a list of "do's and do not's" would be antithetical to his teachings on virtue. However, having noted a common claim that Lao Zi made no distinctions between good behaviour and bad behaviour, the following examples of such distinctions, found in chapters of the *Dao De Jing*, may serve to allay such claims. While many chapters show no concern for any such distinctions, those which do generally echo the guidance found in the following chapters, which may be summarized as:

Ch.2: Do not be conceited or envious. Do not try to show that you're better than others.
Ch.3: Do not stir up trouble between people.
ch. 5: Do not be partial in judgement.
ch. 7: Put others first. Do not be selfish.
ch. 8: Do your best and benefit others.
ch. 9: Do not be greedy.
ch. 17: Do not benefit others only for recognition.
ch. 18: Adhere to the above guidance so that harmony and peacefulness do not break down, for this breakdown necessitates fabricated acts of virtue in order to avoid total chaos.
ch. 19: Do not act "holier than thou."
ch. 20: Do not get so caught up in life that you lose your connection with the Source.

Another common tendency is to deny any reading of kindness in Lao Zi's teachings, or otherwise claim that the perception of kindness in his teachings is merely an implantation of Christian values. This too may be a product of propaganda, likely from both Christian missionaries and the centuries old competition between Buddhists and Daoists. What is most ironic about this assertion is that it so often carries an expressed disdain for Christian imperialism, blaming this imperialism for a perceived projection of Christian values into Daoist literature. These allegations of Christian cultural colonialism, however, curiously overlook the monopoly they concede to Christianity on teachings of love, mercy, kindness, charity, and civility. This only perpetuates the very propaganda that allowed Christian imperialism to turn so many people against their native traditions and cultures despite such blatant evidence of these virtues in their own cultural practices. Teachings of kindness are, in fact, pervasive in the writings of Lao Zi. For example, in his description of Dao's Virtue (De) from chapter 51:

> Dao actuates them
> Virtue takes care of them, extends their lifespans
> Teaches them, completes them
> Tests them, raises them
> And brings them back (to their pure natures)
> Actuates them but does not possess them
> Sets them in motion but does not expect of them
> Extends their lives without ruling and controlling
> This is called Fathomless Virtue

The selflessness of De also proves to be an ideal for the Sage. In chapter 7, for example, Lao Zi states:

> Therefore, sages leave themselves behind
> And they end up in front
> They do not cater to themselves
> Yet they persist
> Is it not because they are without selfishness and wickedness
> That they are able to fulfill themselves?

This virtue of selfless beneficence, and disregard for reciprocity, can be seen throughout the *Dao De Jing*. Surely, Daoists may deny that this kindness is connected to morals, in the common sense, because it is simply an expression of inborn nature. This integral nuance, however, does not change the ultimate reception and benefit of this behaviour as kindness, love, and charity – a beneficence without expectation of reciprocity. Further, English is not the only language with overlays of nuance in these terms. Just as kindness, charity, love, mercy, and civility all fractionally imply each other, so do ci (kindness, compassion), ai (love, care), and ren (benevolence, civility) fractionally imply each other. So, while Lao Zi's teachings arguably transcend ethical rules, one would be completely amiss to overlook his admonishments for kindness, care, and compassion in personifying Fathomless (Mysterious) Virtue – Xuan De.

## The Politics of Lao Zi (added to 2nd edition)

Similar to overlooking his teachings on kindness is the common assertion that Lao Zi was apolitical. If we were to speak of Zhuang Zi, the second most famous Warring States Era Daoist, such an assertion might be correct, but in the case of Lao Zi we simply need to recall that the *Dao De Jing* is quite overtly a political treatise, so much so that some scholars tenaciously maintain this as its central focus. As a Sage, Lao Zi sought to heal society's ills both at the individual spiritual level and at the global political level. Granted, Lao Zi's advice generally rested on being less political, on demonstrating that stability will be attained when political power is employed sparingly and never abused. In expounding on this main tenet, however, he advised rulers in several areas of politics, including corruption, taxes, distribution of wealth, empire building, diplomacy, leadership strategy, lawmaking, punishment, and even, arguably, battle strategy.[11] Nonetheless, Lao Zi taught that, superior to all of these considerations, the Sage's power comes from minimizing desires so that he can hold constantly to Dao and cultivate its Virtue within, knowing that this inner power would express itself in the Sage's harmonious Dao of government.

While Lao Zi's strategy is known as "not doing" (wu wei), he also advocated political reform and laid the groundwork for a strategic pacifism (not to be confused with passivism) based in self-cultivation. These strategies included not inciting competition, avarice, and arrogance amongst people – some of the favourite tools of those who would get others to do their bidding by tempting them with fame, money, and vanity. Lao Zi observed the long term consequences of stirring up these motivations, especially when they corrupted even the ruler. He is very direct with imperatives that dispute and political expansion must be addressed without recourse to war, and that nations and states should work together for mutual benefit.[12] By seeking to benefit smaller nations, larger nations could secure the prosperity and stability of larger trade networks, while the virtue of Daoist rule would make these nations nearly unassailable, winning the loyalty of the common people at home and all around the world who wished to live in such an enlightened nation. While Lao Zi knew that his teachings could heal a great deal of suffering at the individual level, he also knew that if rulers could first heal themselves through inner unity and Virtue, they could bring great healing, prosperity, and vitality to Humanity. Given the damage that human beings are doing even to the Earth and Sky today, sage leaders could indeed transform Heaven, Earth, and Humanity by cultivating the Virtue of Dao and, with minimal resistance, almost unnoticeably instituting this harmony throughout "all under Heaven."

## Dating the Heshang Gong Commentary

Given that The Riverside Elder maintained a prudent level of obscurity, as many ascetic mystics do, scholars have determined a wide variety of possible dates for the writing of his commentary. Tradition suggests around 160 BC, though some scholars suggest the 3rd or 4th century AD, while others suggest closer to the turn of the second century AD.

The primary evidence that Heshang Gong did not write his commentary around 160 BC is a single use of the term "the ten directions"[13] in chapter ten. This may suggest Buddhist influence because, previous to Buddhist contact in China (mid first-century AD), the directions were referred to as "the eight directions 八極,"[14] "the

---

[11] While examples of these topics appear throughout the text, they are most apparent in chapters 61 to 81.
[12] See chapter 61
[13] Inherited by Buddhism from the Hindu tradition, they include the 8 octagonal directions (north, northeast, etc.), plus above and below
[14] Eight octagonal directions

four corners 四方,"[15] or "the six boundaries (of the universe) 六合."[16] It was common to mention "the four corners and the six boundaries" in the same sentence to refer to both earthly and celestial space; however, Heshang Gong would have been the first to group these two designations together as "the ten directions."

Heshang Gong also uses the term "the five natures, 五性" which begins to appear in texts around the middle of the first century AD. In chapter 34, he uses the term "ai yang, 愛養, loving and nurturing/raising" ("(Dao) loves and raises the myriad things"). Ai yang was later changed in this stanza to "yi yang, 衣養, clothing and nurturing/raising." Ai yang 愛養 was not a very commonly used term, but does appear in other texts from around the turn of the first century AD.

For the above reasons, it appears that Heshang Gong wrote his commentary no earlier than 100AD.

Heshang Gong's commentary includes references to mystical concepts and terms which began to develop in much greater detail during the 3rd and 4th century, and this has led some scholars to date his commentary to this time period. Some also believed that Heshang Gong edited earlier versions of the *Dao De Jing* according to changes made by Wang Bi, the editor of what is now the most commonly used *Dao De Jing* text, and who lived between 226-249 AD.

All of this in consideration, it seems safe to date Heshang Gong around 130 AD, thanks to a rather mythological tale about him written by Ge Xuan (164–244 AD),[17] in which Heshang Gong is sought out along the banks of the Yellow River by Emperor Wen of Han (202–157 BC), who was seeking instruction in the *Dao De Jing*. In this story, Heshang Gong floats up into the air, and admonishes the emperor's attempt to ply him with wealth and honour before giving the emperor his written commentary.

Ge Xuan is a highly revered figure in Daoism, as is his paternal grandnephew, Ge Hong (283–343 AD), both of whom were prominent in the development of Daoist Internal Alchemy (Nei Dan). This story shows that Heshang Gong was already a mythological figure by Ge Xuan's time, and so could not have based his edits to the *Dao De Jing* on those of Wang Bi. To put Heshang Gong somewhere after the arrival of Buddhism in China, and long enough before Ge Xuan (164–244 AD) that local stories of him had faded into the wind, it is most probable that Heshang Gong studied near the banks of the Yellow River in and around 130 AD.

---

[15] The northern, southern, eastern, and western directions of the earth. This may also refer to the same four directions as they divide the moon's path through "28 celestial mansions/constellation."
[16] north, south, east, west, above, and below, not limited to the earth
[17] Alan Chan's "Two Visions of the Way," which compares excerpts and concepts from the Wang Bi and Heshang Gong commentaries, describes disputes as to the authorship of this story. Based on the information provided by Chan, these disputes rely on the strong likelihood that the received version of Ge Xuan's story developed out of a similar story which appears in "Lives of Immortals," written by his grandnephew, Ge Hong. While this appears to be the case, given Ge Hong's close affiliation and scholarship with his granduncle, it would also appear likely that Ge Xuan taught Ge Hong this "history."

## Dating the Dao De Jing, and its Author(s)

The true historical identity of Lao Zi (老子, Venerable Master), the author of the *Dao De Jing* (道德經, The Classic of [Nature's] Way and Virtue), has been widely contested for over two thousand years. The earliest possible author is said to be Li Erh, posthumously known as Li Dan. According to historian Sima Qian (circa 100 BC), Li Erh was an official librarian in the court of Zhou, an elder contemporary of Confucius, and was said to have instructed Confucius in the Rites of Zhou. Whether refutations of this history are incontrovertible will be discussed in the following paragraphs.

The fact that some chapters differ widely in style and terminology has lead scholars to conclude that the *Dao De Jing* was written by various authors. The *Dao De Jing* is also believed by many to be a compilation of songs from an oral tradition, as many chapters have an obvious rhyming, lyrical, quality to them. These two theories are mostly in agreement.

In the *Dao De Jing*, Lao Zi often quotes ancient sayings which reveal the workings of Dao in nature. If the *Dao De Jing* was written close to 500 BC, then these sayings, variously either folk saying or attributed to "the ancients,"[18] could potentially go back at least as far as King Wen and the Duke of Zhou, who are attributed with writing the original accompanying text for the Yi Jing (I Ching) hexagrams, circa 1100 BC. If Lao Zi was an expert in the Rites of Zhou, as the above story about Confucius suggests, then it stands to reason that these sayings were part of the ancient Zhou tradition.

Many also say that the criticism of Confucian morals in the *Dao De Jing* proves that it must have been written after the time of Confucius. What this theory does not account for, however, is that Confucius received his formal moral education in school before he went on to teach these morals on a more profound level. Given that such morals were already a well established part of the education received by middle to upper class youth, it was not necessary for Confucius to have written on these subjects before Lao Zi could comment on them.

The main reason it is so difficult to date the *Dao De Jing* is because all books which criticized tyrannical rule were burned in 213 BC by Qin Shi Huang, the first emperor of the Qin dynasty, while following the guidance of Chancellor Li Si.

The earliest surviving copy of the *Dao De Jing*, from before this time, was found in the Guodian tomb, in 1993. This copy, dated to around 300 BC, appears to be an early manuscript which was later reconfigured and added to other writings to create the *Dao De Jing* as we know it today. This theory suggests that there was indeed more than one author of the *Dao De Jing*.

It may be possible, however, that the inhabitant of the Guodian tomb, a noble scholar and teacher to a crown prince of Chu, did not have the entire collection of the *Dao De Jing* chapters in his possession. Most of the other bamboo slips found in this tomb are from the Confucian school, so those who brought these slips may have

---

[18] Most descriptions of the Sage seem to suggest an existing culture; however, more explicit mention of ancient or traditional sayings can be found in chapters 15, 22, 41, 50, 57, 62, and 78.

only selected, or taught, excerpts from the *Dao De Jing* which were not in contradiction to their own beliefs, nor in contradiction to the goals of their emperors.

One notable difference in the Guodian text versus the "complete" text is that, while the Guodian text does contain a few stanzas warning against haphazard conquest, it is missing all of those which are most critical of conquest, namely the second half of chapter 48, and all of chapters 29, 69, 74, and 75. It could be speculated that such ideas within this text made it a less than welcome addition to the curriculum taught to an emperor's child. This would explain why, in this case, only essential excerpts were kept in writing.

Another possible explanation for missing verses, or the less than full acceptance of the *Dao De Jing* in the collection of this teacher, is the fact that it was found accompanied by the *Tai Yi Sheng Shui (The Great One Gave Birth to Water)*. Modern scholars generally agree that the similarities in this text to ideas in the *Dao De Jing* show that it was also part of an early development of the *Dao De Jing*. This may be the case, but it should be considered that the *Dao De Jing* may otherwise have been a relatively recent reformation of the ideas in the Tai Yi Sheng Shui, which had not yet been accepted by traditionalists.

Either theory might account for the fact that all chapters in the *Dao De Jing* that diverge from the cosmogony of the Tai Yi Sheng Shui are absent in the Guodian text. Of the eight chapters which mention Virtue as a nurturing cosmic force,[19] none of them appear in the Guodian. Of the chapters which mention virtue as a character trait, four of nine[20] appear in the Guodian. When the missing chapters which refer to Virtue as a cosmic force are added to the text, the meaning of the word in all cases takes on a new significance by showing how cosmic Virtue reflects itself in people, giving all instances of the word a more mystical tone.

It might be that the cosmogony in the *Dao De Jing* was as influenced by the Tai Yi Sheng Shui, as it was reformative of it in re-writing its account of creation, much as the *Dao De Jing* was reformative of dominant ideas about the value of moral epistemology, and the value of conquest. This shift may have begun long before the Tai Yi Sheng Shui lost favour with the majority of scholars and traditionalists, and long before the Guodian scholar's time.

While the Tai Yi Sheng Shui speaks briefly of a cosmic Dao, has a number of parallels to the cosmogony of the *Dao De Jing*, and may have predated the *Dao De Jing*, this is not certain proof that the missing chapters of the *Dao De Jing* did not exist before 300 BC. If scholars at the time were faithful to the *Tai Yi Sheng Shui*, and loyal to the intellectual pursuit of virtue, then many chapters of the *Dao De Jing* would have contradicted some of their most sacredly held beliefs, and even put the value of their knowledge and professions in danger. This speculation is no certain proof as to why the Guodian *Dao De Jing* text was incomplete, but it is enough to say that there were compelling reasons for less than half of the text to be circulated amongst traditional scholars and teachers, beyond the fundamental difficulty of transporting

---

[19] Chapters 10, 21, 23, 28, 51, 55, 60, and 65
[20] Chapters 41, 54, 59, and 63 (in Guodian text) plus 27, 38, 49, 68, 73, and 79 (not in Guodian text)

heavy bamboo scrolls in ancient times.

## Translating the Dao De Jing

The *Dao De Jing* is considered today to be the second most translated book in the world, second only to the Bible. Given the practice of translating the *Dao De Jing* as a way to study it, however, if all of these translations were to be published they would likely surpass the number of translations of the Bible, especially those made from the original Biblical Hebrew and Biblical Aramaic. Regardless, the relative size of the *Dao De Jing* makes it that such a comparison is not well matched.

The mysterious and terse language within the *Dao De Jing* offers many new discoveries to those who take up translating this text for themselves, even into modern Mandarin.

Because the ancient Chinese dialects are no longer spoken, "expert opinions" on correct translation can in many cases never be more than "opinions." The way in which certain words are used to convey meaning in Classical Chinese do not correlate with the way by which these same words are used to convey meaning in English, or modern Mandarin.

The grammatical rules of Classical Chinese are very different from modern languages. For example, the subject of a sentence, articles, and specification as to whether a word is meant as a noun, verb, or adjective, may all be included or left out, often depending on style rather than grammar. To convey the same meaning between Classical Chinese and English may require a translator to add verbs, nouns, and articles which have been implied but omitted. Without which, English sentences will lack any definitive meaning, and thus fail to transmit intended meanings. Some later editors of the *Dao De Jing* even removed hundreds of words in order to make the text exactly 5000 characters. Given this ancient custom and style of reading and writing with minimal word usage, translators must be able to fill in the blanks while accurately conveying the original words and ideas of the text.

## Notes on the Translation and Translator's Commentary

My commentary appears with the intention to consolidate the teachings of each chapter so as to make these teachings more accessible, and easier to implement in one's life. As with all comments on the Dao De Jing, these comments are limited to their own scope and should serve only as an offering, a starting point, an appetizer if you will, to begin one's own relationship with these teachings.

To differentiate authors, the format and fonts in each chapter will appear as follows:

> Dao De Jing
> Full chapter
> By Lao Zi

老子河上公章句
"Line from Dao De Jing"
Commentary on line by Heshang Gong

One to several paragraphs of commentary by Dan G. Reid
This commentary may be anywhere from 50 to 800 words.

Due to the limitations of English pronouns, I have generally chosen "he" where pronouns for the Sage are required; however, the Sage (sheng ren) is not a gender specific term. I have also capitalized "the Sage" as an honourific; however, an equal argument could be made that "sage" is simply a description of character.

Spaces will appear in the translated commentary where I've added line breaks within the *Dao De Jing* chapters so as to create paragraphs within the text.

This translation has been created with the intention that it will appeal to the casual sinologist, as well as those with an understanding of Daoist meditation, mysticism, and parlance.

# The Heshang Gong Commentary on Lao Zi's Dao De Jing

老子河上公章句

# Volume One
## Dao: The Way (of Nature)

# ~ 1 ~

The path that can be told
Is not the Eternal Path
The name that can be named
Is not the Eternal Name
The Nameless is the origin of Heaven and Earth
The Named is the mother of the myriad things
Thus, always without desires
Observing its inner subtlety
Always with desires
Observing its outer surface
These two were born together, yet differ in name
Together, they are called Fathomless Mystery
This mystery, ever more mystifying
Is a multitude of gates
All leading to the subtlety within

## Chapter One
體道 Form and Dao

道可道，謂經術政教之道也。
"The path that can be told"
This refers to the way in which classic texts, the arts, and statecraft, are taught.
非常道。非自然生長之道也。常道當以無為養神，無事安民，含光藏暉，滅跡匿端，不可稱道。
"Is not the Eternal Path"
It is not the Path of natural spontaneity and long life. The Eternal Path nourishes the spirit with effortlessness. Taking no initiative, it brings peace to the people. It envelops light, conceals radiance, leaves no tracks, and hides its periphery. It is not possible to give a proper name to Dao.
名可名，謂富貴尊榮，高世之名也。
"The name that can be named"
This refers to the name which is the most lofty, honourable, venerable, and glorious, in the world.
非常名。非自然常在之名也。常名當如嬰兒之未言，雞子之未分，明珠在蚌中，美玉處石間，內雖昭昭，外如愚頑。
"Is not the Eternal Name"
(This loftiness) is not the name of eternal spontaneity. The Eternal Name can only

be like that of a child who has not yet spoken; like baby chicks which have not come out of their eggs; like a brilliant and precious pearl which is still within its oyster; like beautiful jade which is still between the rocks. Internally, it is bright and luminous, while externally, it seems dull and dim. [21]

無名，天地之始。無名者謂道，道無形，故不可名也。始者道本也，吐氣布化，出於虛無，為天地本始也。

*"The Nameless is the origin of Heaven and Earth"*

"The nameless" refers to Dao. Dao is without form. This is why it cannot be named. "The origin" is Dao – the root. It springs forth energy-breath, covering and transforming. It comes out of emptiness and nothingness. It is the root from which Heaven and Earth began.

有名，萬物之母。有名謂天地。天地有形位、有陰陽、有柔剛，是其有名也。萬物母者，天地含氣生萬物，長大成熟，如母之養子也。

*"The Named is the mother of the myriad things"*

"The named" refers to Heaven and Earth. Heaven and Earth are the seat of form. They are yin and yang, soft and hard. This is why they have names. They are the mother of the myriad things because Heaven and Earth accumulate energy-breath and give birth to the myriad things, maturing their great and lasting completion like a mother supports her child.

故常無欲，以觀其妙；妙，要也。人常能無欲，則可以觀道之要，要謂一也。一出布名道，讚敘明是非。

*"Thus, always without desires, observing its (inner) subtlety"*

The "subtlety," here, means the key. People who maintain the absence of desire will be able to observe the key to Dao. "The key" is Oneness. Oneness sends forth and proliferates the names of Dao, to which people sing praises for having clarified right from wrong.

常有欲，以觀其徼。徼，歸也。常有欲之人，可以觀世俗之所歸趣也。

*"Always with desires, observing its outer surface"*

The "outer surfaces" are what people return to. By maintaining the desires that people commonly have, you can observe the ways of their time and place, to which they continually return.

此兩者，同出而異名，兩者，謂有欲無欲也。同出者，同出人心也。而異名者，所名各異也。名無欲者長存，名有欲者亡身也。

*"These two were born together, yet differ in name"*

"These two" refers to the presence of desire, and the absence of desire. They are born together because they are both born in people's hearts. They differ in name because each one has a different reputation. The reputation of the absence of desire is that it brings long life. The reputation of the presence of desire is that it destroys the body.

---

[21] The earlier Mawangdui copies have the Dao volume following the De volume. Thus, chapter one proceeded from chapter 81's "True words are not beautified…"

同謂之玄，玄，天也。言有欲之人與無欲之人，同受氣於天也。
"Together, they are called Fathomless Mystery"
Xuan (Fathomless) refers to Heaven. This is to say that people who have desires, and people who have no desires, both receive energy-breath from Heaven.

玄之又玄，天中復有天也。稟氣有厚薄，得中和滋液，則生賢聖，得錯亂污辱，則生貪淫也。
"(This) mystery, ever more mystifying"
Returning to the center of Heaven, there is another Heaven. It dispenses energy-breaths which can be potent or weak. Obtaining harmonious fertile fluid from its center, this gives birth to the worthy and wise; If one receives polluted, chaotic, and aberrant (energies), this gives birth to greed and licentiousness.

眾妙之門。能之天中復有天，稟氣有厚薄，除情去欲守中和，是謂知道要之門戶也。
"(Is a) multitude of gates, all leading to the profound subtlety (within)"
Heaven can return to the Heaven within itself, and dispense energy-breaths which are either potent or weak. Eliminating strong emotions, abandoning desires, and guarding harmony within: this is called "knowing the gate-key to the door of Dao."

ONE

Heshang Gong explains that Dao cannot be named with lofty names because Dao is pure simplicity. These lofty names would suggest that Dao is something elegant and refined when, in reality, it is natural and perfectly unrefined. Beyond name and beyond erudition, Dao is cultivated through awareness and experience, both internal and external.

In the absence of desire, one can develop an unfiltered relationship with the present. As chapter one speaks to purifying the heart-mind, washing desires from the heart-mind will bring about the harmonizing balance of Oneness,[22] opening the gate to Dao within, and creating a pathway to the potent energies of Heaven.

On observing inner subtlety, Lao Zi's chapter 52 may offer additional guidance with its instructions for a Daoist meditation known as "turning the light around." With slightly different language than chapter one, chapter 52 states:

> The world has an origin
> Known as the Mother of All Under Heaven

(In chapter one, "the Nameless" is the *mother* of both Heaven and Earth)

> Having known the Mother, know the Son

---

[22] See in the introduction "Dao, De, and Oneness in Heshang Gong's Commentary" for an explanation of how Heshang Gong equates De and Oneness.

> Having known the Son, guard the Mother within

(Heshang Gong comments in chapter 52 that the Mother refers to Dao, while the Son refers to Oneness)

> With no self, there is no danger

(As Dr. Michael Saso explains in regards to the Daoist Priest, Master Zhuang, "standing before the Imperial Throne of Heaven… the Daoist is the mediator between Heaven and Earth, the man or woman who in meditation can stand before the Eternal Dao because the Daoist has emptied himself or herself of all selfish desires and all thoughts."[23])

> Seal the doors
> Close the gate
> By opening the doors
> And increasing pursuits
> There will be no help for you in later years

The gates and doors, in this case, are generally understood to refer to the sense doors of the body. The "multitude of gates" referred to in chapter one may be contextualized in innumerable ways, but seeing the juxtaposition of themes between chapter 52 and chapter one, it may be that chapter one also suggests inwardly focusing the sense doors, as described in the following lines from chapter 52:

> Seeing what is small is called "seeing clearly"
> Maintaining suppleness is called "strengthening"
> Use this light
> Turn this clear vision back to its source
> And you will not lose the body to illness
> This is called "studying the Eternal"

"Seeing what is small" through this internal gazing appears to introduce later Buddhist mindfulness (vipissana) meditation, where meditators observe subtle changes of emotion, thought, feeling, and internal energies. This sensory observation, however, is what Daoist's call a "post-heaven" practice, dealing with

---

[23] Dr. Saso, Michael. "Master Zhuang". Filmed circa 1970. YouTube video, 6m47sec. Posted April 10, 2010. https://www.youtube.com/watch?v=Qsp33JiO6D8&feature=youtu.be.
In giving me permission to quote the above video, Dr. Saso asked that I note:
This video is a representation of the Zhengyi Orthodox Daoist tradition. Grade Five and above ordination, Grade Two Qing Wei Wu-Wei and Grade Three Beidou registers are also a part of the tradition. See the ordination manual of the Longhu Shan Celestial Masters for verification.

subtleties of the material world (see above, "always without desires, observing its inner subtlety; always with desires, observing its outer surface"), rather than transcending the post-heaven and approaching the "pre-heaven," perhaps what Lao Zi refers to in chapters one and 52 as "the Mother." In any case, "observing the subtlety within," as described in chapter one, offers the essence of the inner practices – "internal gazing (nei guang)" and "turning the light around (hui guang)" – found in chapter 52.

# ~ 2 ~

When the whole world knows the pleasing to be pleasing
This ends in despising
When all know the good to be good
In the end there is "not good"

Thus, existence and non-existence are born together
Difficulty and ease result in each other
Long and short are compared to each other
Above and below are opposites of each other
Noise and tone are harmonized by each other
Front and back accompany each other
Therefore, sages handle affairs with non-action

They practice wordless instruction
And the myriad things all take their places
Without responding

Given life, but not possessed
Acted for, but not expected of
Perfection is cultivated, and not dwelled upon
Surely, what is not dwelled upon
Does not leave

# Chapter Two
## 養身 Self-Cultivation

天下皆知美之為美，自揚己美，使彰顯也。
"When the whole world knows the pleasing to be pleasing"
When the beautiful praise themselves, they put themselves on display.
斯惡已；有危亡也。
"This ends in despising"
They are in danger of being killed.
皆知善之為善，有功名也。
"When all know the good to be good"
When people are known to have accomplishments and fame
斯不善已。人所爭也。
"In the end there is 'not good'"
Others compete and fight with them.

故有無相生，見有而為無也。
"Thus, existence and non-existence are born together"
Seeing existence, people determine non-existence
難易相成，見難而為易也。
"Difficulty and ease result in each other"
Seeing what is difficult, people determine what is easy.
長短相較，見短而為長也。
"Long and short are compared to each other"
Seeing what is short, people determine what is long.
高下相傾，見高而為下也。
"Above and below are opposites of each other"
Seeing what is high, people determine what is low.
音聲相和，上唱下必和也。
"Noise and tone are harmonized by each other"
When a superior sings, those below him must harmonize.
前後相隨。上行下必隨也。
"Front and back accompany each other"
When superiors advance, those below them must follow.
是以聖人處無為之事，以道治也。
"Therefore, sages handle affairs with non-action"
They allow Dao to bring order.

行不言之教，以身師導之也。
"They practice wordless instruction"

They make themselves a guiding example.
萬物作焉，各自動也。
"And the myriad things all take their places"
Each one moves by themselves.
而不辭，不辭謝而逆止。
"Without responding"
They do not respond, or thank the Sage for his instruction, but rebellions come to an end.

生而不有，元氣生萬物而不有。
"Given life, yet not possessed"
The original energy-breath (yuan qi) gives birth to the myriad things, but does not possess them.
為而不恃，道所施為，不恃望其報也。
"Acted for, but not expected of"
Dao is the giver of action, but it does not expect any reciprocal offering.
功成而弗居。功成事就，退避不居其位。
"Perfection is cultivated, and not dwelled upon"
(Sages) bring things to completion as situations arrive, and then withdraw. They do not remain in positions of authority.
夫唯弗居，夫惟功成不居其位。
"Surely, what is not dwelled upon"
(Sages) cultivate perfection and do not linger in positions of authority.
是以不去。福德常在，不去其身也。此言不行不可隨，不言不可知疾。上六句有高下長短，君開一源，下生百端，百端之變，無不動亂。
"Does not leave"
The blessing of Virtue will always remain, and not leave (such) a person. Those who do not advance cannot be followed. Those who do not speak cannot have their weaknesses known. The above six phrases speak of high and low, and long and short, because when the ruler creates one opening, those below give rise to one hundred extremes. This requires one hundred adjustments, (and creates a situation where) there is nothing which is not in confusion.


TWO
Heshang Gong's comments on chapter two highlight the balancing nature of antagonistic polarities, and how this antagonistic nature plays out amongst human beings. Trying to convince others of our worthiness, we invite their scorn. Trying to show our merits, we invite comparisons to those against whom we could never measure up. Wishing to appear great, we invite derision. By trying to exalt ourselves, we in fact humiliate ourselves, but if we humble ourselves, we may gradually and naturally accrue such recognition. In this wu wei, our talents

may be recognized and promotions may be secured, without the obfuscation of self-promotion.

## ~ 3 ~

Do not exalt the worthy
And the people will not fight
Do not praise goods which are difficult to obtain
And the people will not steal
Do not display what is desirable
And their hearts will not be in chaos

Therefore, the Sage's government
Empties the heart and enriches the stomach
Softens the will and strengthens the bones
People then remain uncontrived and without desires
While the scheming do not dare to act
Act by not acting
And everything will fall into place

## Chapter Three
安民 Bringing Peace to The People

不尚賢，賢謂世俗之賢，辯口明文，離道行權，去質為文也。不尚者，不貴之以祿，不貴之以官。
"Do not exalt the worthy"
"The worthy" refers here to those who are deemed by a generation's customs to be worthy. Their mouths are eloquent and their appearances are glorious, but they leave Dao and chase power and authority. They discard (real) substance and fabricate appearances. "Do not exalt," here, means do not honour them with high salaries or positions.
使民不爭。不爭功名，返自然也。
"And the people will not fight"
They will not fight for merit and fame, but will return to their natures.
不貴難得之貨，言人君不御好珍寶，黃金棄於山，珠玉捐於淵也。
"Do not praise goods which are difficult to obtain"
This is to say that rulers should not ride about in chariots embedded with precious

jewels. They should put their gold back in the mountains and throw their jewels and jade into the abyss.

使民不為盜。上化清靜，下無貪人。
"And the people will not steal"
When those above are clear and tranquil, there will be no greedy men below them.

不見可欲，放鄭聲，遠美人。
"Do not display what is desirable"
Get rid of licentious music and send away tantalizers.

使心不亂。不邪淫，不惑亂也。
"And their hearts will not be in chaos"
Where there is no wickedness and licentiousness, there is no chaos and confusion.

是以聖人之治，說聖人治國與治身同也。
"Therefore, the Sage's government"
The Sage governs the nation in the same way that he governs his body.

虛其心，除嗜欲，去亂煩。
"Empties the heart"
By eliminating cravings and desires, he banishes chaos and trouble.

實其腹，懷道抱一守，五神也。
"And enriches the stomach"
He carries Dao in his heart, embraces Oneness, and protects the five spirits.[24]

弱其志，和柔謙讓，不處權也。
"Softens the will"
Harmonious and soft, humble, modest, and accommodating, the Sage does not linger in positions of authority.

強其骨。愛精重施，髓滿骨堅。
"And strengthens the bones"
He cherishes his vital essence and takes seriously what was bestowed upon him (by Heaven, Earth, and his parents). Thus, his bone marrow is full, and his bones are strong.

常使民無知無欲。返樸守淳。
"People then remain uncontrived and without desires"
They return to the unaltered state (by) guarding simplicity within.

使夫知者不敢為也。思慮深，不輕言。
"While the scheming do not dare to act"
They become concerned and think deeply. They do not speak carelessly.

為無為，不造作，動因循。
"Act by not acting"
Do not create more work. Move when there is reason to do so.

---

[24] The five spirits are discussed in chapter six

則無不治。德化厚，百姓安。
*"And everything will fall into place"*
Virtue will bring about great transformation, and all people will become peaceful.


THREE
While chapter two cautions against enticing others to praise oneself, as this invites competition and jealousy, chapter three cautions against enticing people to envy and compete with each other. Leaders often instigate a competitive atmosphere in an attempt to increase the output of their group, but too often this is done by manipulating the base desires of people to fear and conquer each other. This results in an unmanageable situation where the common unity dissolves and a leader must then lead many competing factions, rather than a single functioning organism.

An intriguing correlation to Chinese medicine and Daoist internal alchemy is notably present in Lao Zi's description of emptying the mind, enriching the stomach, softening the will, and strengthening the bones. Guan Zi's *Art of the Heart-Mind* texts explain that to clear the mind is to return to intent, as intent precedes thought.[25] Intent (yi) is also related to the stomach as intent is said to be housed in the spleen. In Daoist meditation, while emptying the heart-mind, intent is focused on the lower dantien – the gravitational center of the body's energy – located just below the navel. Doing so nourishes the basic energy of life. This gravitational center is associated with the "life gate" (ming men) located behind the kidneys, and the kidneys themselves, which are said in Chinese medicine to house the will (zhi) and nourish the bones. So, by emptying the mind, enriching the lower dantien, and not taxing the kidneys by overuse of the will, the kidneys can in turn strengthen the bones. Thereby, one "empties the mind, enriches the stomach, softens the will, and strengthens the bones." While Lao Zi may or may not have known about these connections,[26] their application is no less evident in his theory of governing the nation and, ostensibly, the body.

---

[25] Intent (yi) can be understood as the central cohesive force of the mind that allows for focus. This is also maintained in the correlation of intent with the central and unifying earth element of the spleen. For Guan Zi's Art of the Heart-Mind texts, see: Reid, Dan G. *The Thread of Dao: Unraveling Early Daoist Oral Traditions in Guan Zi's Purifying the Heart-Mind (Bai Xin), Art of the Heart-Mind (Xin Shu), and Internal Cultivation (Nei Ye)*. Montreal: Center Ring Publications, 2017.

[26] The authorship of the *Nei Jing* (*Classic of Internal Medicine*) is uncertain, but the text is said by scholars to have appeared around 200 BC, compiling a variety of writings connected to early Daoist communities as evidenced by philosophical similarities in the *Guan Zi*, *Zhuang Zi*, and *Dao De Jing*.

# ~ 4 ~

Dao is a container
Though used again and again
It is never full
Profound! As though the ancestor of all things
Rounding the points
Untying the knots
Softening the glare
Unifying the dust

Tranquil! As though having a life of its own
I do not know whose child it is
It precedes any concept of a sovereign

## Chapter Four
無源 Without Origin

道沖而用之，沖，中也。道匿名藏譽，其用在中
"Dao is a container. Though used"
"A container"[27] means that it is "within." Dao hides its name and conceals its fame. Its use is found within.
或不盈，或，常也。道常謙虛不盈滿。
"Again and again, it is never full"
"Again," here, means "always." Dao is always humble and empty, and never full or self-satisfied.
淵乎似萬物之宗。道淵深不可知，似為萬物知宗祖。
"Profound! As though the ancestor of all things"
Dao is so deep that its depths cannot be known. (Trying to know it) is like the myriad things trying to know their first ancestors.
挫其銳，銳，進也。人欲銳精進取功名，當挫止之，法道不自見也。
"Rounding the points"
"Points" refer to pushing forward. People wish to direct their vital essence toward receiving merit and fame. They should dull this (desire) until it has stopped, and follow the example of Dao by not displaying themselves.

---

[27] Usually translated as "empty," 沖 chong suggests an empty vessel, and literally means "immersion," made up of the radicals for "water" and "within." In ancient classics, chong appeared in compound words for youth (沖人, 沖子) and so may have alluded to inexhaustible youth, and the 'eternal child' in this chapter.

解其紛，紛，結恨也。當念道無為以解釋。
"Untying the knots"
"The knots" refers to knots of hatred. Giving your thoughts to the effortlessness of Dao, untie and release them.

和其光，言雖有獨見之明，當知闇昧，不當以擢亂人也。
"Softening the glare"
Lao Zi is saying that if you are the only person who sees with brilliant and illuminated vision, you should obscure your knowledge and not draw others into confusion.[28]

同其塵。當與眾庶同垢塵，不當自別殊。
"Unifying the dust"
You should associate with the multitudes in the same dirt and dust. You should not separate and differentiate yourself from them.

湛兮似若存。言當湛然安靜，故能長存不亡。
"Tranquil! As though having a life of its own"
This is to say that you should find tranquility and stillness at the depths of your nature. Then you will be able to endure and not die.

吾不知誰之子，老子言：我不知，道所從生。
"I do not know whose child it is"
Lao Zi is saying: "I do not know from whom or what the Dao was born."

象帝之先。道自在天帝之前，此言道乃先天地之生也。至今在者，以能安靜湛然，不勞煩欲使人修身法道。
"It precedes any concept of a sovereign"
Dao existed before Heaven's first ruler. This means that Dao was born before Heaven and Earth. To arrive at Dao today, people can simply find the tranquility and stillness residing in the depths of their nature. When not beckoned by the calls of desire, they can cultivate themselves and follow the example of Dao.


FOUR

In chapter four, Heshang Gong explains that 'Dao as a container' is a metaphor for humility. Dao is the empty vessel which can never be overfilled. It can accomplish all things, provide all things, and create all things, yet it never shows itself and never seeks recognition. People, on the other hand, are filled up quite quickly, brimming over with their accomplishments and seeking to show how full they have become. The Sage, like the Dao, remains empty. For in doing so, they remain unlimited in capacity.

---

[28] Chapter 20 may illustrate this concept.

# ~ 5 ~

Heaven and Earth are not (willfully) benevolent
The myriad things are treated no differently
Than grass for dogs
Sages are not (willfully) benevolent
The hundred clans are treated no differently
Than grass for dogs

The gate of Heaven and Earth
Is it not like a bagpipe?
Empty yet not finished
It moves, and again more is pushed forth

To speak countless words is worthless
This is not as good as guarding balance within

## Chapter Five
### 虛用   Utilizing Emptiness

天地不仁,天施地化,不以仁恩,任自然也。
"Heaven and Earth are not (willfully) benevolent"[29]
Heaven bestows, and Earth transforms. It is not because of benevolence or mercy that they do this, but simply because it is in their nature (zi ran)
以萬物為芻狗。天地生萬物,人最為貴,天地視之如芻草狗畜,不責望其報也。
"The myriad things are treated no differently than grass for dogs"
Heaven and Earth gave birth to the myriad things. People are highly valued, (yet) Heaven and Earth see them as they see grass and straw (for) dogs and farm animals. Heaven and Earth do not value people with expectations of being treated the same way in response.
聖人不仁,聖人愛養萬民,不以仁恩,法天地行自然。
"Sages are not (willfully) benevolent"
Sages love and take care of the myriad people. It is not because of benevolence or mercy that they do so, but because they follow the example of Heaven and Earth and act according to natural spontaneity.
以百姓為芻狗。聖人視百姓如芻草狗畜,不責望其禮意。
"The hundred clans are treated no differently than grass for dogs"
Sages see the hundred clans as they see grass and straw for dogs and farm animals.

---

[29] Please see "Straw-Dogs, Benevolence, and Chapter Five of the Dao De Jing," in the appendix.

They do not honour people with any expectation of reciprocal courtesy in their minds.

天地之間，天地之間空虛，和氣流行，故萬物自生。人能除情欲，節滋味，清五臟，則神明居之也。

*"The gate of Heaven and Earth"*

The gate of Heaven and Earth is hollow and empty. Harmonious energy-breath flows forth from it. Thus, the myriad things arise spontaneously. By eliminating desires and strong emotions, and abstaining from ingesting too many flavours, the five organs will be purified. Spiritual intelligence will then remain.

其猶橐籥乎。橐籥中空虛，人能有聲氣。

*"Is it not like a bagpipe?"*

The center of a bagpipe[30] is hollow and empty, yet people can obtain musical energy from it.

虛而不屈，動而愈出。言空虛無有屈竭時，動搖之，益出聲氣也。

*"Empty yet not finished. It moves, and again more is pushed forth"*

This means that, though hollow and empty, it has not been exhausted. By moving it back and forth, more musical energy comes out of it.

多言數窮，多事害神，多言害身，口開舌舉，必有禍患。

*"To speak countless words is worthless"*

Having too many duties harms the spirit. Speaking too many words does harm to oneself. When the mouth is open and the tongue cleaves to the roof of the mouth, there is sure to be misfortune and worries.

不如守中。不如守德於中，育養精神，愛氣希言。

*"This is not as good as guarding balance within"*

It is not as good as guarding De within. Nurture and support your spiritual vitality, cherish your energy-breath, and speak infrequently.[31]

## FIVE

In chapter five, Heshang Gong continues to illustrate the natural self-reliance of Heaven and the Sage. Benevolence is often thought of as an act requiring self-sacrifice and willpower, but for Heaven and the Sage, it is simply a genuine expression of their pure nature. They are not humane and kind out of duty and social expectations, and they do not feel the need to parade such behaviours about in debates about proper conduct and courtesies. Being of good service to

---

[30] Literally "bag-flute." Heshang Gong's commentary seems to suggest a musical instrument, perhaps similar to the sheng.

[31] Heshang Gong may also use jing-shen (spiritual vitality) to refer to the organ spirits mentioned in chapter six. Jing-shen is somewhat like a derivative of shen (spirit), and should not be confused with the shen, which refers to the spiritual consciousness as a whole.

others does not require a convincing motivation for Heaven or the Sage, so they find little reason to spend time explaining it.

A great deal of confusion has persisted in regards to the seeming meaning of the first lines of chapter five: "Heaven is not benevolent; it treats all people as sacrificial straw dogs."[32] In summary, benevolence (ren) formerly suggested a hierarchy of disciplined care and concern, beginning with one's closest relatives and eventually reaching to strangers. So "not benevolent" here actually suggested "impartial." Thanks to an anecdote by the great Daoist writer Zhuang Zi (Chuang Tzu), sacrificial straw dogs are known to have been discarded and trampled on by those leaving the sacrficial ceremony; however, Zhuang Zi also describes how they were treated with the utmost care and attention before and during the ceremony, when they were presented as offerings to Heaven. It is this care and attention, treating *all* people as sacred, that Lao Zi seems more likely to have meant in this chapter.

A similar treatment to that of the straw dogs can be found in practices of Daoist and folk herbalism, where prayers and intentions will be infused into the medicine. When the medicinal properties have been absorbed, the dregs will be thrown onto the road "thus symbolically casting the disease out of the house, there to be crushed by the wheels of passing buses and trucks."[33] The end treatment of the medicine is, of course, not the ultimate reflection of how these herbs are used. Prayers and intentions are infused into the medicine in hopes that they will bring peace and harmony to the patient, much as the prayers and intentions infused into the straw dogs were believed to foster peace and harmony in Heaven, and consequently on Earth and amongst Humanity. We may take from this that the Sage, therefore, does not simply tell people how to act and how to care for those closest to him, but puts his best attention and intention to all people, as though they were the mediums through which he would communicate his love and reverence for De and Dao. One might say that when proven devoid of any virtue, people would be considered as potentially disease carrying rubbish; however, this would seem in great contradiction to chapter 27:

> … the wise of unrelenting virtue rescue people
> Therefore nobody is abandoned
> Unrelenting virtue saves things
> Therefore nothing is abandoned
> This is called "capturing light"
> Therefore, those who are excellent
> Are models for those who are not excellent
> Those who are not excellent
> Are valued as assets by those who are excellent

---

[32] See in the Appendix, "Straw-Dogs and Benevolence in Chapter Five of the Dao De Jing."
[33] Bob Flaws and Honora Lee Wolfe. *The Successful Chinese Herbalist*. Boulder: Blue Poppy Press, 2005. p. 50

Those who do not value their teachers
Those who do not care for their assets
To consider these people wise would be a great illusion…

For a more extensive analysis of chapter five, please see in the appendix below: "Straw-Dogs and Benevolence in Chapter Five of the Dao De Jing."

## ~ 6 ~

The valley with a spirit does not die
This is called the Fathomlessness of the Female
The gate to the Fathomlessness of the Female
Is called the Root of Heaven and Earth
Soft and gentle
This is her way of existence
To engage her is not laborious

## Chapter Six
成象 Formation and Image

谷神不死，谷，養也。人能養神則不死也。神，謂五臟之神也。肝藏魂，肺藏魄，心藏神，腎藏精，脾藏志，五藏盡傷，則五神去矣。
"The valley with a spirit does not die"
A valley is nourishing. People have the power to nourish the spirit and not die. "Spirit" refers to the five organ spirits. The liver hides the ethereal (hun) spirit; the lungs hide the corporeal (po) spirit; the heart hides the mind (shen) spirit; the kidneys and sexual organs hide the essence (jing) spirit; and the spleen hides the will (zhi) spirit.[34] If these five hidden spirits are exhausted and injured, they will leave.
是謂玄牝。言不死之有，在於玄牝。玄，天也，於人為鼻。牝，地也，於人為口。天食人以五氣，從鼻入藏於心。五氣輕微，為精、神、聰、明、音聲五性。其鬼曰魂，魂者雄也，主出入於人鼻，與天通，故鼻為玄也。地食人以五味，從口入藏於胃。五味濁辱，為形、骸、骨、肉、血、脈六情。其鬼曰魄，魄者雌也，主出入於人口，與地通，故口為牝也。
"This is called the Fathomlessness of the Female"
What cannot die are the Fathomless and the Female. The Fathomless is of Heaven.

---

[34] Heshang Gong diverges here from the *Yellow Emperor's Classic on Internal Medicine*, which places intention (yi) in the spleen and will (zhi) in the kidneys.

In people, this is the nose. The Female is of the Earth. In people, this is the mouth.

Heaven feeds people with the five energy-breaths. They go in through the nose, and are stored in the heart. The five energy-breaths are refined to make the vital essence, shen-spirit, intelligence, clear vision, vocal expression, and the five intrinsic natures.[35] Their entity is the ethereal spirit (hun). This entity is male. It controls the outflow and inflow of a person's nose so that Heaven can pass through them. Thus, the nose is the Fathomless.

Earth feeds people with the five flavours. They go in through the mouth and are stored in the stomach. The five flavours are mixed and compacted to create the form, the bones, the skeletal framework, the muscles, the blood, the blood channels, and the six emotions.[36] Their entity is the corporeal spirit (po). This entity is female. It controls the outflow and inflow of a person's mouth, so that Earth can pass through them. Thus, the mouth is the Female.

玄牝之門，是謂天地根。根，元也。言鼻口之門，是乃通天地之元氣所從往來也。

"The gate to the Fathomlessness of the Female is called The Root of Heaven and Earth"

The root is the origin. This means that the original energy-breaths (yuan qi) of Heaven and Earth are sent out and drawn in through the gates of the nose and the mouth.

綿綿若存，鼻口呼噏喘息，當綿綿微妙，若可存，復若無有。

"Soft and gentle. This is her way of existence"

The nose and mouth exhale and inhale, breathe in deeply and let the breath out slowly. (The breath) should be soft and gentle, unnoticeable and subtle, returning to be as though not there.

用之不勤。用氣當寬舒，不當急疾勤勞也。

"To engage her is not laborious"

Use of the breath should be wide, spacious, open, stretched, easy, and comfortable. It should not be quick and urgent, difficult, overzealous, or laborious.


## SIX

As Heshang Gong shows in chapter six, Daoist strategies for harmonious living are not simply meant to avoid calamity, but also to nourish divine essence – spirit – and thereby improve wellbeing on every level of our existence. What connects us to the original qi of Heaven and Earth, according to Heshang Gong, is our nose and mouth which allow us to ingest this qi and transform it into divine essence (spirit), manifested in our character and body as virtue and health.

---

[35] "The five intrinsic natures" refer to the natural states of the human spirit before they are disturbed by the six emotions. The five intrinsic natures correspond to the five organs as follows: benevolence 仁(ren)/liver, propriety 礼(li)/heart, trustworthiness 信(xin)/spleen, loyalty 忠(zhong)/lungs, wisdom 智(zhi)/kidneys.

[36] The six emotions are: like 好(hao), dislike 惡(wu), excitement 喜(xi), anger 怒(nu), sorrow 哀(ai), and pleasure 樂(le).

While many of the early Chinese philosophers discussed the true meanings and cultivation of benevolence, propriety, trustworthiness, loyalty, and wisdom, Heshang Gong also taught the benefits of mindful breathing, ingesting the yuan qi of Heaven and Earth, and thereby nourishing the internal organs and their positive expressions of health. These positive expressions of health could be simply described as "feeling good." By feeling good, we will find benevolence, propriety, trustworthiness, loyalty, and wisdom a more natural part of our nature. This feeling good begins with the breath, for by our very own nose and mouth we can breathe in the original breath (yuan qi) of Heaven and Earth (天地之元氣), the subtle nutrients producing the inception of all life on Earth.

On the topic of breath, it may be helpful to look at the role of the lungs according to ancient Chinese medical theory. In the earliest Chinese canon of medicine, the *Yellow Emperor's Classic of Internal Medicine*, Plain Questions (*Nei Jing*, Su Wen), chapter eight, the lungs are described as the prime minister and grand tutor to the emperor (the heart) bringing "order and moderation." At the level of emotion and consciousness, the role of the lungs can be illustrated with a number of intriguing correlations in five elemental phase theory, as shown in the following reasoning:

The metal phase, pertaining to the lungs, is "dominated/corrected" by the fire phase (fire is the grand-parent of metal), with fire pertaining to the heart-mind. Note that the lungs are the only internal organs that we can easily control with our minds. Thus, the heart-mind-emperor can use the lungs-prime-minister to direct the other internal organ-officials. One of the most precarious officials in a polity can be the general who holds sway over the army. In the nation-body metaphor of the *Nei Jing*, this is the liver, pertaining to the wood phase and the emotion of anger. The metal phase of the lungs, however, dominates the wood phase. Similarly, if one finds themselves overcome by anger, the best way to overcome this rising energy is to breathe deeply so that the lungs massage the liver, moderating and bringing order to this insurgence.

Another relationship to consider here is that between the lungs and the kidneys – the kidneys pertaining to water phase and the emotion of fear. The water phase draws from the metal phase (metal is the parent of water), and can thereby weaken it, much as fear can stop us from breathing properly, even causing hyperventilation.

On the other side of the metal phase is the earth phase, pertaining to the spleen,[37] which gives birth to and nourishes the metal phase (earth is the parent of metal). Note that cultivating the calm stillness of the earth will restore deep and bountiful breathing. With this calm stillness, we give rise to the ingestion of

---

[37] *Nei Jing*, chapter eight states: "The spleen and stomach hold the office in charge of grain storage; They bring forth the five tastes (flavours)." Just as the lungs draw in Heavenly qi, the spleen and stomach draw in Earthly grains.

Heavenly qi in our lungs, associated with the flexibility of the metal phase. It would appear similarly relevant, within this circle of five phases, that in the eight natural powers of Feng Shui (Water, Mountain, Thunder, Wind, Fire, Earth, Lake, and Heaven), Heaven is also associated with the metal phase. Thus, in the lungs and spleen, paired in the "tai yin" meridian system of acupuncture, we find the interactions of Heaven and Earth taking place in our very own bodies.

## ~ 7 ~

Heaven has longevity, Earth has continuity
Heaven and Earth have the power of longevity and continuity because they do not live for themselves
This is how they can live for so long

Therefore, sages leave themselves behind
And they end up in front
They do not cater to themselves
Yet they persist

Is it not because they are without selfishness and wickedness
That they are able to fulfill themselves?

## Chapter Seven
韜光 Sheathing Light

天長地久，說天地長生久壽，以喻教人也。
"Heaven has longevity, Earth has continuity"
Heaven and Earth live for a long time, and are thus used as an example to instruct people.
天地所以能長且久者，以其不自生，天地所以獨長且久者，以其安靜，施不求報，不如人居處，汲汲求自饒之利，奪人以自與也。
"Heaven and Earth have the power of longevity and continuity because they do not live for themselves"
Heaven and Earth continue to exist because they are peaceful and gentle. They give and do not seek reciprocation. This is not how people live. People draw and draw (from the world), and seek abundant profit for themselves. They take from others and give to themselves.

故能長生。以其不求生，故能長生不終也。
"This is how they can live for so long"
Because they do not seek after life, they can extend their lives endlessly.

是以聖人後其身，先人而後己也。
"Therefore, sages leave themselves behind"
They put others first, and themselves behind.

而身先，天下敬之，先以為長。
"And end up in front"
The world respects them, and they lead by having endured the longest.

外其身，薄己而厚人也。
"They do not cater to themselves"
They do without, and enhance others.

而身存。百姓愛之如父母，神明祐之若赤子，故身常存。
"Yet they persist"
All people love them like their own mothers and fathers. The spiritual lights (shen ming)[38] protect them like a newborn child. Thus, they always remain.

非以其無私邪。聖人為人所愛，神明所祐，非以其公正無私所致乎。
"Is it not because they are without selfishness and wickedness"
Sages act with love toward people and are protected by the spiritual lights. Is this not because they are fair, upright, and without selfishness?

故能成其私。人以為私者，欲以厚己也。聖人無私而己自厚，故能成其私也。
"That they are able to fulfill themselves?"
People who act with selfishness wish to enhance themselves. Sages are without selfishness, yet they enhance themselves. As a result, they are able to fulfill themselves.


SEVEN
Seeking only to benefit oneself, people lose their connection to the source of benefit, be that their connection to Dao, or their connection to others. People thrive in harmonious communities where they can grow as individuals and secure livelihoods by fulfilling a role as part of the interconnected organism of society. Seeking only to serve oneself in the inescapable circumstances of human society leaves a person disconnected from the greater good and, according to ancient Chinese thought, offends the higher spiritual powers that can put them on the path of success or failure.

---

[38] The shen ming are also mentioned in the Tai Yi Sheng Shui, and texts by Zhuang Zi, Confucius, and Mo Tzu. They are considered as emissaries of Heaven which determine fortune and misfortune according to the purity of one's virtue. Shen ming can also mean spiritual intelligence, or "brilliance of the spirit."

# ~ 8 ~

The highest excellence is like water
The excellence of water benefits all things
And does not fight against them
It dwells in the places that people detest
How close it is to Dao!

Such excellence in dwelling can be found in the Earth
Such excellence in the heart can be found in its depths
Such excellence in giving can be found in benevolence
Such excellence in speech can be found in truthfulness
Such excellence in alignment can be found in order
Such excellence in professionalism can be found in competence
Such excellence in action can be found in appropriate timing

Simply because it does not fight
(Water) has no enemy

## Chapter Eight
易性 The True Nature of Ease

上善若水。上善之人，如水之性。
"The highest excellence is like water"
People of highest excellence resemble the nature of water.
水善利萬物而不爭，水在天為霧露，在地為源泉也。
"The excellence of water benefits all things, and does not fight against them"
Water exists in the sky as mist and dew, and in the earth as springs.
處眾人之所惡，眾人惡卑濕垢濁，水獨靜流居之也。
"It dwells in the places that people detest"
The people all detest places that are low, damp, dirty, and muddy. Only water quietly circulates and lives there.
故幾於道。水性幾於道同。
"How close it is to Dao!"
The nature of water is similar to Dao.

居善地，水性善喜於地，草木之上即流而下，有似於牝動而下人也。
"Such excellence in dwelling can be found in the earth"
The nature of water excels in loving the earth. Plants and trees immediately spring up

when it flows down to them. It resembles how females put themselves below males.
心善淵，水深空虛，淵深清明。
"Such excellence in the heart can be found in its depths"
At the depths of water there is emptiness. Its depths are pure and clear.
與善仁，萬物得水以生。與虛不與盈也。
"Such excellence in giving can be found in benevolence"
The myriad things obtain water for life. It gives where there is emptiness and not where there is fullness.
言善信，水內影照形，不失其情也。
"Such excellence in speech can be found in truthfulness"
Water shows the reflections and shadows of forms but does not lose its own essential character.
正善治，無有不洗，清且平也。
"Such excellence in alignment can be found in order"
Everything it cleans becomes pure and peaceful.
事善能，能方能圓，曲直隨形。
"Such excellence in professionalism can be found in competence"
It can be square, it can be circular, it can be bent, and it can be straight. It can follow any form.
動善時。夏散冬凝，應期而動，不失天時。
"Such excellence in action can be found in appropriate timing"
In summer it disperses; in winter it freezes. It abides by the time when going into action; it does not neglect Heaven's schedule.

夫唯不爭，壅之則止，決之則流，聽從人也。
"Simply because it does not fight"
Stop it and it halts; direct it and it flows. It complies with people.
故無尤。水性如是，故天下無有怨尤水者也。
"(Water) has no enemy"
Because the nature of water is like this, there is nothing in the world which has any hatred or enmity toward it.


EIGHT
Like qi reaching the lungs, water reaches the shore and rolls over its banks, effortlessly pushing and pulling sediment back into the ocean, washing everything it touches, and nourishing every cell. It does not fight, it does not force, it does not resist, nor can it be fought, forced, or resisted.

    As Heshang Gong points out, "*The people all detest places that are low, damp, dirty, and muddy. Only water quietly circulates and lives there.*" Like water, "people of highest excellence" effortlessly take the position of humility and reach out to those in the humblest of situations. They do not exalt themselves above others but naturally find their place as close to the earth as possible. They may in truth rise up to the clouds, but they never make a show of it, and soon find their way back to the lower or supporting roles, even if they in fact lead from beneath.

Another image in water's reflection of virtue is that people of highest excellence, or "utmost goodness," like water, will flow and break and fall as they travel through life without losing their intrinsic nature. As the kidneys are associated with both water phase and courage,[39] courage is this ability to try and fall and get back up. Courage is not stuck in the fear of change and of the unknown; it adapts and accepts even the low muddy ruts. It is without fear of losing the shape of its ego, for this shape is but a movement of its intrinsic nature. This intrinsic nature is what water keeps intact at all times, not the transitory shapes that it takes on in the course of life's myriad channels. Further, like the Sage, water does not dwell on itself, and so its shan (善, goodness, skill, excellence) never diminishes.

In describing the excellence of water, Lao Zi describes excellence in human character:

Grounded: Water always flows downwards, into the ground, the center, the earth. Those with virtue like water persistently gravitate to being grounded, and finding the center within.

Depth: A heart with immeasurable depth has immeasurable patience, empathy, and love.

Benevolence: It is the nature of water to selflessly benefit others. As such, it is beneficial to all, without discrimination.

Sincerity: With water, you always get water. It does not use artifice, deceit, and flattery. It is always completely water, and reliably acts as such.

Order: Water always returns to being level and even. It fills what is low and washes down what is high, while feeding life all around it. As such it is like good government.

Competence: A highly competent professional can handle all situations of their profession. While things may temporarily obstruct them, it is only a matter of time until they adapt to changing situations. In the same way, water fits any cup, flows down every channel, and adapts to every change.

---

[39] In Chinese medicine, kidney pathologies are associated with fear, while healthy kidneys prevent fear from arising. While the kidneys supply the resiliance of courage, the liver and gallbladder supply its determination.

Timing: Good timing depends on taking action when opportunity presents itself. Water does not hesitate. It always flows in accordance with the stream, and reaches its destination.

# ~ 9 ~

To take hold and continue filling
Is not as good as coming to a stop
If you obsessively refine a spear
It will not be long enough to protect you
If gold and jade fill the court
Nothing can hold onto them
When fortune and wealth bring arrogance
They bring the misfortune of their own loss

When achievements are completed
Their recognition should continue
But the individual should withdraw
This is the way of Heaven

## Chapter Nine
### 運夷 Fortune Through Evenness

持而盈之，不如其已。盈，滿也。已，止也。持滿必傾，不如止也。
"To take hold and continue filling is not as good as coming to a stop"
What is continually filled becomes full. To come to a stop means to desist. To hold something and continue filling it ensures that it will overflow. This is not as good as stopping ahead of time.
揣而梲之，不可長保。揣，治也。先揣之，後必棄捐。
"If you obsessively refine a spear,[40] it will not be long enough to protect you"
This obsessive refining refers to governing. If (the spear or nation) is obsessively refined, it will later be discarded.
金玉滿堂，莫之能守。嗜欲傷神，財多累身。
"If gold and jade fill the court, nothing can hold onto them"
A weakness toward desires injures the spirit. Abundant valuables cause worry for a person.

---

[40] Zhuo (梲) is often translated as "blade," but refers to a wooden joist or weapon, as indicated by the radical for wood at the left side of this character.

富貴而驕，自遺其咎。夫富當賑貧，貴當憐賤，而反驕恣，必被禍患也。
*"When fortune and wealth bring arrogance, they bring the misfortune of their own loss"*
The rich should help the poor and the noble should sympathize with the abject. They should not become proud and indulgent. Otherwise, they will surely be met with suffering and misfortune.

功成、名遂、身退，天之道。言人所為，功成事立，名跡稱遂，不退身避位，則遇於害，此乃天之常道也。譬如日中則移，月滿則虧，物盛則衰，樂極則哀。
*"When achievements are completed, their recognition should continue, but the individual should withdraw. This is the Way of Heaven"*
This refers to when people accomplish things while serving the throne. When they seek fame and renown, and do not step back so as to avoid vying for the throne, they bring great danger to themselves. This is brought about by Heaven's enduring Dao. For example, when the sun reaches its height at mid-day, it then moves downwards. When the moon reaches fullness, it then diminishes its light. Things flourish and then decline again. Music reaches its climax, and then becomes nostalgic.

NINE
Once optimal sharpness has been reached, to continue sharpening will only reduce the implement itself. Trying to do the right thing, trying not to do the wrong thing, there is a point at which one must recognize that they can simply do by not-doing. Removing the drive to do right and avoid doing wrong, one can learn to forget these efforts and follow the effortless course of Dao. As Heshang Gong shows, this principle applies to talents and abilities, as well as any efforts to appear talented or worthy.

# ~ 10 ~

Guard the fortress of your bodily spirits
Embrace Oneness
Can you do this without letting them flee?
Gather together the energy-breath and become soft
This is the power of an infant

Looking deeply
Purify and eliminate
Can you be without flaw?

Caring for the people and governing the nation
Can you be without effort?
Heaven's gate opens and closes
Can you act the part of the female?
With your awareness shining on every corner
Can you be without knowledge?
Giving them life and cultivating them
Giving them life yet not possessing them
Acting for them yet not expecting of them
Leading them forward but not managing them
This is called Fathomless Virtue

# Chapter 10
## 能為 Potential and Action

載營魄，營魄，魂魄也。人載魂魄之上得以生，當愛養之。喜怒亡魂，卒驚傷魄。魂在肝，魄在肺。美酒甘肴，腐人肝肺。故魂靜志道不亂，魄安得壽延年也。

"Guard the fortress of your bodily (po) spirits"
The fortress of bodily spirits refers to one's ethereal spirits (hun) and bodily spirits (po). People carry their ethereal and bodily spirits in order to live. They should cherish them.

    Over-excitement and anger kills the ethereal spirits; over-exertion and fear injure the bodily spirits. The ethereal spirits are in the liver; the bodily spirits are in the lungs. Those who enjoy alcohol and delicacies suffer deterioration of the liver and lungs. When the ethereal spirits are tranquil and focused on Dao, there is no confusion; when the bodily spirits are peaceful, one obtains old age and delays the aging process.

抱一，能無離乎，言人能抱一，使不離於身，則長存。一者，道始所生，太和之精氣也。故曰：一布名於天下，天得一以清，地得一以寧，侯王得一以為正平，入為心，出為行，布施為德，摠名為一。一之為言，志一無二也。

"Embrace Oneness. Can you do this without letting them flee?"[41]
People who can embrace Oneness, and not let it leave them, extend their lives. In Oneness, Dao began to situate life by the supreme harmony of the vital energy-breaths.[42] Therefore it is said: "Oneness covered the world with names."

    Heaven attained Oneness and became clear. Earth attained Oneness and became

---

[41] Li, 離, contains imagery of a rare bird, meaning "flee" like a startled bird, rather than simply "leave, 去, qu."

[42] In Chinese medicine, jing-qi (精氣) generally refers to the energetic essence of a particular organ or phenomena, such as the jing-qi of Heaven, or the jing-qi of the kidneys or lungs, etc. (see *Nei Jing, Ling Shu Jing*, ch. 17). Heshang Gong, uniquely, also refers to the jing-qi of Dao (see chapters 21 and 25).

serene. Lords and kings attained Oneness and became upright and peace-loving. Going within, it is mind; going outwards it is actions; in covering all with its blessing, it is Virtue. All the names together are One. Referring to Oneness, it is said: "In a unified consciousness, there is no division (or doubt)."[43]

專氣致柔，專守精氣使不亂，則形體能應之而柔順。
*"Gather together the energy-breath and become soft"*
Gather and embrace the vital energy-breaths within. Then they will not be chaotic and the body will become soft and pliant.

能嬰兒。能如嬰兒內無思慮，外無政事，則精神不去也。
*"This is the power of an infant"*
Have the power of an infant. Be, internally, without a thought or worry, and externally, without official duties. Then the spiritual vitality will not leave.

滌除玄覽，當洗其心，使潔淨也。心居玄冥之處，覽知萬事，故謂之玄覽也。
*"Looking deeply, purify and eliminate"*
One should wash the heart-mind until it is clean and pure. The heart-mind lives in the fathomless depths of emptiness. Investigate. Know its myriad engagements. This is called "investigating the fathomless."

能無疵。不淫邪也，淨能無疵病乎。
*"Can you be without flaw?"*
Do not be licentious or evil. When purified, one can be without flaw or sickness.

愛民治國，治身者，愛氣則身全；治國者，愛民則國安。
*"Caring for the people and governing the nation"*
Those who govern the body cherish energy-breath and their bodies are thereby maintained. Those who govern the nation cherish the people and the nation is thereby stable and peaceful.

能無為。治身者呼吸精氣，無令耳聞；治國者，佈施惠德，無令下知也。
*"Can you be without effort?"*
Those who govern the body breathe out, and breathe in vital energy-breath without commanding their ears to hear it. Those who govern the nation share kindness and Virtue without commanding those below to know about it.

天門開闔，天門謂北極紫微宮。開闔謂終始五際也。治身：天門謂鼻孔，開謂喘，息闔，謂呼吸也
*"Heaven's gate opens and closes"*
"Heaven's gate" refers to the Purple Point Palace near the North Star. Opening and closing, here, refers to the ending and beginning of the five directions.[44]

In regards to governing the body: Heaven's gate corresponds to the nostrils. To take in a deep breath is "opening." To rest after this is "closing." This refers to exha-

---

[43] Undivided" usually meant "無貳爾心 without doubt (without two) in your heart," but suggests the literal meaning here as well.
[44] The five directions with their elements are: wood/east, fire/south, earth/center, metal/west, and water/north

lation and inhalation.

能為雌。治身當如雌牝，安靜柔弱，治國應變，合而不唱也。
*"Can you act the part of the female?"*
Those who govern the body should be like a female (bird on its nest eggs) – peaceful, still, soft, and gentle. Those who govern the nation should adapt to changes and unite (with the people), rather than sing songs (of conquest and try to appear dominant like the male bird).

明白四達，言達明白，如日月四通，滿於天下八極之外。故曰：視之不見，聽之不聞，彰布之於十方，煥煥煌煌也。
*"With your awareness shining on every corner"*
Pure awareness is like the sun and moon which shine on every corner of the world. They fill the eight directions to the utmost distance. This is called "observing without seeing, and listening without hearing." Their presence covers the ten directions in luminous brilliance.

能無知。無有能知道滿於天下者。
*"Can you be without knowledge?"*
It is not possible to understand how Dao permeates the world.

生之、畜之。道生萬物而畜養之。
*"Giving them life and cultivating them"*
Dao gives birth to the myriad things, cultivates them, and supports them.

生而不有，道生萬物，無所取有。
*"Giving them life yet not possessing them"*
Dao gives birth to the myriad things but does not take ownership of them.

為而不恃，道所施為，不恃望其報也。
*"Acting for them yet not expecting of them"*
The Dao gives, yet does not seek any reciprocation.

長而不宰，道長養萬物，不宰割以為器用。
*"Leading them forward but not managing them"*
Dao leads the myriad things toward longevity; it supports them but does not decide where they must stop. It simply makes them into useful vessels.

是謂玄德。言道行德，玄冥不可得見，欲使人如道也。
*"This is called Fathomless Virtue"*
This is to say that Dao advances a Virtue which is unfathomable. One cannot obtain a glance of it and so should only desire to accord with Dao.

## TEN

As Heshang Gong explains in chapter ten, it was through the supreme harmony of vital qi (太和之精氣) that Dao gave rise to all things. This vital essence unites all things, and is within all things. To embrace the supreme harmony of vital essence is to, as Lao Zi says, "embrace oneness" and thereby hold onto the yin spirits (po) that preserve our earthly bodies. To do this, according to Heshang Gong, we must be unified in our resolve – to be of one mind. As shown throughout Heshang Gong's commentary, and other Classical Daoist literature,[45] desires will give rise to emotions and scatter the will. The term *zhi* means will and resolve, while also consciousness, and even *emotions* in early Chinese medical texts. When the *zhi* is unified, it is not divided up into emotions, and the consciousness holds to oneness.

# ~ 11 ~

Thirty spokes join together on one hub
Because the hub is empty
The cart can be used
The surrounding clay makes a pot
And by its emptiness
The pot is used
Door frames and windows are carved out to make a room
And in this emptiness
The room is used
So, substance is gained
And emptiness is used

## Chapter 11
無用 Utilizing Nothingness

三十輻共一轂，古者車三十輻，法月數也。共一轂者，轂中有孔，故眾輻共湊之。治身者當除情去欲，使五藏空虛，神乃歸之。治國者寡能，摠眾弱共使強也。

"Thirty spokes join together on one hub"
The ancient carts had thirty spokes in each wheel, following the average of a lunar month. Together they form one wheel with a hole at the center where the spokes all come together.

When governing the body, one should eliminate strong emotions and abandon desires, so that the five organs are hollow and empty, and their spirits can return.

When governing a nation, a humble ruler can assemble the masses and, by their

---

[45] See, for example, Guigu Zi's "Seven Techniques of Yin Talisman" in Reid, Dan G. *The Thread of Dao: Unraveling Early Daoist Oral Traditions in Guan Zi's Purifying the Heart-Mind (Bai Xin), Art of the Heart-Mind (Xin Shu), and Internal Cultivation (Nei Ye)*. Montreal: Center Ring Publications, 2017.

collective acquiescence, make a powerful nation.

當其無，有車之用。無，謂空虛。轂中空虛，輪得轉行，輿中空虛，人得載其上也。

"Because the hub is empty, the cart can be used"
Nothingness means hollowness and emptiness. Where the center of the wheel is hollow and empty, the wheel is able to turn and move forward. Where the carriage is empty, people can ride in it.

埏埴以為器，埏，和也。埴，土也。和土以為飲食之器。

"The surrounding clay makes a pot"
The periphery, here, refers to harmony. Clay is from the earth. By bringing a harmonious order to the clay, you can make a vessel to drink and eat from.

當其無，有器之用。器中空虛，故得有所盛受。

"And by its emptiness, the pot is used"
The vessel's center is hollow and empty. Thus when something is obtained, there is a space to receive and be filled.

鑿戶牖以為室，謂作屋室。

"Door frames and windows are carved out to make a room"
This refers to building the rooms of a house.

當其無有室之用。言戶牖空虛，人得以出入觀視；室中空虛，人得以居處，是其用。

"And in this emptiness, the room is used"
Doors and windows are made hollow and empty so that people can enter, leave, and look out to see what is there. Rooms are made empty so that people can sit and live in them. This is how they are used.

故有之以為利，利，物也，利於形用。器中有物，室中有人，恐其屋破壞，腹中有神，畏其形亡也。

"So, substance is gained"
We gain things. Things which have form are useful. Within vessels, there are things. Within rooms, there are people who worry that the home will fall to ruin. Within the belly, there is a spirit which fears the form will die.

無之以為用。言虛空者乃可用盛受萬物，故曰虛無能制有形。道者空也。

"And emptiness is used"
That which is empty and hollow can be used. It can receive, and be filled with innumerable things. Thus, it is said: "Empty nothingness can establish the existence of forms." Dao is this hollowness.


ELEVEN
According to the ancient Chinese, the heart holds the mind, and the body is inextricably affected by the heart-mind. When the mind and emotions are full, the physical body suffers, with certain emotions putting stress on particular organs. For example, anger burdens the liver, euphoria burdens the heart, excessive

thinking burdens the spleen, sadness burdens the lungs, and fear burdens the kidneys. According to Daoist teachings, the root of emotion is craving, for emotions generally arise from either a fear of loss, the sadness of loss, thinking to avoid loss, the euphoria of attaining what one craves, or anger for not attaining what one craves. Thus, Heshang Gong explains in chapter 11: "When governing the body, one should eliminate strong emotions and abandon desires, so that the five organs are hollow and empty, and their spirits can return."

Perhaps the best way to understand the organ-spirits is as the intrinsic intelligence of the organs. An organ's effortless mastery of role and function requires the continued fulfillment of its intrinsic, spontaneous, nature. When a person is disturbed by emotions, they may feel "not themselves," and exhibit dysfunctional behaviours as though their spirit has become occupied elsewhere. If they find the time to relax and move on from whatever inflamed their emotions, they will again feel "themselves" and respond to things from a more integrated, centered, and balanced mental-emotional state. Similarly, when the organs are burdened by emotions, they may not "act themselves," and as a result become dysfunctional. Alleviating the burden of emotions, they may once again function peacefully, harmoniously, and for the benefit of the whole organism. Clarifying the body and organs, as Heshang Gong points out, is a fitting inference when Lao Zi says "Thirty spokes join together on one hub," referring to the empty center of a wheel that represents both the body and the universe. If the center was not empty, the cart's axle could not attach to it, and the cart could not move.

# ~ 12 ~

The five colours blind the eyes
The five tones deafen the ears
The five flavours numb the mouth
The intensity of the hunt
Makes the mind go mad
Goods which are difficult to obtain
Interfere with one's journey
Thus, sages are guided by their stomachs
And not by their eyes
Leaving that
They take this

# Chapter 12
## 檢欲 Examining Desires

五色令人目盲；貪淫好色，則傷精失明也。
"The five colours blind the eyes"
Greed and lust for beautiful appearances cause injury to the vital essence and loss of brilliance.

五音令人耳聾；好聽五音，則和氣去心，不能聽無聲之聲。
"The five tones deafen the ears"
If one longs to hear the five notes, harmonious energy-breath leaves the heart and they cannot hear the sound of the soundless.

五味令人口爽；爽，亡也。人嗜於五味於口，則口亡，言失於道也。
"The five flavours numb the mouth"[46]
They excite and destroy it. People who have a weakness for the five flavours end up destroying their mouths. This is to say that they lose Dao.

馳騁畋獵，令人心發狂，人精神好安靜，馳騁呼吸，精神散亡，故發狂也。
"The intensity of the hunt makes the mind go mad"
People's spiritual vitality loves tranquility and stillness. Quickly breathing in and out in haste causes the spiritual vitality to scatter and die. A person then becomes insane.

難得之貨，令人行妨。妨，傷也。難得之貨，謂金銀珠玉，心貪意欲，不知厭足，則行傷身辱也
"Goods which are difficult to obtain interfere with one's journey"
Interfere, here, means to injure. "Goods which are difficult to obtain" refers to gold, silver, precious stones, and jade. The heart-mind which is greedy, and thinks about what it desires does not know how to be content when it has enough. This causes one's journey to suffer and their character to be insulted.

是以聖人為腹，守五性，去六情，節志氣，養神明。
"Thus, sages are guided by their stomachs"
By guarding the five intrinsic natures, abandoning the six emotions,[47] and uniting the energy-breath of the will,[48] spiritual intelligence is cultivated.

不為目，目不妄視，妄視泄精於外。
"And not by their eyes"

---

[46] The commentary here suggests that a great desire for these things makes one no longer able to perceive them.
[47] See footnote in chapter six for an explanation of the five intrinsic natures and the six emotions.
[48] 志 Zhi, intention, will, resolve, consciousness.
There are also "five wills, 五志 (wuzhi)." These are emotional states associated with the five organs, which can exist in balance, but cause the six emotions when imbalanced.
The five wills and their correspondences are: vigor/anger 怒(nu) in the liver, love/over-excitement 喜(xi) in the heart, contemplation/worry 思(si) in the spleen, nostalgia/sorrow 悲(bei) in the lungs, and awe/fear 恐(kong) in the kidneys.

The eyes should not look frantically. Regarding frantically leaks out vital essence.
故去彼取此。去彼目之妄視，取此腹之養性。
"Leaving that, they take this"
They leave frantic looking, and take the cultivation of pure nature (xing) by way of the stomach.[49]

TWELVE
Following his comments in chapter 11 on the absence of desire and emotion, Heshang Gong explains that chapter 12 speaks to the consequences of desire and emotion. Seeking only what we crave, it is easy to miss the adequacy of what is available. Learning to "leave that and take this," nearly everything can be appreciated for the deeper experience of life that it affords. Doing so, however, requires that we first become "empty," and open to "this."

# ~ 13 ~

Favour and disgrace are both startling
Appreciate the great worrying
That both of these cause in your body
What is meant by favour and disgrace?
To be disgraced is to be put down
Winning is startling
Losing is startling
This means that favour and disgrace are both startling

What does it mean to say "Appreciate the great worrying
That both of these cause in your body?"
The reason I have great worries is because I have a self
If I did not have a self, what worries would I have?

Therefore, those who make the world to be their own self
And value it as such
On them the world can rely
Those who make the world to be their own self
And care for it as such
To them the world can be entrusted

---
[49] May refer to the "dantien" energy center below the navel

# Chapter 13
## 厭恥 Detest and Humiliation

寵辱若驚，身寵亦驚，身辱亦驚。
"Favour and disgrace are both startling"
When a person is favoured, they are startled. When they are disgraced, they are also startled.

貴大患若身。貴，畏也。若，至也。謂大患至身，故皆驚。
"Appreciate the great worrying that both of these cause in your body"
Appreciate, here, means fear. Cause, here, means bring. This means that great suffering is brought to the person, and so they should both be feared.

何謂寵辱。問何謂寵，何謂辱。寵者尊榮，辱者恥辱。及身還自問者，以曉人也。
"What is meant by favour and disgrace?"
What is favour? What is disgrace? To be favoured is to be respected and honoured. To be disgraced is to be shamed and humiliated. In regards to self (cultivation), one examines themselves when they are exposed to others.

辱為下，辱為下賤。
"To be disgraced is to be put down"
To be disgraced is to be lowered and devalued.

得之若驚，得寵榮驚者，處高位如臨深危也。貴不敢驕，富不敢奢。
"Winning is startling"
Obtaining favour and honour is startling. Maintaining high position is like constantly approaching dangerous depths. The honoured should never dare to be proud, and the rich should never dare to be extravagant.

失之若驚，失者，失寵處辱也。驚者，恐禍重來也。
"Losing is startling"
To lose, here, means to lose favour and be ashamed. Being startled, here, means to fear danger and concern oneself with its approach.

是謂寵辱若驚。解上得之若驚，失之若驚。
"This means that favour and disgrace are both startling"
Summarizing the above, to obtain them is startling and to lose them is startling.

何謂貴大患若身。復還自問：何故畏大患至身。
"What does it mean to say "appreciate the great worrying that both of these cause in your body?""
Going back to reflect on the question: "for what reason do fear and worry arrive in oneself?"

吾所以有大患者，為吾有身。吾所以有大患者，為吾有身。有身憂者，勤勞念其飢寒，觸情從欲，則遇禍患也。

*"The reason I have great worries is because I have a self"*
The reason I have great worries is because I have a self. Having a self causes one to have grief, to focus laboriously on thoughts about starving and freezing, to be stricken with strong emotions, and to be compelled by desires. This is how one approaches misfortune and worries.

及吾無身，吾何有患。使吾無有身體，得道自然，輕舉昇雲，出入無間，與道通神，當有何患。

*"If I did not have a self, what worries would I have?"*
If I did not have a body, I could obtain the natural spontaneity of Dao; I could be light enough to ascend peacefully into the clouds; I could leave and enter without there being any opening; I could follow Dao's urgings to my spirit. What trouble, then, would I have?

故貴以身為天下者，則可寄天下，言人君貴其身而賤人，欲為天下主者，則可寄立，不可以久也

*"Therefore, those who make the world to be their own self, and value it as such – on them the world can rely"*
Lao Zi is saying that rulers who appreciate themselves, while not others, have the desire to be king of the world. Though they might take the throne, they cannot keep it for long.

愛以身為天下，若可託天下。言人君能愛其身，非為己也，乃欲為萬民之父母。以此得為天下主者，乃可以託其身於萬民之上，長無咎也。

*"Those who make the world to be their own self, and care for it as such – to them the world can be entrusted"*
Lao Zi is saying that rulers who are able to cherish themselves, but not act for themselves, will desire to be father and mother of the myriad people. As a result, they can obtain kingship of the world. They can be trusted to put the selves of the myriad people above their own, and so will lead without error.


THIRTEEN
Heshang Gong explains that being content with oneself, rather than envying the power, prestige, privilege, personality, or possessions of others, is indispensable to the Dao of Lao Zi. Such envy moves away from "this" in search of the ephemeral "that."[50] A moment of praise is startling to Lao Zi because it puts him at risk of clinging to the idea of "self," placing himself above others, and seeking external assurances and satisfaction for this self. Thus, the final lines of chapter thirteen read, more literally, "When he values himself as he values the world, the world can rely on him. When he loves himself as he loves the world, the world can be entrusted to him." The world is endangered by leaders who are unable to

---

[50] See chapter 12

find this value and love within themselves, for rarely will someone truly value and love people they've never met if they lack this value and love for themselves. These last lines also differentiate between valuing and loving (caring) because valuing something doesn't necessarily mean that we always take care of it. We may even harm it in an effort to possess it. Thus the Sage, beyond simply valuing his or her body, takes care of it, loves, nourishes, and cherishes it.

Paradoxically, to take care of the shen (身), simultaneously meaning *self*, *body*, and *character*, one must transcend it. Craving too many external things, one inevitably neglects themselves at their most basic levels, leading to the blind pursuit of wealth, glory, pride, and pleasure in an attempt to assuage a deepening sense of lack or failure. As explained in chapter 72:

> Therefore, the Sage knows himself
> But does not display himself
> Loves and cares for himself
> But does not overestimate himself
> He abandons that and chooses this

The love, *ai*, that Lao Zi refers to here is compassionate, heartfelt, accepting, nurturing, forgiving, and beneficent. Such traits embody the Sage as much as those of modesty and equanimity; thus, holding such feelings toward oneself is as good a place to start as any. From this foundation, they may expand and grow in power until reaching those close to us, and in due time to the rest of humanity. As expressed in chapter 81: "Sages do not hoard. Having helped others, oneself gains more; having given to others, oneself continues to gain." By dismantling our urges to dominate others, we can begin to shed the obfuscations of egotism.

# ~ 14 ~

By looking, it is not seen
It is known as Clear
By listening, it is not heard
It is known as Inaudible
What cannot be obtained when seized
Is known as Infinitesimal
These three things cannot be inspected
And are merged into one

Above, it is not bright
Below, it is not dark
Immeasurable and unnameable

It is again nothing
This is called "having no form or appearance"

Without a materialized image
This is called "absent-minded"
Greet it and you do not see its front
Follow it and you do not see its rear
Hold to the ancient Dao and ride it until you possess the present
Then you can know the ancient beginning
This is called "the thread of Dao"

# Chapter 14
## 贊玄 Assistance from the Fathomless

視之不見名曰夷，無色曰夷。言一無采色，不可得視而見之。
"By looking, it is not seen. It is known as Clear."
What is without colour and appearance is called Clear. This is to say that Oneness is without accumulated colour and appearance. It cannot be inspected or observed.
聽之不見名曰希，無聲曰希。言一無音聲，不可得聽而聞之。
"By listening, it is not heard. It is known as Inaudible."
What is without sound is called Inaudible. This is to say that Oneness is without tone and pitch. It cannot be listened to or heard.
搏之不得名曰微。無形曰微。言一無形體，不可搏持而得之。
"What cannot be obtained when seized is known as Infinitesimal"
What is without form is called Infinitesimal. This is to say that Oneness is without form or body. It cannot be touched or held.
此三者不可致詰，三者，謂夷、希、微也。不可致詰者，夫無色、無聲、無形，口不能言，書不能傳，當受之以靜，求之以神，不可問詰而得之也。
"These three things cannot be inspected"
"These three" refers to the Clear, Inaudible, and Infinitesimal. It is not possible to inspect what has no colour or appearance, no sound, and no form; no mouth that can speak, nor a book which can transmit. You should receive it by stillness and seek it by the spirit. You cannot attain it through interrogation.
故混而為一。混，合也。故合於三名之為一。
"And are merged into one"
To be merged is to be combined. These three names are combined to make one.

其上不皦，言一在天上，不皦。皦，光明。
"Above, it is not bright"
Oneness in the Heavens is not bright. It is not bright, shining, or brilliant.
其下不昧。言一在天下，不昧。昧，有所闇冥。

"Below, it is not dark"
Oneness in the world is not dark. It is not dark, dismal, or gloomy.

繩繩不可名，繩繩者，動行無窮極也。不可名者，非一色也，不可以青黃白黑別，非一聲也，不可以宮商角徵羽聽，非一形也，不可以長短大小度之也。

"Immeasurable and unnameable"
What is immeasurable continues on without stopping. It cannot be named because it has not even a single colour; thus, it cannot be named blue, green, yellow, white, black, or any other colour. It has not even a single pitch, and so it cannot be named after (any of the five pitches) doh, ray, me, so, or la, which may be heard. It has not even a single form, and so cannot be named long, short, large, small, or any other measurement.

復歸於無物。物，質也。復當歸之於無質。

"It is again nothing"
"Nothing," here, means without any substance. As it also returns, one should return to it in nothingness.

是謂無狀之狀，言一無形狀，而能為萬物作形狀也。

"This is called 'having no form or appearance'"
Oneness is without any form or appearance, yet can cause the myriad things to take on their own forms and appearances.

無物之象，一無物質，而為萬物設形象也。

"Without a materialized image"
Oneness is without any materialized substance, yet it can cause the myriad things to display their own forms and images.

是謂惚恍。一忽忽恍恍者，若存若亡，不可見之也。

"This is called 'absent-minded'"
Oneness is sudden, abrupt, and seemingly absent-minded. It is as though existing, and as though not existing. It cannot be seen.

迎之不見其首，一無端末，不可預待也。除情去欲，一自歸之也。

"Greet it and you do not see its front"
Oneness is without any end or beginning, so you cannot welcome it. Eliminate strong emotions and abandon desires. Oneness will then return of its own accord.

隨之不見其後，言一無影跡，不可得而看。

"Follow it and you do not see its rear"
Oneness has no tracks or shadows. It cannot be obtained by tracking it.

執古之道，以御今之有，聖人執守古道，生一以御物，知今當有一也。

"Hold to the ancient Dao and ride it until you possess the present"
Sages hold and embrace the ancient Dao which gave birth to Oneness and allowed them to commandeer things. Understand the present by holding onto Oneness.

能知古始，是謂道紀。人能知上古本始有一，是謂知道綱紀也。

"Then you can know the ancient beginning. This is called the thread of Dao"

People are able to know the foundation and beginning of the highest antiquity by holding Oneness. This is called "knowing the thread of Dao."

FOURTEEN
Just as health is forgotten when illness disappears, and shoes are forgotten when they are well fitting, we reside in the Oneness of non-differentiation when the harmony of Dao naturally returns. Likes and dislikes, distractions and uncertainty, anger, sadness, euphoria, anxiety, and fears, are all born of our ability or inability to attain the objects of our desires. While these experiences may eventually encourage us to find the harmony of Dao and reveal to us its importance, in their absence, Dao alights, though its very presence makes us unable to detect it. This limited capacity to express the notion of Dao may be hinted at in DDJ chapter one – "always without desires, observing its inner subtlety; always with desires, observing its outer surface."

As Heshang Gong shows in his last two comments on chapter 14, holding to this Oneness, we are able to become the active, rather than reactive, party in our own lives. The *Nei Ye* ("*Internal Cultivation*," c. 350 BC) also explains this role of Oneness as being the precursor to bringing about creation and change:

> With Oneness, things can be transformed. We call this spirit.
> With Oneness, situations can be changed. We call this wisdom.
> Transforming (things) without altering breath,
> Changing (situations) without altering wisdom:
> Only the junzi who maintains Oneness can do this.
> Holding Oneness and not losing it,
> They can preside over the myriad things.
> The junzi then conducts things,
> And is not conducted by things,
> (Having) attained the principle of Oneness.

# ~ 15 ~

Ancient and knowledgeable masters
The subtle mystery in them explored the fathomless
Unfathomably deep
They cannot be comprehended
So I will try to describe their appearances

Patient! As though crossing a stream in winter

Blending in! As though fearing neighbours from all directions
Respectful! As though guests in another's house
Flowing! Like thawed ice
Candid and sincere! Plain as wood
Broad and open! Like a valley
United! Like muddy water
Who, by the power of their stillness
Can make clouded water slowly become clear?
Who, by the power of their serenity
Can long sustain this progress until life slowly arises?
Those who maintain this Dao do not desire fullness
It is because they are not full that they can remain covered
And not let what is new come to an end

# Chapter 15
顯德 Manifestions of Virtue

古之善為士者，謂得道之君也。
"Ancient and knowledgeable masters"
This refers to rulers who obtained Dao.
微妙玄通，玄，天也。言其志節玄妙，精與天通也。
"The subtle mystery in them explored the fathomless"
The fathomless, here, means "Heaven." Lao Zi is saying that their will joined with the fathomless mystery, and their vital essence followed the urgings of Heaven.
深不可識。道德深遠，不可識知，內視若盲，反聽若聲，莫知所長。
"Unfathomably deep"
Dao's Virtue is of such great depth that it is unknowable. To look for it within, one is as though blind. To listen back for it, one is as though deaf. Its length cannot be known.
夫唯不可識，故強為之容。謂下句也。
"They cannot be comprehended, so I will try to describe their appearances"
Referring to the following sentences.

與兮若冬涉川；舉事輒加重慎與。與兮若冬涉川，心難之也。
"Patient! As though crossing a stream in winter"
When taking up affairs, they took great caution. Patient! As though crossing a stream in winter, they were mindful of difficulty.
猶兮若畏四鄰；其進退猶猶如拘制，若人犯法，畏四鄰知之也。
"Blending in! As though fearing neighbours from all directions"
When advancing or retreating, they would blend in as though adhering to an estab-

lished system, or like a person committing a crime who is afraid that his neighbours will find out.

儼兮其若客；如客畏主人，儼然無所造作也。
"Respectful! As though guests in another's house"
As though guests in the house of a fearsome and powerful person, they were naturally respectful and not obsequious.

渙兮若冰之將釋，渙者，解散。釋者，消亡。除情去欲，日以空虛。
"Flowing! Like thawed ice"
That which disperses (flows) is loosened and then scattered. When ice releases water, it melts away until completely gone. Remove strong emotions and abandon desires until there is emptiness and hollowness.

敦兮其若樸，敦者，質厚。樸者，形未分。內守精神，外無文采也。
"Candid and sincere! Plain as wood"
Those who are candid and sincere are of real substance; plain wood has a form which has not been altered. Internally, hold on to your spiritual vitality; externally, be without learned accumulations.

曠兮其若谷；曠者，寬大。谷者，空虛。不有德功名，無所不包也。
"Broad and open! Like a valley"
That which is broad is vast and open; a valley is empty and hollow – it does not have virtue, achievement, or fame, yet there is nothing it does not embrace.

渾兮其若濁。渾者，守本真，濁者，不照然。與眾合同，不自專也。
"United! Like muddy water"
That which is united embraces the foundation of reality. It is not the nature of muddy water to shine. (The ancient masters) associated with the masses and united as one with them. They were not concerned only with themselves.

孰能濁以靜之，徐清。孰，誰也。誰能知水之濁止而靜之，徐徐自清也。
"Who, by the power of their stillness, can make clouded water slowly become clear?"
Who can know how to make disturbed water stop and become still – to slowly and quietly clarify oneself?

孰能安以久動之，徐生。誰能安靜以久，徐徐以長生也。
"Who, by the power of their serenity, can long sustain this progress until life slowly arises?"
Who has the power to remain stable and clear – to slowly and calmly lengthen life?

保此道者，不欲盈。保此徐生之道，不欲奢泰盈溢。
"Those who maintain this Dao do not desire fullness"
Protecting this quiet calm is the Dao of (cultivating) life. Do not desire to be extravagant or exalted, to fill up and spill over.

夫惟不盈，故能蔽不新成。夫為不盈滿之人，能守蔽不為新成。蔽者，匿光榮也。新成者，貴功名。

*"It is because they are not full that they can remain covered, and not let what is new come to an end"*

Those who do not fill to overflowing can remain covered up and not let what is new come to an end. Those who conceal, hide their light from glory; those who do not let what is new come to an end, accomplish praiseworthy things without becoming famous.

## FIFTEEN

The first adjective applied here to the ancient masters, Yu (與), generally has a grammatical function of showing compliance or connection between elements, with a more literal meaning of companionship. It appears to suggest, in this instance, that the sages were attentive and adaptive in their interactions with others, not rushing over them but rather being soft and accomodating. This is like unifying with the frozen stream and adapting to the exchange of pressure between one's feet and the water under the ice. As river ice is never very thick, one must be careful not to apply any pressure to the ice until they are sure it is safe. Such wisdom may also apply in precarious interpersonal situations.

Heshang Gong explains that the ancient masters (literally "the ancient scholar-gentlemen of excellence") did not display their skill and power. Like King Yu the Great (c. 2100 BC), who worked alongside his people to irrigate the land and transform the yearly floods into a blessing for the interior villages, these masters were able to overcome any sense of self-importance. Having conquered this shortcoming, so common in powerful leaders, few would even recognize their nobility.

Holding to Dao, desires eventually melt away (see Heshang Gong's comment on "Flowing! Like thawed ice"). In the same way that desires melt away, so must the assumed authority of ego. This refining and purifying eventually reveals the nameless pearl within,[51] and so these masters did not latch on to any such achievements or merits, even transcending attachment to namelessness when the need for a doctor, strategist, scholar, or king, arose.

The cleansing of self-importance is not only effective in spiritual-cultivation, but also supports one's physical-cultivation – two sides of the same coin for Daoists – as it allows one to process situations without becoming emotionally wrapped-up in egoic obsessions that disturb the jing-qi (vital energy-breaths) and jing-shen[52] (spiritual vitality). As Heshang Gong states in regards to *desiring fullness* (second-last line): "Protecting this quiet calm is the Dao of (cultivating) life. Do not desire to be extravagant or exalted, to fill up and spill over."

---

[51] See HSG's comments on "the eternal name" in chapter one.
[52] In *Rooted in Spirit: The Heart of Chinese Medicine*, Claude Larre and Elisabeth Rochat de la Valee explain jing-shen as the combined essences of the kidney's essence and heart's spirit. See footnote in chapter 10, above, for an explanation of jing-qi.

# ~ 16 ~

Arrive at supreme emptiness
Embrace deep silence
Myriad creatures arise together
I thereby observe them returning
So many things blossoming
And each returns back to its roots

Returning to the roots is called silence
This means returning to one's destiny-life-force (ming)
Returning to one's destiny-life-force is called eternality
Understanding eternality is called enlightenment
Oblivious to eternality, one is reckless
And author of their own misfortune

Know how to embrace eternality
This embrace shows the way of impartiality
The way of impartiality shows the way of a king
The way of a king shows the way of Heaven
The way of Heaven shows the way of Dao
The way of Dao shows the way of longevity
And for the body to be without peril

## Chapter 16
歸根 Return to the Root

致虛極，得道之人，捐情去欲，五內清靜，至於虛極。
"Arrive at supreme emptiness"
Become a man of Dao. Give up strong emotions and discard desires. Then the five internal organs will be clear and tranquil, arriving at supreme emptiness.
守靜篤，守清靜，行篤厚。
"Embrace deep silence"
Hold onto clarity and tranquility until it is deep and substantial.
萬物並作，作，生也。萬物並生也。
"Myriad creatures arise together"
Arise, here, means they are born. The myriad creatures are born side by side.
吾以觀復。言吾以觀見萬物無不皆歸其本也。人當念重其本也。
"I thereby observe them returning"
Lao Zi is saying "I watch and observe the myriad creatures, and there is not one

which does not return to the root foundation." People should consider the heaviness of the foundation.[53]

夫物芸芸，芸芸者，華葉盛也。
"So many things blossoming"
Blossoming refers to abundant flowers and leaves.

各復歸其根，言萬物無不枯落，各復反其根而更生也。
"And each returns back to its roots"
There is not one of the myriad things which does not dry out and fall. Each returns back to the root, and then many more are born.

歸根曰靜，靜謂根也。根安靜柔弱，謙卑處下，故不復死也。
"Returning to the roots is called silence"
Silence is another word for the root. The root is peaceful and still, soft and pliant. Modestly and humbly, it remains below. Thus, it does not return to death.

是謂復命。言安靜者是為復還性命，使不死也。
"This means returning to one's destiny-life-force (ming)"
Lao Zi is saying that peace and stillness are the correct way to return to pure nature (xing) and the destiny-life-force (ming). Then one will not die.

復命曰常。復命使不死，乃道之所常行也。
"Returning to one's destiny-life-force is called eternality"
By returning (to) the destiny-life-force, one will not die but will follow Dao eternally.

知常曰明；能知道之所常行，則為明。
"Understanding eternality is called enlightenment"
Knowing how to follow Dao at all times is to be enlightened.

不知常，妄作凶。不知道之所常行，妄作巧詐，則失神明，故凶也。
"Oblivious to eternality, one is reckless, and author of their own misfortune"
Not knowing how to follow Dao at all times, people recklessly work on developing deceptive skills. As a result, they lose spiritual intelligence. Disaster then befalls them.

知常容，能知道之所常行，去情忘欲，無所不包容也。
"Know how to embrace eternality"
Know how to follow Dao at all times. Leave strong emotions and forget desires. Then there will be nothing which is not wrapped in this embrace.

容乃公，無所不包容，則公正無私，眾邪莫當。
"This embrace shows the way of impartiality"[54]
When there is nothing which is not wrapped in this embrace, there is impartiality, uprightness, and unselfishness. No wickedness can obstruct it.

公乃王，公正無私，可以為天下王。治身正則形一，神明千萬，共湊其躬也。

---

[53] See chapter 26, "The Virtue of Heaviness."
[54] 公 (gong) means both "elder" (as in Heshang Gong) and "impartial," as in serving the public, rather than private, interest.

*"The way of impartiality shows the way of a king"*
Impartial, honourable, and unselfish, one can become king of all under Heaven. By governing and aligning the body, form is unified. Countless spiritual lights then assemble in the body.

王乃天，能王，德合神明，乃與天通。
*"The way of a king shows the way of Heaven"*
Being a king, here, means that Virtue will gather spiritual lights and allow you to communicate with the Heavens.

天乃道，德與天通，則與道合同也。
*"The way of Heaven shows the way of Dao"*
When Virtue allows communication with the Heavens, you follow Dao and become united as one with it.

道乃久。與道合同，乃能長久。
*"The way of Dao shows the way of longevity"*
Following Dao and becoming united with it, one can endure indefinitely.

沒身不殆。能公能王，通天合道，四者純備，道德弘遠，無殃無咎，乃與天地俱沒，不危殆也。
*"And for the body to be without peril"*
If one can follow the way of impartiality and kings, they communicate with Heaven and unite with Dao. These four things prepare one for Dao and Virtue to expand immensely. One will be without misfortune and without error. Then they can be a companion of Heaven and Earth until both have disappeared, yet they will not be endangered.

## SIXTEEN

Ancient Chinese doctors observed that the kidneys, liver, heart, spleen, and lungs were harmed by fear, anger, euphoria, anxiety, and sadness, respectively.[55] Heshang Gong shows in chapter 16 that silence-and-stillness (jing, 靜) is the root from which the nourishment of Heaven, Earth, Virtue, and Dao reaches the body and mind. By abstaining from strong emotions and moving away from desires, we clear the paths through which this nourishment will travel. By connecting to this root, we also reconnect with the spiritual intelligence (shen ming), housed within the heart-mind. This spiritual intelligence allows the heart-mind to gain sovereignty over the emotions and thereby establish itself as the active leader in our lives – rather than a reactive head, and leader in name only.

---

[55] While moderate yet prolonged emotions can have this effect, it is generally intense and frantic emotions that bring about pathologies related to the respective organs. For example, intense and frantic euphoria will quickly wear out the heart, while general happiness is excellent for overall health and immunity. The wood phase of the liver may express itself healthfully in the strength of the muscles and in one's determination; however, if one becomes upset with circumstances and lashes out in anger, this weakens the liver. The weakened liver may then make it more difficult to express the wood phase healthfully as determination, and result in its unhealthy expression as anger.

This clarity of spirit allows for the impartiality, broader consideration and non-differentiation suggested in the word gong (公), otherwise translated as public – the opposite of private (私, si). Gong also means respected elder, as in Heshang Gong (Riverside Elder). Such an elder is a "man of the people." He sees his community as his family, and the community knows they can trust him with their welfare, for his interests are public rather than private, or selfish (私). In this way, gong also means "impartial." Heshang Gong explains that the way of the gong (elder) is impartial, honourable (upright), and without selfishness (公正無私). Without selfishness, leadership becomes effortless as people naturally cooperate with someone who truly seeks their benefit.

By connecting to the root (silence and stillness), one becomes peaceful like the gong, thereby attaining the sovereignty of the heart-mind. As such, they no longer act out of likes and dislikes, fears, or desires, and so move with the Way of Heaven and the unencumbered nature of Dao. As Lao Zi says in chapter 25:

> Man is regulated by Earth
> Earth is regulated by Heaven
> Heaven is regulated by Dao
> Dao is regulated by its own spontaneous nature (zi ran)

No longer reacting and following the fears and desires of the body, the heart-mind follows the way of Heaven and the spontaneous nature of Dao, leading one back to their pure nature (xing) and destiny-life-force (ming). Reaching pure nature and destiny-life-force, one is sure to live a long and vibrant life.

# ~ 17 ~

The forefathers of the empire
Were simply known to exist by those below
Next were those with a wide reputation for being loved
Next were those who were feared
Next were those who were reviled
Their sincerity was insufficient!
Of the consequence of words, take great heed!
When accomplishments are completed and left behind
The hundred families all say "We did it naturally"

# Chapter 17
## 淳風 (The Sounds of) Simplicity in the Wind

太上，下知有之。太上，謂太古無名之君。下知有之者，下知上有君，而不臣事，質朴也。

"The forefathers of the empire were simply known to exist by those below"

"The forefathers of the empire" refer to the most ancient rulers who are now unknown.[56] "Are simply known to exist by those below" means that the lower classes knew of a ruler above them but not of his ministers' works. (This is because) things remained in their unaltered states.

其次，親之譽之。其德可見，恩惠可稱，故親愛而譽之。

"Next were those with a wide reputation for being loved"

Their virtue could be seen, and their charity and kindness could be recognized. Thus, they were loved and praised.

其次畏之。設刑法以治之。

"Next were those who were feared"

They governed by establishing punishments and laws.

其次侮之。禁多令煩，不可歸誠，故欺侮之。

"Next were those who were reviled"

To have many prohibitions causes many troubles. The nation could not return to sincerity and truth, so the people were not honest with these rulers, but secretly reviled them.

信不足焉。君信不足於下，下則應之以不信，而欺其君也。

"Their sincerity was insufficient!"

When the ruler's sincerity is not sufficient toward those below him, those below him follow his example, act insincerely, and try to cheat the ruler.

猶兮其貴言。說太上之君，舉事猶，貴重於言，恐離道失自然也。

"Of the consequence of words, take great heed!"

The forefathers of the emperor measured their actions against this standard. They honoured the seriousness of words for fear of moving away from Dao and losing their natural spontaneity.

功成事遂，謂天下太平也。

"When accomplishments are completed and left behind"

This refers to the peace which existed during the time of the forefathers.

百姓皆謂我自然。百姓不知君上之德淳厚，反以為己自當然也。

"The hundred families all say 'we did it naturally'"

When the hundred families do not know of the ruler's superior virtue and authenticity,

---

[56] "太上" also appears in various ancient books with the meaning "great antiquity" (trans. Legge) Given its reference to ancient rulers here, taishang may have suggested Taishang Huang: "太上皇 Emperor's Father; 'Puppet Master.'" Please also see footnote in chapter 19 regarding the Three Sovereigns.

they rediscover the natural spontaneity within themselves.

SEVENTEEN
Like the Dao itself, the legendary ancient leaders did not use harsh controls to maintain peace. They simply arranged society in a way that would serve humanity and provide what was needed for people to pursue their means. Consequently, none had to struggle hopelessly to meet their ends, crime and punishment were unnecessary, and people enjoyed the richness of living cooperatively and appreciating all the little miracles that make existence possible. They did not feel obligated to acknowledge the throne but simply went about life as water rolling down the stream. Heshang Gong alludes to this in chapter 10 when he writes:

> Those who govern the body breathe out, and breathe in the vital energy-breaths without commanding their ears to hear it. Those who govern the nation share kindness and Virtue without commanding those below to know about it.

We could take the first rulers in chapter 17 as a metaphor for spiritual intelligence (shen ming). When the individual is regulated by the spontaneous nature of Dao, they no longer feel the limitations of mind, nor a necessity for the mind to follow and dictate. They can do without doing and know without knowing, for the one who sits in the throne is not so obsessed, and possessed, by their authority.

# ~ 18 ~

When the peacefulness of Dao is abandoned
Benevolence and righteousness appear
When learnedness and intelligence are brought forth
Great deceit appears
When the six family relations are out of harmony
Filial piety appears
When the nation is on the eve of chaos
Loyal ministers appear

# Chapter 18
## 俗薄 The Frailty of Social Custom

大道廢，有仁義。大道之時，家有孝子，戶有忠信，仁義不見也。大道廢不用，惡逆生，乃有仁義可傳道。

*"When the peacefulness of Dao is abandoned, benevolence and righteousness appear"*

During times when there is peace and Dao, children obey their parents and there is loyalty and sincerity in the home. Benevolence and righteousness are not seen. When the peacefulness of Dao is abandoned rather than utilized, hatred and disobedience arise. Then benevolence and righteousness appear in order to restore Dao (in the home).

智慧出，有大偽。智慧之君賤德而貴言，賤質而貴文，下則應之以為大偽姦詐。

*"When learnedness and intelligence are brought forth, great deceit appears"*

When the ruler is knowledgeable and intelligent, he disdains virtue, and values words; he disdains substance, but values ornamentation. The lower classes then follow his example and act with great deceit, debauchery, and fraudulence.

六親不和，有孝慈。六紀絕，親戚不合，乃有孝慈相牧養也。

*"When the six family relations are out of harmony, filial piety appears"*

When the six family relations are broken, parents and relatives do not gather together. Filial piety is then needed to bring them together and make them help each other.

國家昏亂，有忠臣。政令不明，上下相怨，邪僻爭權，乃有忠臣匡正其君也。此言天下太平不知仁，人盡無欲不知廉，各自潔己不知貞。大道之世，仁義沒，孝慈滅，猶日中盛明，眾星失光。

*"When the nation is on the eve of chaos, loyal ministers appear"*

When official orders do not come from a place of enlightenment, those above and below fight with each other and commit atrocious acts in vying for power. loyal ministers then appear to correct the situation, and re-align the ruler (with Dao).

This is to say that when the world has great peace, there is no knowledge of benevolence. People die without desires and do not know anything about being upright. Each person purifies themselves but does not know about virtue. During times of the great peace of Dao, benevolence and right-conduct are submerged and filial piety disappears. This is similar to the brilliant light of mid-day when the multitude of starlights can no longer be seen.


EIGHTEEN

Just as the anonymous rulers of chapter 17 brought order to the nation in a way that seemed to arise naturally, Dao is pervasive when virtues arise naturally rather than being imposed by rules of conduct.

Departing from the peace of Dao, one may experience frustration, impatience, and the deep sense of disconnection and separation that aggravates our selfish impulses. Realizing again an inner harmony and peace that spreads throughout our spirit and energy, this sense of opposition loses its fuel source. Consequently, righteousness, piety, and dedication are subsumed in this Oneness.

# ~ 19 ~

Quit sageliness
Abandon wisdom
And the people will benefit one hundred fold
Quit benevolence, abandon right-conduct
And the people will return to caring for their parents
Quit cleverness, abandon profit
And robbers and thieves will not exist

These three
Are only ornamental, and not satisfactory
Thus, we have the following:
Observe the natural state
Embrace the unaltered
Minimize self-importance
And have few desires

## Chapter 19
還淳 Return to Simplicity

絕聖,絕聖制作,反初守元。五帝垂象,倉頡作書,不如三皇結繩無文。
"Quit sageliness"
Quit building institutions of sageliness. Return to the beginning and embrace the origin. The five emperors passed down knowledge of the constellations and Cang Jie brought forth literacy, but they were not as good as the Three Sovereigns[57] who notated with knotted cords and had no written characters.
棄智,棄智慧,反無為。

---

[57] The Three Sovereigns are: Fuxi, Nuwa, and Shennong. Nuwa (Fuxi's sister) is sometimes substituted in this group with Huang Di, The Yellow Emperor. Fuxi and Nuwa could be described as a god-like Adam and Eve who are also credited with a number of cultural advancements. Shennong is credited with the invention of agriculture and medicine. Huang Di is considered the father of Chinese civilization.

"Abandon wisdom"
Abandon wisdom and intelligence; return to effortlessness.
民利百倍。農事修，公無私。
"And the people will benefit one hundred fold"
They will study farming and agriculture; they will be fair and without selfishness.
絕仁棄義，絕仁之見恩惠，棄義之尚華言。
"Quit benevolence, abandon right-conduct"
Quit benevolent displays of kindness and charity. Abandon right-conduct that emphasizes superficial speech.
民復孝慈。德化淳也。
"And the people will return to caring for their parents"
Their virtue will become sincere.
絕巧棄利，絕巧者，詐偽亂真也。棄利者，塞貪路閉權門也。
"Quit cleverness, abandon profit"
Quit cleverness, swindling, deceit, and confusing the truth. Abandon profit, block the road to greed, and close the doors to power and authority.
盜賊無有。上化公正，下無邪私。
"And robbers and thieves will not exist"
When those above become fair and upright, those below will be without wickedness and selfishness.

此三者，謂上三事所棄絕也。
"These three"
Meaning the above three actions of quitting and abandoning.
以為文不足，以為文不足者，文不足以教民。
"Are only ornamental, and not satisfactory"
They are ornamental and not satisfactory because what is ornamental does not instruct the people satisfactorily.
故令有所屬。當如下句。
"Thus, we have the following:"
Referring to the sentences which follow.
見素抱樸，見素者，當抱素守真，不尚文飾也。抱朴者，當見其篤朴，以示下，故可法則。
"Observe the natural state, embrace the unaltered"
Seeing the natural state, you should embrace the natural state; hold onto reality rather than ornamentation. Embrace unaltered substance. See the genuine unaltered state when it shows itself in the world so that you can abide by its example.
少私寡欲。少私者，正無私也。寡欲者，當知足也。
"Minimize self-importance and have few desires"
Those who minimize self-importance become honourable and without self-importance. Those who have few desires know satisfaction.

## NINETEEN

Lao Zi and Heshang Gong speak to what Chogyam Trungpa (1939-1987) more recently termed "spiritual materialism." This is the trap of letting the materialistic desire to possess things leak into our spiritual development – using our spiritual development as cultural capital or status symbols, and wearing it like a three-piece suit, showing everyone how successful we have become, and feeding this progress to the ravenous ego rather than allowing it to grow and blossom. Lao Zi and Heshang Gong repeatedly warn of displaying our virtues, in hopes that we learn not to bite the hand (Virtue) that feeds us.

## ~ 20 ~

Stop learning
And there will be no grief
Is reluctant acceptance so different from rejection?
What is the difference between good and evil?
People in a fearful place cannot be without fear
Uncultivated! They have not been centered!
The crowd is joyous and buoyant
As though having caught a massive beast
Or celebrating spring rites
I alone am like the clearness of still water
Alas, in this way, making no predictions
Nor making myself predictable
Like a newborn baby
Not yet able to make these distinctions
Roaming! As though having no home to return to

The people in the crowd all have more than they need
But I alone am as one who has lost everything
I have the mind of a simpleton, indeed
Clouded and muddy!
It is customary for people to have clear and cutting perception
I alone am as though in a twilight of understanding
It is customary for people to be fascinated
I alone am as though distant and forlorn

Quick! I am like the ocean

Drifting! As though without any place to stop
The multitudes of people all have purpose
Yet I alone seem stubborn
And unsophisticated

I alone seem strange to others
For I cherish the nourishment of the mother

# Chapter 20
## 異俗 Strange Customs

絕學，絕學不真，不合道文。
"Stop learning"
Stop learning what is not real; do not mix Dao with superficialities.
無憂。除浮華則無憂患也。
"And there will be no grief"
Eliminate flowery and lofty speech and there will be no grief and worry.
唯之與阿，相去幾何。同為應對而相去幾何。疾時賤質而貴文。
"Is reluctant acceptance so different from rejection?"
Both are necessary responses, yet how do they differ? The problem today is that people do not value the substance, but instead value embellishments and appearances.
善之與惡，相去若何。善者稱譽，惡者諫諍，能相去何如。疾時惡忠直，用邪佞也。
"What is the difference between good and evil?"
Those who are good are praised and awarded titles. Those who are evil are admonished and remonstrated. How can these be so different? The problem today is that evil people are loyal to the upright but use their evil to flatter them.
人之所畏，不可不畏。人謂道人也。人所畏者，畏不絕學之君也。不可不畏，近令色，殺仁賢。
"People in a fearful place cannot be without fear"
People, here, refers to people with Dao. People in a fearful place fear that the emperor will not stop learning (false teachings). They cannot be without the fear that he will order the execution of the benevolent and virtuous.
荒兮其未央哉！言世俗人荒亂，欲進學為文，未央止也。
"Uncultivated! They have not been centered!"
The customs of today's people amount to uncultivated chaos. Their desires for advancement, and their study of superficialities, have never been centered or stopped.
眾人熙熙，熙熙，放淫多情欲也。
"The crowd is joyous and buoyant"
Joyous and buoyant, here, means openly licentious, with many desires and strong

emotions.
如享太牢，如飢思太牢之具，意無足時也。
"As though having caught a massive beast"
As though hungry and preparing to slaughter a massive animal.
如春登臺。春，陰陽交通，萬物感動，登台觀之，意志淫淫然。
"Or celebrating spring rites"
In spring, yin and yang mix and pass through each other. The emotions of the myriad things are stirred, and they travel upwards to look at the stars. Their thoughts and intentions burn with licentiousness.
我獨怕兮其未兆，我獨怕然安靜，未有情欲之形兆也。
"I alone am like the clearness of still water, alas, in this way, making no predictions nor making myself predictable"
I alone am apprehensive, and so calm and tranquil – not yet possessing any form or sign of desires and strong emotions.
如嬰兒之未孩。如小兒未能答偶人時也。
"Like a newborn baby, not yet able to make these distinctions"
Like a small child, not yet able to participate in such festivities.
乘乘兮若無所歸。我乘乘如窮鄙，無所歸就。
"Roaming! As though having no home to return to"
I roam about as though poor and with nowhere that I return to or leave from.

眾人皆有餘，眾人餘財以為奢，餘智以為詐。
"The people in the crowd all have more than they need"
When the masses have too many valuables, they waste them; when they have too much cleverness, they use it to cheat others.
而我獨若遺。我獨如遺棄，似於不足也。
"But I alone am as one who has lost everything"
I alone am as though having lost or discarded everything, seeming to not have enough.
我愚人之心也哉，不與俗人相隨，守一不移，如愚人之心也。
"I have the mind of a simpleton, indeed,"
He does not follow the customs that others all partake in together. He embraces Oneness and does not move. This is like someone who has the mind of a simpleton.
沌沌兮。無所分別。
"Clouded and muddy!"
(He abides in Oneness,) without separation or differentiation.
俗人昭昭，明且達也。
"It is customary for people to have clear and cutting perception"
They clearly perceive and define things.
我獨若昏。如闇昧也。
"I alone am as though in a twilight of understanding"

He is as though in the dark and unable to see.
俗人察察，察察，急且疾也。
"It is customary for people to be fascinated"
They are curious and scrutinizing with an urgency that borders on illness.
我獨悶悶。悶悶，無所割截。
"I alone am as though distant and forlorn"
He seems to be in low spirits, as though he was not given his share.

忽兮若海，我獨忽忽，如江海之流，莫知其所窮極也。
"Quick! I am like the ocean"
I alone am sudden and spontaneous, like the Yangtze river flowing into the ocean.
漂兮若無所止。我獨漂漂，若飛若揚，無所止也，志意在神域也。
"Drifting! As though without any place to stop"
I alone am drifting and floating about, as though high, spreading out, and without any place to stop. My will and intention reside in spiritual realms.
眾人皆有以，以，有為也。
"The multitudes of people all have purpose"
Purpose, here, means to be taking action.
而我獨頑，我獨無為。
"Yet I alone seem stubborn"
I alone am not taking action.
似鄙。鄙，似若不逮也。
"And unsophisticated"
He seems as though un-ambitious.

我獨異於人, 我獨與人異也。
"I alone seem strange to others"
He is the only one amongst them who seems strange.
而貴食母。食，用也。母，道也。我獨貴用道也
"For I cherish the nourishment of the mother"
Nourishment is utilized. Mother, here, means Dao. "I alone cherish the utilization of Dao."[58]

TWENTY
Chapter 20 exemplifies the Daoist veneration of childlike innocence. The ideal state of mind for the Daoist is like that of a tranquil newborn – pure awareness and wonder, receptive and open. Most people go about their day with an assortment of expectations about what it will bring. While this helps us to make sense

---

[58] Dao is empty. Emptiness is used (See chapter 11). To utilize emptiness is to be filled with Virtue (See chapter 22).

of, survive, and even thrive in this world, it also holds us back from appreciating and experiencing life as it spontaneously changes. The newborn simply takes in new things and experiences. It has not yet decided what will come based on its accumulated past experiences. It is simply open, aware, present, curious. Lao Zi describes this absence of the conceit of knowing this and that, free of the arrogance to push these views on others. "Playing the fool," Lao Zi escapes these traps which would serve only to submerge him in the confusion that has carried away so many others. Holding to this openness, he stays with the life giving nourishment of Dao, absorbing the Virtue of Heaven and vital-breath of the Earth.

# ~ 21 ~

Openness is Virtue's form
With your attention on Dao alone
This will arrive

Dao acts on all things spontaneously and suddenly
Sudden! Spontaneous! Within, there is image
Spontaneous! Sudden! Within, there is being
Obscure! Dark! Within, there is essence
This essence of utmost reality
Within it is sincerity

It is ancient and it is modern
Its attributes do not leave
By it, we can examine how the multitudes began
How am I able to know that the multitudes
Began according to this nature of beginnings?
By this

## Chapter 21
虛心 Empty the Heart and Mind

孔德之容，孔，大也。有大德之人，無所不容，能受垢濁，處謙卑也。
"Openness is Virtue's form"
Openness means immense. Those with immense Virtue can take on anything. They can accept the dirt and stains yet remain humble.

唯道是從。唯，獨也。大德之人，不隨世俗所行，獨從於道也。
"With your attention on Dao alone, this will arrive"
To keep focus means to keep a solitary focus. Those of immense Virtue do not follow the ways and practices of the world, but focus only on following Dao.

道之為物，唯恍唯忽。道之於萬物，獨恍忽往來，於其無所定也。
"Dao acts on all things spontaneously and suddenly"
Dao comes and goes in things spontaneously and suddenly. It is not bound to any one place.

忽兮恍兮，其中有象；道唯忽恍無形，之中獨有萬物法象。
"Sudden! Spontaneous! Within, there is image"
Dao is sudden and spontaneous. Within its formlessness, the myriad things conform to their appearances.

恍兮忽兮，其中有物。道唯恍忽，其中有一，經營生化，因氣立質。
"Spontaneous! Sudden! Within, there is being"
Dao is spontaneous and sudden. At its center is Oneness. It passes through barriers to transform life, and uses energy-breath to establish substance.

窈兮冥兮，其中有精，道唯窈冥無形，其中有精實，神明相薄，陰陽交會也。
"Obscure! Dark! Within, there is essence"
The Dao is obscure, dark, and without form. Within it is the essence of reality. Spirit and radiance join together in one thin line. Yin and yang blend together.

其精甚真，言存精氣，其妙甚真，非有飾也。
"This essence of utmost reality"
Lao Zi is talking here about the existence of the [Dao's][59] vital energy-breath, a mystery which is very real. It is not a deception.

其中有信。道匿功藏名，其信在中也。
"Within, it is sincerity"
Dao conceals its skill, and hides itself from being known, yet it is sincere through to the center.

自古及今，其名不去，自，從也。自古至今，道常在不去。
"It is ancient and it is modern. Its attributes do not leave"
Dao follows itself. It is ancient and modern, for Dao is always present. It never leaves.

以閱眾甫，閱，稟也。甫，始也。言道稟與，萬物始生，從道受氣。
"By it, we can examine how the multitudes began"
To examine is to show. To examine the beginning is to find the start. Lao Zi is saying that Dao shows how the myriad things began to arise. While guided by Dao, they received energy-breath.

吾何以知眾甫之然哉。吾何以知萬物從道受氣。

---

[59] See the second-last sentence of Heshang Gong's comments in chapter 21.

"How am I able to know that the multitudes began according to this nature of beginnings?"

(In other words) "How can I know that the myriad things followed Dao to be infused with energy-breath?"

以此。此，今也。以今萬物皆得道精氣而生，動作起居，非道不然。

"By this"

"This" refers to "the present." In this very moment, the myriad things all receive the Dao's vital energy-breath in order to live, to move, to stand up, and to rise to their places. If not by a Path (Dao), this could not have happened.

## TWENTY-ONE

Lao Zi's explanation of creation in chapter 21 can be taken as a precursor to the creation of human beings as described in chapter eight of *The Yellow Emperor's Classic of Internal Medicine, Spiritual Hinge Text* (*Huang Di Nei Jing, Ling Shu Jing*):

> Qi Bo replied:
> That which Heaven gives an individual is De (intrinsic virtue). That which Earth gives an individual is qi (energy-breath). When De and qi intermingle, there is life. From life, what then comes into existence is called jing (essence). When the two jing (of Heaven and Earth) combine and grasp each other, we have what is called shen (spirit).

While it is Virtue from Heaven and the qi of Earth that brings about life, it is the essence of Dao – containing image, being, and all that is real – which makes this possible. This Dao-jing is analogous to the DNA of all existence, with its attributes being present in all images, beings, minds, and spirits. As Lao Zi and Heshang Gong comment above:

> Obscure! Dark! Within, there is essence
>> The Dao is obscure, dark, and without form. Within it is the essence of reality. Spirit and radiance join together in one thin line. Yin and yang blend together.
>
> This essence of utmost reality
> Within, it is sincerity
> It is ancient and it is modern. Its attributes do not leave
> By it, we can examine how the multitudes began

# ~ 22 ~

That which is flexible is preserved
That which is bent is straightened
That which is empty is filled
That which is broken is repaired
That which is lacking acquires
That which is excessive becomes confused
Therefore, the Sage embraces Oneness
So as to bring the world into alignment

He does not look for himself
Thus, he has enlightened vision
He does not claim to be correct
Thus, he is believable
He is not prideful
Thus, he achieves
He does not self-aggrandize
Thus, he endures
Neither agreeing nor quarrelling
Nothing can pull him into dispute
The old saying, "be flexible in order to maintain wholeness"
Are these but empty words?
To those who keep sincerity whole
All things return

## Chapter 22
益謙 Advantages of Humility

曲則全，曲己從眾，不自專，則全其身也。
"That which is flexible is preserved"
Being flexible for the greater good, and not doing things only for oneself, one's body and character are preserved.
枉則直，枉，屈己而伸人，久久自得直也。
"That which is bent is straightened"
Bending, here, means that by bending yourself low in order to stretch others high, over time you will also be straight.
窪則盈，地窪下，水流之；人謙下，德歸之。
"That which is empty is filled"

Where the earth is low, water flows into it. When people humble themselves, Virtue returns to them.

敝則新,自受弊薄,後己先人,天下敬之,久久自新也。

"That which is broken is repaired"

Taking oneself to be wrong and inferior, putting oneself last and others first, the world will respect this. Over time, such a person is made anew.

少則得,自受取少則得多也,天道祐謙,神明託虛。

"That which is lacking acquires"

Those who take only very little for themselves obtain far more. Heaven and Dao protect the humble. Spiritual intelligence requires emptiness.

多則惑。財多者,惑於所守,學多者,惑於所聞

"That which is excessive becomes confused"

Those who possess many valuables are not sure what they have. Those who study too much are confused about what they have heard.

是以聖人抱一為天下式。抱,守也。式,法也。聖人守一,乃知萬事,故能為天下法式也。

"Therefore, the Sage embraces Oneness so as to bring the world into alignment"

Embrace, here, means to guard within. Order, here, means principle. The Sage guards Oneness within and so knows every action to take. Thus, he can bring the world into alignment.

不自見故明,聖人不以其目視千里之外也,乃因天下之目以視,故能明達也。

"He does not look for himself, thus, he has enlightened vision"

The Sage does not use his eyes to look a thousand miles away, but uses the eyes of the empire to investigate. Therefore, he can see clearly and intelligently.

不自是故彰,聖人不自以為是而非人,故能彰顯於世。

"He does not claim to be correct, thus, he is believable"

The Sage does not claim himself to be correct and others to be wrong. Thus, he can be obvious and apparent.

不自伐故有功,伐,取也。聖人德化流行,不自取其美,故有功於天下。

"He is not prideful, thus, he achieves"

To be prideful is to take for oneself. The Sage's Virtue transforms by flowing and circulating. He does not take its beauty to be his own. Thus, his achievements remain in the world.

不自矜故長。矜,大也。聖人不自貴大,故能久不危。

"He does not self-aggrandize,[60] thus, he endures"

To sympathize means to aggrandize. The Sage does not aggrandize his honour; thus, he can endure without danger.

夫惟不爭,故天下莫能與之爭。此言天下賢與不肖,無能與不爭者爭也。

---

[60] 自矜, translated as "self-aggrandize," means literally "to sympathize with oneself."

*"Neither agreeing nor quarrelling, nothing can pull him into dispute"*

When all under heaven deems the Sage to be worthy, he acts as though not this way (worthy). He approaches disputes as though incapable and not disputing..

古之所謂曲則全者，豈虛言哉。傳古言，曲從則全身，此言非虛妄也。

*"The old saying, 'be flexible in order to maintain wholeness' – are these but empty words?"*

Lao Zi transmits the old saying, "Flexibility preserves the body." These words are not empty and foolish.

誠全而歸之。誠，實也。能行曲從者，實其肌體，歸之於父母，無有傷害也。

*"To those who keep sincerity whole, all things return"*

Sincerity, here, means what is real. Those who can practice flexibility and bring the muscles of the body back to their true state of flexibility, as provided by their mother and father, will not injure or damage them.

## TWENTY-TWO

While solidute offers great potential for self-cultivation and realization, for Lao Zi and Heshang Gong, the Sage did not permanently escape the world but lived amongst the people. Rather than escape to the mountains, the Sage lived in such a way that allowed him to maneuver through the conflicts and difficulties of his day without bringing further danger or disharmony to himself or others. Doing so, he would inadvertently show another way, another path. Understanding the danger of "standing on tiptoes," or even being raised above others, the Sage accomplished his ends by remaining below others, even if they tried to raise him up above themselves. This is not the way of man, but the way of Heaven, the way of water.

This way of the Sage is also described in *The Yellow Emperor's Classic of Internal Medicine, Plain Questions (Huang Di Nei Jing, Su Wen)*, chapter one:

> Next were the Sages who dwelled in the harmony of Heaven and Earth and accorded with the principles of the eight winds. Their cravings and desires were suited to the era and local customs, and they had no hatred or anger in their hearts. In their activities they had no desire to avoid the world. In their dress and manner, they had no desire to be elevated and admired by popular people. Externally, they did not over-exert their bodies with endeavours; internally, they did not worry and speculate in their thoughts. They considered enjoying tranquility to be the highest application of oneself, and self-realization to be achievement. Physically, they did not deteriorate, and their spiritual vitality did not dissipate.

A brilliant example of the humility Heshang Gong describes can also be found in the Nordic "Law of Jante," encapsulated in Aksel Sandemose's book *A Fugitive*

*Crosses His Tracks*.[61] The Law of Jante states:

1. You're not to think you are anything special.
2. You're not to think you are as good as we are.
3. You're not to think you are smarter than we are.
4. You're not to convince yourself that you are better than we are.
5. You're not to think you know more than we do.
6. You're not to think you are more important than we are.
7. You're not to think you are good at anything.
8. You're not to laugh at us.
9. You're not to think anyone cares about you.
10. You're not to think you can teach us anything.

# ~ 23 ~

To speak rarely is natural
Gusting wind does not last in the early morning
Sudden rainstorms do not last all day

Who acts in this way? Heaven and Earth
If Heaven and Earth cannot continue in such a way
What then, should be the case for men?
They should follow the method of Dao!

(To be a person of) Dao, be one with Dao
(To be a person of) Virtue, be one with Virtue
(To be a person of) loss, be one with loss

Those who are one with Dao
Dao is also happy to have them
Those who are one with Virtue
Virtue is also happy to have them
Those who are one with loss
Loss is also happy to have them

Where faith and trust is not satisfactory
There will be no faith and trust

---

[61] Sandemose, Aksel; Eugene Gay-Tifft (trans.). *A Fugitive Crosses His Tracks*. New York: A.A. Knopf, 1936.

# Chapter 23
虛無 Emptiness and Nothingness

希言自然。希言者,謂愛言也。愛言者,自然之道。
"To speak rarely is natural"
To speak rarely means to hold words precious. To hold words precious is natural to the Dao.
故飄風不終朝,驟雨不終日。飄風,疾風也。驟雨,暴雨也。言疾不能長,暴不能久也。
"Gusting wind does not last in the early morning. Sudden rainstorms do not last all day"
Gusting wind refers to the winds of illness. "Sudden rainstorms" refers to raining down violence. Illness cannot last. Violence cannot continue.

孰為此者?天地。孰,誰也。誰為此飄風暴雨者乎?天地所為。
"Who acts in this way? Heaven and Earth"
Who causes these gusting winds and violent rainstorms? Heaven and Earth.
天地尚不能久,不能終於朝暮也。
"If Heaven and Earth cannot continue in such a way"
If they cannot go on like this from morning until night
而況於人乎?天地至神合為飄風暴雨,尚不能使終朝至暮,何況人欲為暴卒乎。
"What then, should be the case for men?"
Heaven and Earth combine their spirits to make gusting winds and violent rainstorms, yet cannot make them go on from morning until night. Given this, why should men wish to drive their armies forward?
故從事於道者,從,為也。人為事當如道安靜,不當如飄風驟雨也。
"They should follow the method of Dao!"
Follow, here, means "act." People should conduct affairs like the Dao, in peace and stillness, and should not conduct affairs like gusting winds and violent rainstorms.

道者同於道,道者,謂好道人也。同於道者,所謂與道同也。
"(To be a person of) Dao, be one with Dao"
"Of Dao" refers to those who love Dao. "One with Dao" means that they follow Dao and unify with it.
德者同於德,德者,謂好德之人也。同於德者,所謂與德同也。
"(To be a person of) Virtue, be one with Virtue"
"Of Virtue" refers to those who love Virtue. "One with Virtue" means that they follow Virtue and unify with it.
失者同於失。失,謂任己而失人也。同於失者,所謂與失同也。

"(To be a person of) loss, be one with loss"
"Of loss" means that they follow only themselves, and so lose others. "One with loss" means that they follow loss and unify with it.

同於道者，道亦樂得之。與道同者，道亦樂得之也。
"Those who are one with Dao, Dao is also happy to have them"
Those who encounter Dao, and are one with it, Dao is also happy to have them.
同於德者，德亦樂得之，與德同者，德亦樂得之也。
"Those who are one with Virtue, Virtue is also happy to have them"
Those who encounter Virtue, and are one with it, Virtue is also happy to have them.
同於失者，失亦樂得之。與失同者，失亦樂失之也。
"Those who are one with loss, loss is also happy to have them"
Those who encounter loss, and are one with it, loss is also happy to lose them.

信不足焉，君信不足於下，下則應君以不信也。
"Where faith and trust is not satisfactory"
Rulers who do not sufficiently trust those below them are not trusted by those below them.
有不信焉。此言物類相歸，同聲相應，同氣相求。雲從龍，風從虎，水流濕，火就燥，自然之類也。
"There will be no faith and trust"
This explains that things which are of the same type return to each other. Notes resonate together, energy-breaths seek each other, clouds follow the dragon, wind follows the tiger, water drifts toward what is wet, fire approaches what is dry. This is the spontaneous nature of types.[62]

## TWENTY-THREE

Though calamities and misfortunes may arise, one should not give up Dao and Virtue. Losing faith in Dao and Virtue, speaking at length of despair and hopelessness: this invites further misfortune. Lao Zi and Heshang Gong remind us that words are powerful and so should not be given to these losses. One may talk about seeming failures for hours on end, but if they instead save their words, have faith in Dao and Virtue, and wait for the storm to pass, Dao and Virtue will return.[63]

Heshang Gong explains that chapter 23 expresses the concept of "resonance response" (gan ying), quoting an early commentary (the *Wenyan*) on the *Yi Jing* (*I Ching*), chapter one (Heaven, line 5) which describes the mutual attraction that

---

[62] Chapter 23 can be understood as an explanation of ganying 感應 (lit. "feeling response," aka "resonance response"), a term which appears in numerous ancient Chinese texts of various traditions, and which correlates closely to the modern term "the law of attraction."

[63] See my comments on chapter 39 for more on these ideas as they appear in chapter 23.

occurs between things of the same type. Another early text that speaks to this concept is the Huainan Zi, chapter 6, which states:

> Now, the way things adhere to others that share mutual categories is a most profound and subtle mystery. Knowledge cannot determine it, nor can eloquence unravel it. So (it is said), "when the east wind blows, the wine overflows. When the silkworms are rolled into thread, the second lute string (made of silk) breaks. Somehow it resonated. Drawing a picture in the ashes, moonlight hits the watchtower. A whale dies, and a star then falls out of the sky. Something moved them."
>
> When a Sage holds the throne, keeping Dao in his breast without a word, his grace reaches the myriad people. When the ruler and his minister have thoughts of deceiving each other, images of "back-to-back" show their craftiness in the sky. Spirit and energy-breath share a call and response.[64]

# ~ 24 ~

Those who stand on tiptoes are not established
Those who straddle do not stride
Those who display themselves are not brilliant
Those who claim to be correct are not believable
Those who boast are without achievement
Those who sympathize with themselves do not endure
When Dao remains, people say "surplus food goes foul"
All creatures are untrusting of that which appears foul
To hold on to Dao, these things must be avoided

## Chapter 24
苦恩 Hardship and Mercy

企者不立，企，進也。謂貪權慕名，進取功榮，則不可久立身行道也。
"Those who stand on tiptoes are not established"
Standing on tiptoes, here, refers to status seekers. Greedy for position and longing for fame, status seekers chase after glory and so cannot endure in establishing themselves on the path of Dao.

---

[64] Translated by Dan G. Reid

跨者不行，自以為貴而跨於人，眾共蔽之，使不得行。
"Those who straddle do not stride"
Those who try to bring honours and glory to themselves by sitting above others will be blocked by others and not gain any ground.

自見者不明，人自見其形容以為好，自見其所行以為應道，殊不知其形醜，操行之鄙。
"Those who display themselves are not brilliant"
Some people display themselves, believing their appearance to be pleasant. Some display their actions, believing them to be in accord with the Dao. Finding themselves extraordinary, they do not know when they are disgraceful but carry on their petty ways.

自是者不彰，自以為是而非人，眾共蔽之，使不得彰明。
"Those who claim to be correct are not believable"
Those who claim themselves to be correct, and others to be wrong, will be blocked by others. (Thus,) they will not attain a clear perspective.

自伐者無功，所謂輒自伐取其功美，即失有功於人也。
"Those who boast are without achievement"
Those who try to load themselves with claims about their own achievements and refinement soon lose others' esteem about any such achievements.

自矜者不長。好自矜大者，不可以長久。
"Those who sympathize with themselves do not endure"
Those who are pleased with themselves and proudly aggrandize themselves cannot endure for long.

其在道也，曰：餘食贅行。贅，貪也。使此自矜伐之人，在治國之道，日賦斂餘祿食以為貪行。
"When Dao remains, people say 'surplus food goes foul'"
Surplus, here, refers to greed. Proud men will aggrandize themselves and, if governing a state, will extract excessive taxes when there is surplus. Greed is then perpetuated (amongst the people).

物或惡之。此人在位，動欲傷害，故物無有不畏惡之者。
"All creatures are untrusting of that which appears foul"
Those who hold the throne, yet are perverted by a desire to injure and kill, will be feared and despised by all creatures.

故有道者不處。言有道之人不居其國也。
"To hold on to Dao, these things must be avoided"
Lao Zi is saying that men of Dao will not stay in nations like this.

## TWENTY-FOUR
Lao Zi continues to illustrate the necessity for balancing strong and soft, high and low. While one should strive for excellence, they must balance this excellence by

remaining humble. If the skilled warrior is not kind and compassionate, if the wealthy person does not moderate their desires, if those holding great authority do not develop tolerance, they will suffer greatly from the pull of this power.

# ~ 25 ~

Something exists, random and chaotic
Yet perfect and complete
Existing before Heaven and Earth were born
Still and serene, desolate and empty, it stands alone
Unchanged, it travels in circles and is not hazardous
It can thereby serve as Heaven and Earth's mother

I do not know its name, but write its name as Dao
Impelled to name it, I call it Vast Greatness
Vast and great, I call it Drifting
Drifting, I call it Spreading Out
Spreading Out, I call it Returning

Therefore, Dao is immense, Heaven is immense
Earth is immense, and the Emperor is also immense
From the periphery to the center
There exists the Four Immensities
And the Emperor represents their unification
Man is regulated by Earth
Earth is regulated by Heaven
Heaven is regulated by Dao
Dao is regulated by its own spontaneous nature

## Chapter 25
象元 Image and Origin

有物混成，先天地生。謂道無形，混沌而成萬物，乃在天地之前。
"Something exists, random and chaotic, yet perfect and complete, existing before Heaven and Earth were born"
This means that Dao is without form. It is stirred up and chaotic, yet completes the myriad things. It existed before Heaven and Earth.
寂兮寥兮，獨立而不改，寂者，無音聲。寥者，空無形。獨立者，無匹雙。

不改者，化有常。
"Still and serene, desolate and empty, it stands alone, unchanged"
What is still and serene has no sound or voice. What is empty is hollow and without form. What stands alone is not paired. (Dao) does not change because its transformations are constant.

周行而不殆，道通行天地，無所不入，在陽不焦，託陰不腐，無不貫穿，而不危殆也。
"It travels in circles and is not hazardous"
Dao passes over, and through, Heaven and Earth. There is nothing it does not go into. It brings yang into being, but is not burned. It supports yin but does not wear out. There is nothing it does not go through. Further, it is never idle or dangerous.

可以為天下母。道育養萬物精氣，如母之養子。
"It can thereby serve as Heaven and Earth's mother"
Dao gives birth to, and nurtures, the myriad things, giving them its vital energy-breath like a mother raising children.

吾不知其名，字之曰道，我不見道之形容，不知當何以名之，見萬物皆從道所生，故字之曰道。
"I do not know its name, but write its name as Dao"
(Lao Zi says) "I do not see Dao's form or appearance, and so do not know what to call it. Seeing that the myriad things follow a path toward life, I therefore call it the Path (Dao)."

強為之名曰大。不知其名，強曰大者，高而無上，羅而無外，無不包容，故曰大也。
"Impelled to name it, I call it Vast Greatness"
(Lao Zi says) "I do not know its name, but if forced, I would call it Vast Greatness. So high that nothing is above it; its net is so wide that nothing is outside of it. There is nothing that it does not enwrap and cover. Therefore, I call it Vast Greatness."

大曰逝，其為大，非若天常在上，非若地常在下，乃復逝去，無常處所也。
"Vast and great, I call it Drifting"
Its reach is vast. Unlike Heaven, which is always above; unlike Earth, which is always below; it comes and goes, never residing in only one place.

逝曰遠，言遠者，窮乎無窮，布氣天地，無所不通也。
"Drifting, I call it Spreading Out"
Spreading out, it has nothing, yet there is nothing it does not have. Covering Heaven and Earth with energy-breath, there is nothing it does not pass through.

遠曰反。言其遠不越絕，乃復反在人身也。
"Spreading Out, I call it Returning"
Spreading out, it does not go on without stopping, but also returns and exists in the human body.

故道大，天大，地大，王亦大。道大者，包羅天地，無所不容也。天大者，無所不蓋也。地大者，無所不載也。王大者，無所不制也。

"Therefore, Dao is immense, Heaven is immense, Earth is immense, and the Emperor is also immense"

Dao is immense. It wraps Heaven and Earth in its net. There is nothing it does not enclose. Heaven is immense. There is nothing it does not cover. Earth is immense. There is nothing it does not carry. The Emperor is immense. There is nothing he does not overpower.

域中有四大，四大，道、天、地、王也。凡有稱有名，則非其極也。言道則有所由，有所由然後謂之為道，然則是道稱中之大也，不若無稱之大也，無稱不可而得為名，曰域也。天地王皆在乎無稱之內也，故曰域中有四大者也。

"From the periphery to the center, there exists the Four Immensities"

The Four Immensities are Dao, Heaven, Earth, and the Emperor. Together, this is their name. This is not to say that they are The Ultimate (Ji). Lao Zi is saying that because Dao exists, a cause exists. Because this cause is in nature, what it leaves behind are called "the creations of Dao." In nature, this Dao is called The Immensity Within. This is not the same as calling it The Nameless Immensity – The nameless which cannot be given a name is called The Ultimate. Heaven, Earth, and the Emperor all have the nameless within them!  For this reason, it is said: "from the periphery to the center, The Four Immensities exist."

而王居其一焉。八極之內有四大，王居其一也。

"And the Emperor represents their unification"

Within the extremes of the eight directions, there are Four Immensities, and the Emperor represents their unification.

人法地，人當法地安靜和柔也，種之得五穀，掘之得甘泉，勞而不怨也，有功而不置也。

"Man is regulated by Earth"

Man should follow the example of Earth's peacefulness, stillness, harmony, and softness. People sow seeds and obtain the five grains. They dig and obtain sweet springs. Though they work the Earth, the Earth is not resentful. It provides bounteous results and does not abandon its dependents.

地法天，天澹泊不動，施而不求報，生長萬物，無所收取。

"Earth is regulated by Heaven"

Heaven is an anchor of tranquility that does not move. It provides and does not seek anything in return. It extends the lives of the myriad things without collecting anything from them.

天法道，道清靜不言，陰行精氣，萬物自成也。

"Heaven is regulated by Dao"

The Dao is clear, tranquil and does not speak. Yin circulates vital energy-breaths, and the myriad things complete themselves.

道法自然。道性自然，無所法也。

"Dao is regulated by its own spontaneous nature"

The nature of Dao is self-sufficient. It is without any regulator.

## TWENTY-FIVE

Following Heshang Gong's commentary, the last four lines of chapter 25 could be translated *"Man should follow the example of Earth, for Earth follows Heaven, and Heaven follows Dao. Dao is regulated by its own spontaneous nature."*

As all things constantly change and transform according to Dao, Dao cannot be described. How can something that encompasses all changes and transformations, constantly doing so in accordance with past, present, and future, infinite times at any given moment, yet never itself changing whatsoever, be described? Within it, images exist, beings exist; yet it precedes the existence of any shape, colour, or attribute. Thus, it is without name. Heshang Gong animates Lao Zi's thought process: "I do not see Dao's form or appearance, and so do not know what to call it. Seeing that the myriad things follow a path toward life, I therefore call it the Path (Dao)."

This path toward life is natural, spontaneous: *zi ran*. Part of the yin-yang dichotomy is moving toward life (yang) and moving toward death (yin); however, if one is too forceful in striving for yang, they inevitably fall out of balance and cannot resist the pull of yin. Spontaneity allows a natural balance to be achieved, like the fluctuations of yin and yang that maintain homeostasis in a body or ecosystem. The closer one gets to spontaneous nature (zi ran), the more tranquil and empty they become (like Heaven); the more peaceful, quiet, harmonious, and adaptive they become (like Earth). This, as Lao Zi often explains,[65] is the path of life.

## ~ 26 ~

Heaviness brings lightness back to the root
Calm stillness rules restlessness
Therefore the prince walks all day
Without parting from his luggage cart
Even when there are glorious things to behold
And comfortable places to stay
He overcomes his urges
And what about the master of ten thousand chariots
If he himself is light (ungrounded)
And easily carried away by the world?
As a result of this "lightness," his ministers are lost

---

[65] For example, in chapter 76

*As a result of their restlessness, rulers are lost*

# Chapter 26
## 重德 The Virtue of Heaviness

重為輕根，人君不重則不尊，治身不重則失神，草木之花葉輕，故零落，根重故長存也。

"Heaviness brings lightness back to the root"
Rulers who do not remain (grounded and) "heavy" are not respected. Ruling the body without this "heaviness" results in loss of the spirit. The flowers and leaves of plants and trees are light, thus they all fall off. Their foundations are heavy, and thus survive a long time.

靜為躁君。人君不靜則失威，治身不靜則身危，龍靜故能變化，虎躁故夭虧也。

"Calm stillness rules restlessness"
When a ruler is not calm, he loses his powerful appearance. When people who govern their bodies are not calm, they put their bodies in danger. Dragons remain calm, and are therefore able to adapt and change. Tigers are restless, and so perish early.

是以聖人終日行，不離輜重。輜，靜也。聖人終日行道，不離其靜與重也。

"Therefore the prince walks all day without parting from his luggage cart"
"His luggage cart" refers to his calm stillness. Sages do not stop practicing Dao at any time. They do not part from their calm stillness, but rather exemplify this "heaviness."

雖有榮觀，燕處超然。榮觀，謂宮闕。燕處，后妃所居也。超然，遠避而不處也。

"Even when there are glorious things to behold, and comfortable places to stay, he overcomes his urges"
"Glorious things to behold" refers to palatial towers. "Comfortable places to stay" refers to the residences of (foreign) queens. "He overcomes his urges" means that he stays far away from them, and does not spend any time there.

奈何萬乘之主，奈何者，疾時主傷痛之辭。萬乘之主謂，王者。

"And what about the master of ten thousand chariots"
The injuries committed during his era would be spoken of painfully. The master of ten thousand chariots refers to the ruler.

而以身輕天下？王者至尊，而以其身行輕躁乎。疾時王奢恣輕淫也。

"If he himself is light, (ungrounded,) and easily carried away by the world?"
Will rulers be venerated if they are "light," (ungrounded,) and easily carried away by restlessness? Their era will suffer if they are extravagant and indulgent, ungrounded, and licentious.

輕則失臣，王者輕淫則失其臣，治身輕淫則失其精。

"As a result of this 'lightness,' his ministers are lost"

Rulers who are flippant and licentious lose their ministers. To become "light" and licentious while governing the body results in loss of vital essence.

躁則失君。王者行躁疾則失其君位，治身躁疾則失其精神也。

*"As a result of their restlessness, rulers are lost"*

Rulers who become restless will lose the throne. To become restless while governing the body results in loss of spiritual vitality.

TWENTY-SIX

In Chapter 26, Heshang Gong again shows the tradition of internal medicine and health preservation that surrounded many of the early teachings found in the *Dao De Jing*. Rulers and ministers are shown to represent the mind and body, much as they were throughout the *Huang Di Nei Jing*. "Heaviness brings lightness back to the root" also pertains to chapter 16 and the practice of sitting in silence and stillness[66] as a way to reconnect with one's pure nature and destiny-life-force. By allowing our energies, organs, and thereby emotions, to settle, we can secure the essences and spiritual vitalities that will scatter when disturbed by strong emotions and desires. This nourishes both the mind and body, fostering a greater capacity to correlate information and be successful in one's endeavours[67] – all important capacities for a leader, whether as a leader of others or of one's own life.

## ~ 27 ~

Excellent walking leaves no trail of footprints
Excellent speech is without fault or blame
Excellent counting does not use counting devices
Excellent closing requires no bolts
Yet the seal cannot be broken
Excellent binding requires no rope to secure it
Yet cannot be unbound

In this way the wise of unrelenting virtue rescue people
Therefore nobody is abandoned

---

[66] Chapter 16 explains that "the root" refers to silence and stillness (靜, jing)

[67] Accroding to Chinese medicine, our mind and spirit are housed in the heart, while competence (zhi) and essence are housed in and supported by the kidneys. The interrelationship and balance between the heart and kidneys, paired in the shao yin meridian system, is integral to the vitality of all of these capacities.

Unrelenting virtue saves things
Therefore nothing is abandoned
This is called "capturing light"
Therefore, those who are excellent
Are models for those who are not excellent
Those who are not excellent
Are valued as assets by those who are excellent
Those who do not value their teachers
Those who do not care for their assets
To consider these people wise would be a great illusion
It is correct to say that this is essential to the secret of life

# Chapter 27
## 巧用 Employing Skill

善行無轍迹，善行道者求之於身，不下堂，不出門，故無轍迹。
"Excellent walking leaves no trail of footprints"
Those who are excellent at walking the Dao seek it in themselves, and do not go down to the hall or out of the gates. Thus, they leave no trail of footprints.

善言無瑕讁，善言謂擇言而出之，則無瑕疵讁過於天下。
"Excellent speech is without fault or blame"
Excellent speech means choosing words and imparting them without the world finding fault or blame in them.

善數不用籌策，善以道計事者，則守一不移，所計不多，則不用籌策而可知也。
"Excellent counting does not use counting devices"
Those who are excellent at finding a strategy to attain Dao simply guard Oneness within and do not shift from it. Their strategies are not numerous, and so they do not use counting devices to know them all.

善閉無關楗而不可開，善以道閉情欲、守精神者，不如門戶有關楗可得開。
"Excellent closing requires no bolts yet the seal cannot be broken"
For excellence in the way of sealing off desires and strong emotions, guard the spiritual vitality within and do not be like gates and doors. Locked bolts can be opened.

善結無繩約而不可解。善以道結事者，乃可結其心，不如繩索可得解也。
"Excellent binding requires no rope to secure it, yet cannot be unbound"
Achieve excellence by tying Dao into your usual affairs. Then you can tie it to your heart. This is to not use ropes and cords, which can be untied.

是以聖人常善救人，聖人所以常教人忠孝者，欲以救人性命。
"In this way the wise of unrelenting virtue rescue people"

Sages always teach (the selflessness of) loyalty and filial piety, hoping to rescue people's pure nature (xing) and destiny-life-force (ming).

故無棄人;使貴賤各得其所也。
"Therefore nobody is abandoned"
Both rich and poor are employed.

常善救物,聖人所以常教民順四時者,欲以救萬物之殘傷。
"Unrelenting virtue saves things"
Sages always teach people to obey the four seasons, desiring to save the myriad things from injury and waste.

故無棄物。聖人不賤名而貴玉視之如一。
"Therefore nothing is abandoned"
Sages do not take common things for granted while cherishing what is precious, but rather, they see them equally as one.

是謂襲明。聖人善救人物,是謂襲明大道。
"This is called 'capturing light'"
Sages are good at rescuing people and things. This is called capturing the light of the Great Dao.

故善人者,不善人之師;人之行善者,聖人即以為人師。
"Therefore, those who are excellent are models for those who are not excellent"
People who practice excellence are quick to follow the Sages' teachings.

不善人者,善人之資。資,用也。人行不善者,聖人猶教導使為善,得以給用也。
"Those who are not excellent are valued as assets by those who are excellent"
Valued as assets, here, means that they are useful. Those who do not practice excellence, the sages teach and guide, making them excellent so that they can be useful.

不貴其師,獨無輔也。
"Those who do not value their teachers"
Who leave them alone and without assistance.

不愛其資, 無所使也。
"Those who do not care for their assets"
Who do not put them to good use.

雖智大迷,雖自以為智。言此人乃大迷惑。
"To consider these people wise would be a great illusion"
If people such as this still consider themselves wise, Lao Zi says that they have deluded themselves.

是謂要妙。能通此意,是謂知微妙要道也。
"It is correct to say that this is essential to the secret of life"
If you can penetrate this idea, this is what it means to know the subtlest mystery and essential secret of Dao.

## TWENTY-SEVEN

The skills described in the beginning of chapter 27 may symbolize the Sage's vital yet undetectable influence as a leader and teacher. He crosses someone's path but does not entice them to follow him (travelling without footprints); corrects a person's thinking without their realizing they were corrected (speaking without blame); reveals many faults without mentioning them (counting without counting devices); gets a person to change their behaviour without stifling their freedom (locking without bolts); does not force his own influence, yet this influence is inescapable (tying without ropes).

These skills are necessary for the Sage to steer proud and powerful people away from their chosen path, and entice them to choose one that serves the greater good. It was often the job of a Sage to give their council to people with thousands of soldiers at their beckon call. To point out such a person's errors would always be like dancing on the foot of a cliff; yet, doing so was at least as important as it was dangerous, and so the self-restraint, wisdom, and genuine virtue of a Sage was of great importance to traversing these precipices successfully.

Zhuang Zi (c. 300 BC), in one of his many fictional tales, tells the story of an envoy seeking advice from Confucius on how to avoid punishment when meeting with such a dangerous and tyrannical king:

> Yan Hui said: "… By doing what other's do, they have no basis to blame me. This is called being a fellow disciple. Maintaining the ways of antiquity is to be a disciple of antiquity. Though my words of instruction may point out the ruler's errors, they will be the words of antiquity and not my own. As such, though being direct, they will not be insulting. This is called being a disciple of the ancients. Will this suffice?"
> Confucius replied: "Most certainly not! You have too many conditions and policies. You plan to go to [the tyrannical ruler of Wei] having yet to learn anything about him. Though your plan is firm, you will only avoid transgression. Stopping at that, how can you successfully convert him? You are only using your mind as the teacher."

Having mercy on Yan Hui, Confucius imparts the way of "heart-mind fasting" (xin zhai), one of the basic practices of Daoist meditation that helps to absorb the influence of Virtue and thereby increase spiritual intelligence (shen ming). It may be this power and influence, gained through purifying the heart-mind, that Lao Zi refers to when describing the Sage's mysterious methods in chapter 27. Confucius continues:

> "… You must be of singular focus. Do not listen with the ears, but listen with the heart-mind; do not listen with the heart-mind, but listen with the breath. Listening (then) stops in the ears, and the heart-mind stops in its verifications. As for the breath, it is the emptiness which receives all

things, and it is Dao which brings (all things) toward emptiness. *Emptiness is the fasting of the heart-mind.*"[68]

As Heshang Gong comments above:

> Those who are excellent at finding a strategy to attain Dao simply guard Oneness within and do not shift from it. Their strategies are not numerous, and so they do not use counting devices to know them all.

# ~ 28 ~

Knowing the masculine, guard the feminine
And be a valley under Heaven
Be a valley under Heaven
And Virtue will never flee
But will return to her infant son

Knowing the white, guard the black
And be a guide for the world
Be a guide for the world
And Virtue will remain without wavering

Return to Wuji, Supreme Nothingness
Knowing glory, hold fast to humiliation
And be a valley under Heaven
Being a valley under Heaven
Virtue will always fulfill you

Return to your unaltered substance
Unaltered wood is shaped into vessels
Sages make use of this model
When acting in positions of leadership
Thereby, the greatest establishment is undivided

---

[68] From *Zhuang Zi*, chapter four. Translated by Dan G. Reid.

# Chapter 28
## 反朴 Return to the Unaltered State

知其雄，守其雌，為天下谿。雄以喻尊，雌以喻卑。人雖自知其尊顯，當復守之以卑微，去雄之強梁，就雌之柔和，如是則天下歸之，如水流入深谿也。
"Knowing the masculine, guard the feminine, and be a valley under Heaven"
The male is a metaphor for receiving honour. The female is a metaphor for being humble. While it may be obvious that they are venerated, people should hold onto humility and smallness. Leave the male's power and rigidity, and approach the female's gentle harmony. Then all under Heaven will return to you like water currents flow into deep valleys.

為天下谿，常德不離，人能謙下如深谿，則德常在，不復離於己。
"Be a valley under Heaven, and Virtue will never flee"
In people who can humble and lower themselves like mountain streams, Virtue will always exist and never again leave them.

復歸於嬰兒。當復歸志於嬰兒，慈然而無所知也
"But will return to her infant son"
Return to the intentions of an infant son – his playful nature is without knowledge.

知其白守其黑，為天下式。白以喻昭昭，黑以喻默默。人雖自知昭昭，明白當復守之以默默，如闇昧無所見，如是則可為天下法式，則德常在。
"Knowing the white, guard the black, and be a guide for the world"
White is a metaphor for intense brightness. Black is a metaphor for quiet stillness. Though someone may know that they are full of light, they should understand the white while holding onto quiet stillness, close themselves within a darkness which cannot be seen, and be well aligned (with Dao). This enables them to be a standard and guide for the world. Then Virtue will always be with them.

為天下式，常德不忒，人能為天下法式，則德常在於己，不復差忒。
"Be a guide for the world, and Virtue will remain without wavering"
When someone can be a standard and guide for the world, Virtue will always be with them, unwaveringly.

復歸於無極。德不差忒，則常生久壽，歸身於無窮極也。
"Return to Wuji, Supreme Nothingness"
When Virtue does not waver, it always brings long life and reconnects the body to that which is without any exhaustible limit.

知其榮，守其辱，為天下谷。榮以喻尊貴，辱以喻污濁。人能知己之有榮貴，當復守之以污濁，如是則天下歸之，如水流入深谷也。
"Knowing glory, hold fast to humiliation, and be a valley under Heaven"
Knowing praise refers to respect and honour. Reproof refers to unworthiness. If you can, knowing your own respectability and value, return and hold fast to your un-

worthiness (lit. foul muddiness), all under Heaven will return to you like water currents flow to deep valleys.

為天下谷，常德乃足，足，止也。人能為天下谷，則德乃常止於己。
*"Being a valley under Heaven, Virtue will always fulfill you"*
To be fulfilled is to come to rest. To people who can be (empty, open, and nourishing like) a valley under Heaven, Virtue will always come to rest.

復歸於樸。復當歸身於質樸，不復為文飾。
*"Return to your unaltered substance"*
Return yourself to the unaltered state. Do not go on covering yourself with ornamentation.

樸散則為器，器，用也。萬物之樸散則為器用也。若道散則為神明，流為日月，分為五行也。
*"Unaltered wood is shaped into vessels"*
Vessels are useful. The simplicity of the myriad things is altered to make useful tools. Similarly, the Dao makes alterations in order to create spiritual intelligence, the alterations of day and night, and the separation of the five elemental phases.

聖人用之則為官長。聖人升用則為百官之元長也
*"Sages make use of this model when acting in positions of leadership"*
Using only a few ounces of leadership, the Sage plays the role of one hundred leaders.

故大制不割。聖人用之則以大道制御天下，無所傷割，治身則以大道制御情欲，不害精神也。
*"Thereby, the greatest establishment is undivided"*
The Sage uses (leaders). Thereby, the Great Dao is established in managing all under Heaven without causing harm or division.

In governing the body, when the Great Dao is established it drives out desires and strong emotions (so that they) do not injure the spiritual vitality.

## TWENTY-EIGHT

Only in humility can we know simplicity. Without humility we cannot abstain from ornamenting our personas, and without abstaining from ornamenting our personas, we cannot return to simplicity. Simplicity (pu) is the unaltered state by which one receives Virtue and accumulates spiritual radiance. Without the obstruction of self-ornamentation, without getting in our own way by falling into egoic emotional battles that protect these false ornamentations, original essence (yuan jing) can be transformed to bring about spiritual intelligence and lead us to fulfill destiny.

# ~ 29 ~

The wish to possess all under Heaven
And control it
I see this has no end
The world is an instrument of the gods
It cannot be controlled
Those who try, spoil it
Those who grasp, lose

Hence, sometimes leading, sometimes following
Sometimes breathing in through the nose
Sometimes breathing out through the mouth
Sometimes strong
Sometimes weak
Sometimes chopping down
Sometimes being destroyed

Therefore, the wise abstain from excess, abstain from exaggeration, and abstain from exaltation

## Chapter 29
無為 Effortlessness (Wu Wei)

將欲取天下，欲為天下主也。
"The wish to possess all under Heaven"
The wish to rule all under Heaven.
而為之，欲以有為治民。
"And control it"
The wish to have control of, and govern, the people.
吾見其不得已。我見其不得天道人心已明矣，天道惡煩濁，人心惡多欲。
"I see this has no end"
I see that this cannot be obtained. Heaven's Dao and people's hearts are too intelligent! Heaven's Dao dislikes trouble and contamination. People's hearts dislike too much desire.
天下神器，不可為也。器，物也。人乃天下之神物也，神物好安靜，不可以有為治。
"The world is an instrument of the gods. It cannot be controlled"
The instrument, here, refers to "beings" – humans become spirit beings on the earth. Spirit beings like peace and tranquility; they do not like to be forcibly governed.

為者敗之，以有為治之，則敗其質性。
"Those who try, spoil it"
By trying to force and control the world, they spoil its pure nature and substance.
執者失之。強執教之，則失其情實，生於詐偽也。
"Those who grasp, lose"
If you try to forcibly hold and indoctrinate the population, their true feelings will be lost and they will become artificial and deceitful.

故物或行或隨，上所行，下必隨之也。
"Hence, sometimes leading, and sometimes following"
Superiors lead, and those below must follow them.
或歔或吹，歔，溫也。吹，寒也。有所溫必有所寒也。
"Sometimes breathing in through the nose, and sometimes breathing out through the mouth"
Breathing in through the nose means warming; breathing out through the mouth means cooling. If there is warming, there must be cooling.
或強或羸，有所強大，必有所羸弱也。
"Sometimes strong, and sometimes weak"
When there is strength and greatness, there must also be weakness and adaptability.
或挫或隳。載，安也。隳，危也。有所安必有所危，明人君不可以有為治國與治身也。
"Sometimes chopping down, sometimes being destroyed"
There is both support of peace, and destruction and danger. If there is peace, there must be danger. Enlightened rulers do not try to forcibly control the nation but follow the way of governing the body.

是以聖人去甚，去奢，去泰。甚謂貪淫聲色。奢謂服飾飲食。泰謂宮室臺榭。去此三者，處中和，行無為，則天下自化。
"Therefore, the wise abstain from excess, abstain from exaggeration, and abstain from exaltation"
Excess means wanton and licentious music and prostitutes. Exaggeration means fancy clothes, drinks, and food. Exaltation means lofty towers and pavilions.

By abstaining from these three, remaining internally harmonious and effortless in activity, all under Heaven will reform itself.


TWENTY-NINE
The guidance in chapter 29 is reminiscent of the *Yijing* and Chinese martial strategy: knowing one's limits is of utmost importance when attempting to leverage one's power. A leader seeking harmony within the nation and within themselves must appreciate that dominance and force cannot engender this harmony.

Thereby can they stive toward the Daoist political goal of bringing about voluntary cooperation.

A nation that reflects the ambitions of its people does not need punishments to obtain compliance. The people of such a nation take pride in something they feel they are a part of and helped to create. Knowing this, the sage leader avoids pride and extraneous desires so as to rid himself of any temptation to neglect or abuse the people while aggrandizing himself.

# ~ 30 ~

As for those who use Dao to counsel the king
It is not by weapons that they have power in the world
Such activities are reciprocated
Where troops gather, thorns and brambles appear
Following war, there is sure to be famine and misfortune
Large armies are sure to bring sadness in the future
Achieve your aim well, and then stop
Do not dare to abuse power
Achieve your aim, but do not boast
Achieve your aim, but do not attack again
Achieve your aim, but do not become arrogant
Achieve your aim, but do not claim all the credit
Achieve your aim, but do not abuse power
Things thrive in their prime and then become aged
This is called "not Dao"
What is "not Dao" ends prematurely

## Chapter 30
儉武 Limiting Militancy

以道佐人主者，謂人主能以道自輔佐也。
"As for those who use Dao to counsel the king"
This means that the king can use Dao to protect and counsel himself.
不以兵強天下。以道自佐之主，不以兵革，順天任德，敵人自服。
"It is not by weapons that they have power in the world"
By Dao, the king can counsel himself. Then, without using weapons and armour but by submitting to Heaven and trusting in Virtue, his enemies will surrender themselves.

其事好還。其舉事好還自責，不怨於人也。
"Such activities are reciprocated"
If he accepts responsibility for harmonizing himself, he will not be hated by others.
師之所處，荊棘生焉。農事廢，田不修。
"Where troops gather, thorns and brambles appear. Following war, there is sure to be famine and misfortune"
Agriculture is forgotten and the fields cannot be cultivated.
大軍之後，必有凶年。天應之以惡氣，即害五穀，盡傷人也。
"Large armies are sure to bring sadness in the future"
Heaven responds to this with a malicious breath that destroys the five grains. This exhausts and injures the people.
善有果而已，善用兵者，當果敢而已，不美之。
"Achieve your aim well, and then stop"
With proper employment of the military, results should be won and the campaign then stopped and not indulged in.
不敢以取強。不以果敢取強大之名也。
"Do not dare to abuse power"
Do not, after winning results, try to gain a reputation of great strength.
果而勿矜，當果敢謙卑，勿自矜大也。
"Achieve your aim, but do not boast"
When results have been won, be humble and do not boast and aggrandize yourself.
果而勿伐，當果敢推讓，勿自伐取其美也。
"Achieve your aim, but do not attack again"
When results have been won, move forward or pull back, but do not become proud and conceited.
果而勿驕，驕，欺也。果敢勿以驕欺人。
"Achieve your aim, but do not become arrogant"
Arrogant, here, means deceitful. Achieve results but do not become arrogant and deceitful.
果而不得已，當過果敢至誠，不當逼迫不得已也
"Achieve your aim, but do not claim all the credit"
If you exceed your aim, remain honest. Do not bully anyone, nor claim all the credit.
果而勿強，果敢勿以為強兵、堅甲以欺凌人也。
"Achieve your aim, but do not abuse power"
Achieve your aim without using the power of the military, and do not hide behind your armour to cheat and insult others.
物壯則老，草木壯極則枯落，人壯極則衰老也。言強者不可以久。
"Things thrive in their prime and then become aged"
Grass and trees become fully grown and then dry out and fall; people reach their prime and then decline until death. So it is said, "the forceful cannot live long."
是謂不道。枯老者，坐不行道也。

"This is called 'not Dao'"
Drying out and aging is not how one practices Dao.
不道早已。不行道者早死。
"What is 'not Dao' ends prematurely"
Those who do not practice Dao, die prematurely.

THIRTY
In providing excellent guidance on how to prevent backlash after ending a conflict, Lao Zi draws an image of barren fields. This serves to remind that even "successful" conflicts have consequences. For example, someone may enjoy arguments and pride themselves on their ability to trounce their opponents, but in doing so may alienate everyone around them and end up desolate. Thus, we must be careful not to indulge in contentious impulses, and be careful of how and where we fight our battles, lest we destroy the vitality of our own fields, both internally and externally.

# ~ 31 ~

Elegant weapons are instruments of ill omen
All beings should despise them
Therefore, those who have Dao do not stay with them
The superior man (junzi) prefers to stay on the left
But those who use weapons prefer the right
Weapons are not instruments of good omen
They are not instruments of the junzi
If an attacker cannot be stopped, and weapons are used
To be calm and unemotional is considered most important

If victory is then won, do not be pleased
For to be pleased with this would be to celebrate murder
Anyone who celebrates murder
Is not capable of obtaining the will of the world!

For auspicious matters they [junzi] stay on the left
For ominous matters, (the junzi) stay on the right
When the low ranking officer is on the left
And the high ranking officer is on the right

This is said to observe the rites of mourning
When many people are killed
This is cause for sympathy and mourning
Victory in war
Is also cause for the mourning rites to be observed

# Chapter 31
## 偃武 Putting Away Militancy

夫佳兵者，不祥之器，佳，飾也。祥，善也。兵者，驚精神，濁和氣，不善人之器也，不當修飾之。
"Elegant weapons are instruments of ill omen"
Elegant, here, means decorative. Ill omen, here, means not good. Weapons startle the spiritual vitality and contaminate the energy-breath. They are not the good man's instrument, for he does not cultivate decoration.

物或惡之，兵動則有所害，故萬物無有不惡之者。
"All beings should despise them"
When weapons are employed, they cause injury. This is why the myriad things hate them.

故有道者不處。有道之人不處其國。
"Therefore, those who have Dao do not stay with them"
Those who have Dao do not remain in violent nations.

君子居則貴左，貴柔弱也。
"The superior man (junzi) prefers to stay on the left"
He maintains softness and flexibility.[69]

用兵則貴右。貴剛強也，此言兵道與君子之道反，所貴者異也。
"But those who use weapons prefer the right"
They prefer the rigid and inflexible. This is to say that the way of the soldier moves opposite to the way of the junzi. What they prefer is different.

兵者，不祥之器，兵，革者。不善之器也。
"Weapons are not instruments of good omen"
Weapons and armour are not instruments of good.

非君子之器，非君子所貴重之器也。
"They are not instruments of the junzi"
They are not instruments that the junzi favours.

不得已而用之。謂遭衰逆亂禍，欲加萬民，乃用之以自守。
"If an attacker cannot be stopped, and weapons are used"
This is referring to when the state is in decline and a rebellion then results in chaos

---

[69] The left is the side of life, and yang (please see next footnote).

and disaster – when all the people's desires have multiplied and you must do something to protect yourself.

恬淡為上。不貪土地，利人財寶。
"To be calm and unemotional is considered most important"
Do not be greedy for land, nor profit by taking people's possessions and valuables.

勝而不美，雖得勝而不以為利己也。
"If victory is then won, do not be pleased"
Even though attaining victory, do not take things for yourself.

而美之者，是樂殺人。美得勝者，是為喜樂殺人者也。
"For to be pleased with this would be to celebrate murder"
Those who are pleased after attaining victory act as though they enjoy and celebrate murder.

夫樂殺人者，則不可以得志於天下矣。為人君而樂殺人者，比不可使得志於天下矣，為人主必專制人命，妄行刑誅。
"Anyone who celebrates murder is not capable of obtaining the will of the world!"
Acting as though a junzi yet celebrating murder, one will never be able to obtain the will of the world! Acting like a king requires a human being to establish the will of Heaven. It would be absurd, then, for that person to execute people.

吉事尚左，左，生位也。
"For auspicious matters they [junzi] stay on the left"
The left is the position of life.[70]

凶事尚右，陰道殺人。
"For ominous matters, (the junzi) stay on the right"
The yin side of Dao is deadly.

偏將軍居左，偏將軍卑而居陽者，以其不專殺也。
"When the low ranking officer is on the left"
The low rank of an officer is humble. It resides here in the yang position, and so is not tasked with killing.

上將軍居右。上將軍尊而居陰者，以其專主殺也。
"And the high ranking officer is on the right"
The high rank of an officer is respected. He resides in the yin position here, and so is responsible for the king's execution orders.

言以喪禮處之。上將軍居右，喪禮尚右，死人貴陰也。
"This is said to observe the rites of mourning"
The high ranking officer is on the right. In funeral rites, he customarily stays on the right because the dead prefer yin.

---

[70] In the 'pre-heaven' arrangement of the trigrams (representing natural forces), the yang trigrams are all on the left (Eastern) side, while the yin trigrams are all on the right (Western) side.

殺人之眾，以哀悲泣之；傷己德薄，不能以道化人，而害無辜之民。

"When many people are killed, this is cause for sympathy and mourning"
One does injury to themselves when their Virtue is weak. They cannot reform people by Dao, and they kill people who have committed no crime.

戰勝，以喪禮處之。古者戰勝，將軍居喪主禮之位，素服而哭之，明君子貴德而賤兵，不得以而誅不祥，心不樂之，比於喪也，知後世用兵不已故悲痛之。

"Victory in war is also cause for the mourning rites to be observed"
In ancient times, when a battle was won, a Master of Ceremony conducted official funeral rites. People wore plain clothing and wept. The enlightened junzi valued virtue and not weapons. He did not take up these instruments of ill omen to execute people, and did not celebrate in his heart. These were the funeral rites. They knew that the use of weapons would not stop in the future, and so were sad and mournful.

THIRTY-ONE
"Elegant weapons" symbolize an attempt to treat violence as something attractive and pleasant. This is a dangerous attitude to have, especially for someone leading others, as it makes light of the cost that violence inevitably brings to the lives and culture of those involved.

As Daoists observe and prepare for change, constantly training themselves to adapt, they also have a rich history of martial skills. However, the focus of Daoist martial arts (Tai Ji, Bagua Zhang, Xing Yi) is preserving life. Aside from teaching how to protect oneself from an attacker, they teach ideal body alignment, inner tranquility, and are often taught alongside the healing arts of Chinese medicine. Thus, Daoist training in martial arts does not glorify dominance, but rather self-sufficiency, knowing that while we may occasionally encounter physical threats of violence, the challenge to overcome our inner limitations will be offered every single day.

Just as a Sage does not ornament himself but tries to stay true to his pure nature, he would not try to turn violence into some sort of dazzling and venerable undertaking. Similarly, "If an attacker cannot be stopped, and weapons are used, to be calm and unemotional is considered most important."

# ~ 32 ~

The Way is always without name
Simple, and seemingly insignificant
Nothing in the world can subordinate it
If lords and kings would embrace it

The myriad things would willingly submit to them
Heaven and Earth would unite
And send down sweet dew
The people could be given no commands
As it would fall on each one equally

When the beginning was established, names came into being
When this naming began, it was too late
Even before things are known
Know them
Thereby, you will not be endangered

Just as Dao exists in the world
Valley streams flow into the ocean

## Chapter 32
聖德 Wisdom and Virtue

道常無名，道能陰能陽，能弛能張，能存能亡，故無常名也。
"The Way is always without name"
Dao has the power of yin, the power of yang, the power of looseness, the power of tension, the power of life, and the power of death. Therefore, it is without a constant name.

樸雖小，天下莫能臣也。道樸雖小，微妙無形，天下不敢有臣使道者也。
"Simple, and seemingly insignificant, nothing in the world can subordinate it"
Dao is simple and seemingly insignificant. Infinitesimal and mysterious, it is without form. Nothing in the world dares to subordinate it, and so it is Dao.

侯王若能守之，萬物將自賓。侯王若能守道無為，萬物將自賓，服從於德也。
"If lords and kings would embrace it, the myriad things would willingly submit to them"
If lords and kings could embrace the effortlessness of Dao, the myriad things would willingly submit to them. Their Virtue would then spread far and wide.

天地相合，以降甘露，侯王動作能與天相應和，天即降下甘露善瑞也。
"Heaven and Earth would unite and send down sweet dew"
When lords and kings move into action in accord with Heaven, they ensure harmony. Heaven then descends sweet dew as a most auspicious omen.

民莫之令而自均。天降甘露善瑞，則萬物莫有教令之者，皆自均調若一也。
"The people could be given no commands, as it would fall on each one equally"
Heaven would descend sweet dew as an auspicious omen, then the myriad things would not be guided or commanded as Heaven's dew reached each and every individual equally as one.

始制有名，始，道也。有名，萬物也。道無名能制於有名，無形，能制於有形也。

*"When the beginning was established, names came into being"*

"The beginning" refers to Dao. "Names came into being," refers to the myriad things. Dao is without name, yet can establish what has names. Dao is without form, yet can establish what has forms.

名亦既有，既，盡也。有名之物，盡有情欲，叛道離德，故身毀辱也。

*"When this naming began, it was too late"*

Too late, here, means near the end. Putting names (and reputations) on things leads to desires and strong emotions as a result of them – to rejecting Dao, and abandoning Virtue. Thereby oneself is brought to ruin.

夫亦將知之。人能法道行德，天亦將自知之。

*"Even before things are known"*

People can align with Dao and act in accordance with Virtue. In this way they will know Heaven in themselves.

知之，所以不殆。天知之，則神靈祐助，不復危殆。

*"Know them. Thereby, you will not be endangered"*

When the Way of Heaven is known, spiritual forces bring protection and aid, and there is no return to the dangerous state of neglecting (the Way of Heaven).

譬道之在天下，猶川谷之與江海。譬言道之在天下，與人相應和，如川谷與江海相流通也。

*"Just as Dao exists in the world – valley streams flow into the ocean"*

This is a metaphor to say that Dao's presence in the world brings people together in harmony, just like valley streams flow together into the ocean where they are united.


## THIRTY-TWO

Like the body's ongoing changes toward homeostasis, Dao is not so much a thing as a dynamic process. As such, trying to understand Dao as a thing with a name is akin to referring to the changing balance of hot and cold in a room. We can say "warm" or "cool," but these static descriptions actually refer to a constantly changing process.

    The end of chapter 32 ("When the beginning was established, names came into being") can be read as guidance to clear the mind and know Oneness. Knowing Oneness within, we can be open to, and embrace, all. Virtue (De) nourishes all things and nurtures their fruition. Finding this peace and vitality within, we can practice the way of Virtue.

    Virtue does not distinguish and favour, but brings Dao to all beings and things (if such distinctions can be made). To practice Dao is also to find this Oneness in all things. As such, external practices of Daoism include cultivating forbearance and emotional moderation, accepting that our place may sometimes be low and sometimes be high while acting accordingly and without contempt.

# ~ 33 ~

Those who know others, are wise
Those who know themselves, are clear-sighted
Those who overpower others, have strength
Those who overpower themselves, have fortitude
Those who know contentment, are rich
Those who exercise this fortitude, have will-power
Those who do not lose their station, continue
Those who die but do not disappear, live long

## Chapter 33
辯德 Dispute and Virtue

知人者智，能知人好惡，是為智。
"Those who know others, are wise"
Those who can know others' likes and dislikes are wise.
自知者明。人能自知賢與不肖，是為反聽無聲，內視無形，故為明也。
"Those who know themselves, are clear-sighted"
Those who can know their own worthiness and unworthiness – this is to turn around and listen to what has no voice, and look within at what has no form. This is to be clear-sighted.
勝人者有力，能勝人者，不過以威力也。
"Those who overpower others, have strength"
The ability to overpower others is no more than showing off might and physical strength.
自勝者強。人能自勝己情欲，則天下無有能與己爭者，故為強也。
"Those who overpower themselves, have fortitude"
When a person has overcome their emotions and desires, nothing in the world can make this person contend with them. Hence, they are powerful.
知足者富，人能知足，則長保福祿，故為富也。
"Those who know contentment, are rich"
When a person knows how to be content, they enjoy lasting happiness and blessings. Hence they are rich.
強行者有志，人能強力行善，則為有意於道，道亦有意於人。
"Those who exercise this fortitude, have will-power"
Those who exercise fortitude and strength with good (intentions) put their intention with Dao, while Dao also puts its intention with them.
不失其所者久，人能自節養，不失其所受天之精氣，則可以長久。
"Those who do not lose their station, continue"

Those who can nurture a connection within themselves, and not lose their place to receive Heaven's vital energy-breath, will continue for a very long time.

死而不亡者壽。目不妄視，耳不妄聽，口不妄言，則無怨惡於天下，故長壽。

"Those who die, but do not disappear, live long"

When the eyes do not observe frantically, the ears do not listen frantically, and the mouth does not speak frantically, there will be no blame or hatred of the world. Thus, lifespans will be long.

THIRTY-THREE
Chapter 33 helps to dispel a persistent myth that the cultivation of effortlessness (wu wei) and natural spontaneity (zi ran) amounts to little more than idleness and self-indulgence. Quite to the contrary, Daoist monks and priests exemplify self-restraint in their commitment to spiritual and physical refinement. Attempting to transcend desire, selfishness, intense emotional states, physical limitations, and the ever-present allures of praise and fame, the guiding ropes of one's sail must never slip from the hand of internal awareness.

# ~ 34 ~

Oh how the Great Dao is overflowing
It can go both left and right
When the myriad things trust in it
They live, and are not refused
It accomplishes its work
Yet makes no name for itself
It loves and raises the myriad things
Yet does not act as their master

Always without wants, it can be known by its smallness
All things returning to it yet it does not act as their master
It can be known by its greatness
Therefore, when finishing, Sages' actions are not grandiose
Thus, they can complete what is great

# Chapter 34
任成 Trust and Completion

大道汜兮，言道汜汜，若浮若沉，若有若無，視之不見，說之難殊。
"Oh how the Great Dao is overflowing"
The Dao is flooding; overflowing; covering; submerging; As though present; as though absent. It cannot be seen through observation. To describe it is unusually difficult.

其可左右。道可左可右，無所不宜。
"It can go both left and right"
Dao can be on both the left and the right. It has no place that is out of place.

萬物恃之而生，恃，待也。萬物皆待道而生。
"When the myriad things trust in it, they live"
"Trust," here, means rely. The myriad things all rely on Dao to give them life.

而不辭，道不辭謝而逆止也。
"And are not refused"
Dao does not refuse (the myriad things), nor does it stop (supporting them).

功成不名有，有道不名其有功也。
"It accomplishes its work, yet makes no name for itself"
The Dao does not try to make itself known, though it has accomplishments.

愛養萬物而不為主。道雖愛養萬物，不如人主有所收取。
"It loves and raises the myriad things, yet does not act as their master"
Dao only loves[71] and raises the myriad things. Unlike man, it does not try to act as their master and take possession of them.

常無欲，可名於小。道匿德藏名，怕然無為，似若微小也。
"Always without wants, it can be known by its smallness"
Dao, in concealing its Virtue, hides from notoriety. It seems as though small and afraid to take action.

萬物歸焉而不為主，萬物皆歸道受氣，道非如人主有所禁止也。
"All things returning to it, yet it does not act as their master"
All things return to Dao and receive energy-breath. Unlike man, Dao does not try to master things and keep them from rest.

可名為大。萬物橫來橫去，使名自在，故可名於大也。
"It can be known by its greatness"
Over every land, the myriad things come and go. They make the Dao known by their very existence. Thus it can be known by its greatness.

---

[71] Heshang Gong uses "ai 愛, love" in this stanza, where Wang Bi and Fu Yi have "yi, 衣, clothe." The word "ai 愛, love/care/cherish" appears about three-dozen times in Heshang Gong's commentary, showing that he felt it was a worthy virtue to cultivate along with detachment from desires.

是以聖人終不為大，聖人法道匿德藏名，不為滿大。
*"Therefore, when finishing, Sages' actions are not grandiose"*
Sages follow the way of Dao. They conceal their virtue and hide from notoriety; they are not extravagant.

故能成其大。聖人以身師導，不言而化，萬事修治，故能成其大。
*"Thus, they can complete what is great"*
Sages lead by example. Without having to speak, they reform things, influencing them to study and cultivate balance. Through this potent influence, they complete great things.


## THIRTY-FOUR

The Dao is immeasurable, and thus too is the capacity of its primordial force: De, Virtue. Where the ambition of Daoists may be most present is in modelling their behaviour after the Dao itself, seeking to embody and invest in themselves the effortlessness of its beneficence.

While benevolence in a person requires the desire, meaning, or inclination to do good, Dao benefits life without any desire, meaning, or inclination. It does so simply by doing what Dao does. Thus, it does not expect recognition for doing so any more than we expect to be thanked for running into someone on the street. As such, benevolence does not even apply, yet everything Dao does fulfills the needs of life.


## ~ 35 ~

Hold forth the great image
And all under Heaven will approach
Approaching, unharmed
Tranquility and stability reach their ultimate

Joyful music and sweets entice passing travelers to stop
When Dao appears in the mouth
Like water, it is without taste
Looking at it, it is not seen
Listening to it, it is not heard
Using it, it is not used up

# Chapter 35
## 仁德 The Virtue of Benevolence

執大象，天下往。執，守也。象，道也。聖人守大道，則天下萬民移心歸往之也。治身則天降神明，往來於己也。
*"By holding onto the great image, the world is put into motion"*
"Hold forth," here, means embracing. "Image," here, means Dao. The Sage embraces the Great Dao, and everything in the world shifts its heart to the way things once were. He governs his body and Heaven sends down spiritual lights (shen ming) which go back and forth between his body (and Heaven).

往而不害，安平太。萬民歸往而不傷害，則國家安寧而致太平矣。治身不害神明，則身安而大壽也。
*"Approaching, unharmed, tranquility and stability reach their Ultimate"*
When the myriad people return to the way that things once were, and do not inflict harm, the nation will be tranquil, serene, and arrive at supreme peace. When governing the body, do not harm the spiritual intelligence. Then the body will be peaceful and have a great lifespan.

樂與餌，過客止，餌，美也。過客，一也。人能樂美於道，則一留止也。一者，去盈而處虛，忽忽如過客。
*"Joyful music and sweets entice passing travelers to stop"*
"Sweets" refers to pleasantness. "Passing travelers" refers to Oneness. When people enjoy the pleasantness of Dao, Oneness comes to visit. Oneness leaves fullness, and remains in emptiness, spontaneously and suddenly like the passing traveller.

道之出口，淡乎其無味，道出入於口，淡淡非如五味有酸鹹苦甘辛也。
*"When Dao appears in the mouth, like water, it is without taste"*
When Dao goes into the mouth, it is like water. It is not like the five flavours: sour, salty, bitter, sweet, and pungent.

視之不足見，足，得也。道無形，非若五色有青黃赤白黑可得見也。
*"Looking at it, it is not seen"*
Zu 足 is an alternate of de 得 (which would function here as a grammatical particle). Dao is without form. It does not resemble the five colours: blue, green, yellow, red, white, and black. It cannot be seen.

聽之不足聞，道非若五音有宮商角徵羽可得聽聞也。
*"Listening to it, it is not heard"*
Dao does not resemble the five tones: gong (doh), shang (ray), jue (me), zhi (so), yu (la).[72] It cannot be heard.

---

[72] The names of these tones translate respectively as: the temple, the merchant, the wine vessel, the invitation, and the feather. They are the 1st, 2nd, 3rd, 5th, and 6th degrees of a major scale. This scale also begins on different degrees to create "modes" as in Western music. Note that the name of the 5th

用之不足既。既,盡也。謂用道治國,則國安民昌。治身則壽命延長,無有既盡之時也。

*"Using it, it is not used up"*

This means that when Dao is used to govern a nation, the nation is peaceful and the people are radiant. When Dao is used to govern the body, aging is delayed and one's destined lifespan is extended indefinitely.

## THIRTY-FIVE

Heshang Gong specifies that it is enjoyment of the pleasantness of Dao that brings Oneness to visit a gathering, community, or nation. Dao in this instance may refer to the absence of want – the harmony, ease, and cooperation between individuals, and the presiding radiance of spirit that increases upon the lasting decorum of those assembled.[73] It was, in part, to preserve this unity that Confucius resolved to scrutinize ritual, etiquette, music and harmony, proprieties of social hierarchy, righteousness, and justice. In the *Book of Music*, Confucius establishes:

> Knowing the fluctuations that occur at our deepest roots is the essence of music; the bearing of one's sincerity and abstaining from all artifice is the sacredness of ceremony. Ceremony and music adhere to the essence of Heaven and Earth; they bring forth the virtues of the spiritual lights (shen ming); they bring down and raise up the spirits from above and below; they give substance to what is intangible and tangible, and guide the right relationships between father and son, ruler and minister.[74]

Both Heshang Gong and Confucius share the ancient cosmology that a gathering pervasive with harmony is presided over by fortunate spirits. Confucius notes that sincerity devoid of artifice is integral to true ceremony, much as Lao Zi paints benevolence, etiquette and righteousness as artificial efforts to return to the natural Oneness and harmony of Dao. This sentiment of unpretentiousness, naturalness, and the spirit that presides when people commune as such, might also be reflected in Lao Zi's subtle description of a fortuitous and warm encounter:

> When Dao appears in the mouth,
> Like water, is without taste
> Looking at it, it is not seen
> Listening to it, it is not heard
> Using it, it is not used up

---

degree is "the invitation," resembling the Western theory that a "dominant" chord urges resolution back to the "tonic," here called "the temple."

[73] Note the reference to shen ming in HSGs comments on line one as "spiritual lights," and on line two as "spiritual intelligence/radiance."

[74] Translated by Dan G. Reid

# ~ 36 ~

Those wishing to draw in, first set up expansion
Those wishing for there to be weakness, first set up power
Those wishing for there to be failure, first set up success
Those wishing to rob, first set up allegiance
This is called minimalist intelligence

The soft and yielding win over the rigid and inflexible
Fish should not leave the cover of deep waters
The state's sharp instruments should not be revealed

## Chapter 36
微明 The Intelligence of Minimalism

將欲歙之，必固張之。先開張之者，欲極其奢淫
"Those wishing to draw in, first set up expansion"
If at first they are open and stretched, desires will extend to extravagance and licentiousness.
將欲弱之，必固強之。先強大之者，欲使遇禍患
"Those wishing for there to be weakness, first set up power"
If at first they are great and powerful, their desires will bring about disaster and suffering.
將欲廢之，必固興之。先興之者，欲使其驕危。
"Those wishing for there to be failure, first set up success"
If at first they are successful, their desires will bring about arrogance and danger.
將欲奪之，必固與之。先與之者，欲極其貪心。
"Those wishing to rob, first set up allegiance"
If at first they are accepted, their desires will extend to a greedy mind.
是謂微明。此四事，其道微，其效明也。
"This is called minimalist intelligence"
These four operations use minimalist method and effective intelligence.

柔弱勝剛強。柔弱者久長，剛強者先亡也。
"The soft and yielding win over the rigid and inflexible"
The soft and yielding last the longest; the tough and rigid are first to die.
魚不可脫於淵，魚脫於淵，謂去剛得柔，不可復制焉。
"Fish should not leave the cover of deep waters"
Taking fish out of water refers to abandoning rigidity and attaining softness.[75] Should

---

[75] See previous line.

one not return to this principle?
國之利器，不可以示人。利器者，謂權道也。治國權者，不可以示執事之臣也。治身道者，不可以示非其人也。

*"The state's sharp instruments should not be revealed"*
"Sharp instruments" refers to the Dao of power. Those who govern a nation should not display their political strategies. The Dao of governing the self should not be revealed to the wrong sorts of people.


THIRTY-SIX
Illustrating again the paradoxical effects of self-serving efforts, Lao Zi notes some common political tactics of his day. During the Warring States Period of China (c. 475-221 BC) as throughout history all around the world, states were constantly attacking, aiding, betraying, and aligning with each other, making shrewd diplomacy of utmost value. Though chapter 36 is saturated with Daoist philosophy, the tactics mentioned within it were likely borrowed from commonplace strategies of the day, presented here as evidence that desire is one's greatest vulnerability, and self-aggrandizing efforts one's greatest folly.[76] These examples of self-defeat also show that the best strategy is to simply follow Dao and allow its power – Virtue – to guide success. This means putting aside thoughts of personal gain and acting according to what benefits the greater community – in other words, simply staying out of destiny's way to see what the harmony of Dao will bring.


# ~ 37 ~

*The Dao is always effortless yet without inaction*
*When lords and kings can guard this within*
*The myriad things eventually transform themselves*
*Transforming, yet desiring to do so intentionally*
*I pacify this desire with the simplicity of the nameless*

*The simplicity of the nameless removes all desires*
*When the tranquility of desirelessness is established*
*The world stabilizes itself*

---

[76] See chapter 46.

# Chapter 37
## 為政 Active Government

道常無為而無不為。道以無為為常也。
"The Dao is always effortless yet without inaction"
The Dao's effortlessness is always active.

侯王若能守之，萬物將自化。言侯王若能守道萬物將自化效於己也。
"When lords and kings can guard this within, the myriad things eventually transform themselves"
When lords and kings can hold on to Dao, the myriad things progress and transform themselves by their own power.

化而欲作，吾將鎮之以無名之樸。吾，身也。無明之樸，道德也。萬物已化效於己也。復欲作巧偽者，侯王當身鎮撫以道德也。
"Transforming yet desiring to do so intentionally, I pacify this desire with the simplicity of the nameless"
"I," here, means within his body. Dao and Virtue are invisible in their unaltered simplicity. The myriad things transform themselves by their own power. When the desire to interfere through skillful artifice returns, lords and kings should pacify and soothe it with Dao and Virtue.

無名之樸，夫亦將無欲。不欲以靜，言侯王鎮撫以道德，民亦將不欲，故當以清靜導化之也。
"The simplicity of the nameless removes all desires. When the tranquility of desirelessness is established"
When lords and kings pacify and soothe (the desire to interfere) with Dao and Virtue, the people also stop desiring. Thus, clarity and tranquility must guide their transformation.

天下將自定。能如是者，天下將自正定也。
"The world stabilizes itself"
Those who can be like this, help the world to align and stabilize itself.


## THIRTY-SEVEN
The term *wei* (為, doing, being) suggests acting with *willfulness*, which Dao and De do not have. Thus, Dao is without *wei*, yet always effective. De is Dao's effectiveness, or simply Dao's *effect*, always active like the energy of a cosmic and perpetual energy-source. If people can absorb Dao's energetic essence[77] and follow its spontaneous nature, they can be without desire and willfulness yet perpetually effective. This offers the seeming paradox of removing desire in order

---

[77] "Jing-qi." See chapter 21.

to attain completion and perfection in oneself and in the nation. Such a way of being is described in the Duke of Zhou's comment (c. 1100 BC) on the first line of the first hexagram (Heaven) in the Yi Jing (I Ching): "Heaven moves with vitality. The junzi therefore sturdies himself to ceaseless activity."[78] As Heshang Gong comments in chapter 65, "to follow Heaven is to unite with Virtue."

A common reaction to the idea of transcending personal desires might be, "but if I don't serve my own desires, what am I doing here? I am completely insignificant!" In fact, we may be completely insignificant; no more significant than a mayfly in the grand universal scheme of things, despite the religious cosmologies that help to make us feel important in an inconceivably immense universe.

Paradoxically, this insignificance would only stem from our individuality. While we may be extremely significant to other beings on this planet, as individuals we are inconceivably miniscule in our vast universe. However, by uniting with the Great Dao, we become part of the Dao, we act from the Dao, we express the universe and the universe expresses us. In this way, our lives are connected to the One Existence beyond existence – Dao.

Chapter 25 makes clear how we can live with this connection, showing that humankind follows Earth, Earth follows Heaven, and Heaven follows Dao. Observing the changes that take place in the earth as it adapts to those of Heaven, we can learn how to follow Heaven, and thus Dao. This includes following the seasons and transformations of nature, life, and events, and utilizing the natural leverage afforded to us by the power and effectiveness of Dao – De, Virtue. If we must find meaning in life, we may find it in uniting with the Great Nature (Heaven), the Virtue of Dao, and the spontaneous essentiality of existence. To find our connection to this path, road, or stream, is to find life's ultimate consequence.

---

[78] 天行健，君子以自强不息

# Volume Two
# De: The Virtue (of Nature)

# ~ 38 ~

Highest virtue is not (noticeably) virtuous
Therefore it has Virtue
Lower virtue is unmistakably virtuous
Therefore it is without Virtue

Highest Virtue is without action
It does not exist by its actions
Lower virtue takes action
It exists because of its actions

Highest benevolence takes action
Yet does not exist by its actions
Highest righteousness takes action
And exists because of its actions
Highest etiquette takes action
And when its obligations are not met
People are taken by the arm and forced to obey

Thus, when Dao is lost, virtue appears
When virtue is lost, benevolence appears
When benevolence is lost, righteousness appears
When righteousness is lost, etiquette appears

In etiquette, sincerity and selflessness are lacking
And this is the beginning of chaos
This trajectory can be recognized
When people who don't know
Display flowery appearances of the Dao
And speak as though they know how to recognize what is coming
This is the beginning of idiocy

Therefore, great and noble men stay with what is substantial
And not with what is slight
They stay with the fruit
And not with the flower
They leave that and choose this

# Chapter 38
論德 Discourse on Virtue

上德不德,上德,謂太古無名號之君,德大無上,故言上德也。不德者,言其不以德教民,因循自然,養人性命,其德不見,故言不德也。

"Highest virtue is not (noticeably) virtuous"
This refers to the virtue of the rulers of great antiquity who were without fame or title. Their virtue was great and without superior. Thus, it is called "highest virtue."

To say that it was "not (noticeably) virtuous" means that they did not teach the people virtues, but caused them to follow their natural spontaneity, thereby supporting the development of their pure nature (xing), and destiny-life-force (ming). Their virtue was not put on display. Thus, Lao Zi describes it as "not (noticeably) virtuous."

是以有德。言其德合於天地,和氣流行,民德以全也。

"Therefore it has Virtue"
This refers to the Virtue which unites Heaven and Earth. Its harmonious energy-breath flows and circulates, refining Virtue in the people.

下德不失德,下德,謂號諡之君,德不及上德,故言下德也。不失德者,其德可見,其功可稱也

"Lower virtue is unmistakably virtuous"
Lower virtue refers to that which is signified by an honorary title. This cannot equal the highest virtue, and so is called lower virtue. It is "unmistakably virtuous," which means that such virtue is put on display, and accomplishments are officially recognized.

是以無德。以有名號及其身故。

"Therefore it is without Virtue"
It is but a name attributed to an individual.

上德無為,謂法道安靜,無所施為也。

"Highest Virtue is without action"
This means that the character of Dao is peaceful, still, and without intentional actions.

而無以為,言無以名號為也。

"It does not exist by its actions"
It is without name or recognition for its actions.

下德為之,言為教令,施政事也。

"Lower virtue takes action"
(Lower virtue) acts by teaching, giving commands, and carrying out duties.

而有以為。言以為己取名號也。

"It exists because of its actions"
Its actions create reputations and titles.

上仁為之, 上仁謂行仁之君,其仁無上,故言上仁。為之者,為人恩也。

"Highest benevolence takes action"
"Highest benevolence" refers to the benevolent actions of a ruler. His benevolence has no superior. Thus it is called highest benevolence. He actively treats all people with kindness and charity.

而無以為，功成事立，無以執為。
"Yet does not exist by its actions"
When his achievements have been completed as required by his position, there is no attachment to those actions.

上義為之，為義以斷割也。
"Highest righteousness takes action"
It acts in the name of righteousness by interrupting and dividing.

而有以為。動作以為己，殺人以成威，賊下以自奉也。
"And exists because of its actions"
It moves out of self-interest, kills people to create an air of power, robs those below, and serves only itself.

上禮為之，謂上禮之君，其禮無上，故言上禮。為之者，言為禮制度，序威儀也。
"Highest etiquette takes action"
This refers to the highest etiquette of a ruler without superior(s). Thus it is called highest etiquette. It is active because it standardizes etiquette according to hierarchy and ceremony.

而莫之應，言禮華盛實衰，飾偽煩多，動則離道，不可應也。
"And when its obligations are not met"
This is to say that flowery displays of class and refinement are artificial and create much tension. This moves away from the Dao, and so cannot be necessary.

則攘臂而扔之。言禮煩多不可應，上下忿爭，故攘臂相仍引。
"People are taken by the arm and forced to obey"
Etiquette causes many unnecessary tensions. When people are taken by the arm and forced to obey these rules, it creates hostility and competition between authorities and subordinates.

故失道而後德，言道衰而德化生也。
"Thus, when Dao is lost, virtue appears"
When Dao declines, permutations of Virtue arise.

失德而後仁，言德衰而仁愛見也。
"When virtue is lost, benevolence appears"
When virtue declines, benevolence and love are put on display.

失仁而後義，言仁衰而分義明也。
"When benevolence is lost, righteousness appears"
When benevolence declines, righteousness is clealry distinguished.

失義而後禮。言義衰則失禮聘，行玉帛也。

"When righteousness is lost, etiquette appears"
When righteousness declines, it is lost to etiquette and gifts of jade and silk.

夫禮者，忠信之薄，言禮廢本治末，忠信日以衰薄。
"In etiquette, sincerity and selfless loyalty are lacking"
This implies that etiquette discards the root and focuses on the branches, causing sincerity and selfless loyalty to gradually weaken.

而亂之首。禮者賤質而貴文，故正直日以少，邪亂日以生。
"And this is the beginning of chaos"
Etiquette is of cheap substance and wealthy appearance. As a result, honour gradually declines while wickedness and chaos arise.

前識者，道之華不知而言知為前識，此人失道之時，得道之華。
"This trajectory can be recognized when people who don't know display flowery appearances of the Dao, and speak as though they know how to recognize what is coming"
This is how people lose the right timing of Dao while taking on flowery appearances of Dao.

而愚之始。言前識之人，愚闇之倡始也。
"This is the beginning of idiocy"
This is to say that foolhardy fortune tellers begin to lead people blindly.

是以大丈夫處其厚，大丈夫謂得道之君也。處其厚者，謂處身於敦樸。
"Therefore, great and noble men stay with what is substantial"
"Great and noble people" refers to rulers who have attained Dao. "Staying with what is substantial" means keeping one's character candid and plain.

不居其薄，不處身違道，為世煩亂也。
"And not with what is slight"
They do not keep themselves in opposition to Dao, as this would cause tension and chaos in the world.

處其實，處忠信也。
"They stay with the fruit"
They maintain sincerity and selfless loyalty.

不居其華。不尚華言也。
"And not with the flower"
They are not in the habit of using flowery words.

故去彼取此。去彼華薄，取此厚實。
"They leave that, and choose this"
They leave the flowery and lacking, and choose what is substantial – they choose the fruit.

## THIRTY-EIGHT

Heshang Gong interprets chapter 38 as depicting a ruler's De, and its effect on his or her people. When a ruler's virtue is put on display, it teaches the people to emulate, rather than abide in their own pure nature. Teaching otherwise satisfied people about the superiority of this or that behaviour causes them to take pride in demonstrating their newfound superiority, and lose the true Virtue inherent in their pure nature (xing). To have left them without such knowledge would have saved them from re-evaluating their self-esteem according these demonstrations of newly acquired superior attributes. Now robbed of the pure nature and former wellspring of their simplicity, they focus on shaping themselves according to these new measurements. This opens them up to tarnishing their natural perfection with conceit and foolish pride. Thus, leaders should not put too much effort into teaching people how to emulate heroes, but rather allow them to discover the inborn Virtue of which they are all in possession. Further, if the ruler's virtue is exceptional, it will affect others without having to intentionally demonstrate it.

Chapter 38 also includes what appears to be a reference to divination, expressing incredulity rather than esteem for divination practices presumably connected to the Yi Jing (Book of Changes) – another important book in the Daoist tradition. Lao Zi describes a pattern of departure from Dao and Virtue which eventually reaches the point of reliance on divination to determine how events will turn out. Lao Zi's thoughts, here, would then correlate closely to those found in the *Bai Xin* (*Purifying the Heart-Mind*, attributed to Guan Zi and dated to 700 BC or 350 BC, according to tradition or scholars, respectively[79]):

> "Not by the day or the month, but by how affairs follow (Dao), and not by prophesy or divination, but by how cautiously one follows (Dao), can you know their fortune or misfortune."[80]

This dismissal of diviners may otherwise simply express that these diviners have lost Dao, and so are incapable of such foresights. As Guigu Zi (Master of Ghost-Valley, circa 250 BC) explains in his chapter, *Seven Techniques of Yin Talisman*:

> Consolidating intention refers to contemplative energy. The heart-mind desires peace and quiet. Contemplation desires depth and breadth. When the heart-mind is peaceful and silent, spiritual foresight arises. When contemplation is deep and broad, strategic plans are refined. When spiritual foresight arises, the will should not be disturbed. When strategic plans are refined, success will not be denied.[81]

---

[79] Note that both tradition and the concensus of scholarship date the Bai Xin before the Dao De Jing.
[80] Reid, Dan G. *The Thread of Dao: Unraveling Early Daoist Oral Traditions in Guan Zi's Purifying the Heart-Mind (Bai Xin), Art of the Heart-Mind (Xin Shu), and Internal Cultivation (Nei Ye)*. Montreal: Center Ring Publications, 2017.
[81] Ibid.

# ~ 39 ~

In the beginning was the attainment of Oneness

Heaven attained Oneness
And became clear
Earth attained Oneness
And became serene
Gods attained Oneness
And became spiritually powerful
Valleys attained Oneness
And became full
The myriad things attained Oneness
And were born
Lords and kings attained Oneness
And all under Heaven became loyal

Then occurred the following

Heaven, lacking the cause of its clarity
Began to tremble and split open
Earth, lacking the cause of its serenity
Became fearful and began to gush forth
The gods, lacking the cause of their spiritual power
Became fearful and stopped moving
The valley, lacking the cause of its fullness
Became fearful and began to drain
The myriad things, lacking the cause of their life
Became fearful and began to die out
The lords and kings, lacking the cause of their being praised and elevated
Became fearful and began to fall

Therefore, value the lowest and treat it as the root source
Elevate the low and treat it as the foundation
This is why lords and kings
Call themselves orphans, widows
And "no hub-of-the-wheel"
Is this not treating the lowest as the root source?
Is it not?
Thus, they are sent several palanquins without a palanquin

Have no desires for fine jade

Nor for cheap necklaces and stones

# Chapter 39
## 法本 Guided by the Root

昔之得一者：昔，往也。一，無為，道之子也。
"In the beginning was the attainment of Oneness"
"Begin," here, means "from the outset." Oneness is effortless – a child of Dao.

天得一以清，言天得一故能垂象清明。
"Heaven attained Oneness and became clear"
Heaven attained Oneness and was thereby able to send down images of clarity and brilliance.
地得一以寧，言地得一故能安靜不動搖。
"Earth attained Oneness and became serene"
Earth attained Oneness and was thereby able to remain peaceful and still, not moving or shaking.
神得一以靈，言神得一故能變化無形。
"Gods attained Oneness and became spiritually powerful (ling)"
Gods attained Oneness and were thereby able to transform without form.
谷得一以盈，言谷得一故能盈滿而不絕也。
"Valleys attained Oneness and became full"
Valleys attained Oneness and were thereby able to fill until overflowing without cease.
萬物得一以生，言萬物皆須道以生成也。
"The myriad things attained Oneness and were born"
The myriad things all followed Dao and lived their full lifespans.
侯王得一以為天下貞。言侯王得一故能為天下平正。
"Lords and kings attained Oneness, and all under Heaven became loyal"
Lords and kings attained Oneness and were thereby able to make the entire world peaceful and honourable.

其致之。致，誠也。謂下六事也。
"Then occurred the following"
This is a warning, referring to the following six incidents.
天無以清將恐裂，言天當有陰陽弛張，晝夜更用，不可但欲清明無已時，將恐分裂不為天。
"Heaven, lacking the cause of its clarity, began to tremble and split open"
Heaven has both yin and yang, laxity and tension, day, night, and other workings. It should not want clarity and brilliance without cease, and so became fearful and divided, no longer acting like Heaven.

地無以寧將恐發，言地當有高下剛柔，節氣五行，不可但欲安靜無已時，將恐發泄不為地。
"Earth, lacking the cause of its serenity, became fearful and began to gush forth"
Earth has both high and low, hard and soft, and joins the energy-breaths of the five elemental phases. It should not want only peace and stillness without cease, and so became fearful and began to gush and flow, no longer acting like Earth.

神無以靈將恐歇，言神當有王相囚死休廢，不可但欲靈變無已時，將恐虛歇不為神。
"The gods, lacking the cause of their spiritual power, became fearful and stopped moving"
The gods are both kings and prisoners of an unending death. They should not want to be only spiritually powerful and transforming without cease, so they became fearful and lost their power to move, no longer acting like gods.

谷無以盈將恐竭，言谷當有盈縮虛實，不可但欲盈滿無已時，將恐枯竭不為谷。
"The valley, lacking the cause of its fullness, became fearful and began to drain"
The valleys were full, filling their emptiness with wealth. They should not want to continue filling without cease, and so became fearful and dried out until empty, no longer acting like the valleys.

萬物無以生將恐滅，言萬物當隨時生死，不可但欲長生無已時，將恐滅亡不為物。
"The myriad things, lacking the cause of their life, became fearful and began to die out"
The myriad things followed the seasons of birth and death. They should not want for long life without cease, and so became fearful and began to die out, no longer acting like living things.

侯王無以貴高將恐蹶。言侯王當屈己以下人，汲汲求賢，不可但欲貴高於人無已時，將恐顛蹶失其位。
"The lords and kings, lacking the cause of their being praised and elevated, became fearful and began to fall"
The lords and kings bent themselves down to serve the people, and drank abundantly from the well of Virtue. They should not want to be praised and elevated by the people without cease, and so became fearful, fell from the summit, and lost the throne.

故貴以賤為本，言必欲尊貴，當以薄賤為本，若禹稷躬稼，舜陶河濱，周公下白屋也。
"Therefore, value the lowest and treat it as the root source"
This is to say that it is necessary for those who are highly honoured to treat the weak and low as the root source. This is like King Yu becoming the minister of agriculture and personally sowing the grain, like King Shun digging clay and making pottery, or like the Duke of Zhou humbling himself at simple dwellings.

高以下為基,言必欲尊貴,當以下為本基,猶築牆造功,因卑成高,不下堅固,後必傾危。

*"Elevate the low and treat it as the foundation"*

This is to say that those who are highly honoured must treat the low as the root foundation. This is similar to building a wall. Preparing well, begin low so as to end high. If you do not lend strength to the low, the future will surely overflow with danger.

是以侯王自謂孤、寡、不穀。孤寡喻孤獨,不穀喻不能如車轂為眾輻所湊。

*"This is why lords and kings call themselves orphans, widows, and 'no hub-of-the-wheel'"*

Being an orphan is a metaphor for being alone. Not being the hub of the wheel is a metaphor for not being able to unite the masses like spokes in a wheel.

此非以賤為本邪?言侯王至尊貴,能以孤寡自稱,此非以賤為本乎,以曉人?

*"Is this not treating the lowest as the root source?"*

This is to say that lords and kings attain honour by calling themselves orphans and widows. Is this not treating the low as the root, and thereby understanding others?

非乎!嗟嘆之辭。

*"Is it not?"*

This is an expression of admiration.

故致數輿無輿,致,就也。言人就車數之為輻、為輪、為轂、為衡、為轝,無有名為車者,故成為車,以喻侯王不以尊號自名,故能成其貴。

*"Thus, they are sent several palanquins without a palanquin"*

"Sent," here means that they approach. This is to say that one approaches (the making of) a cart by making spokes, making wheels, making wheel hubs, making measurements, and taking blame for errors; yet, those who make the cart have no fame. Thus, completing the construction of a cart is a metaphor for lords and kings who, by not giving themselves reverential titles and names, make themselves worthy of praise.

不欲琭琭如玉,珞珞如石。琭琭喻少,落落喻多,玉少故見貴,石多故見賤。言不欲如玉為人所貴,如石為人所賤,當處其中也。

*"Have no desires for fine jade, nor for cheap necklaces and stones"*

Fine jade is a metaphor for scarcity, while cheap necklaces are a metaphor for surplus. Jade is scarce and thus is seen as valuable. Stones are abundant and thus they are seen as cheap. This is to say that we should not want to be like jade, which people value highly, nor like stones which people find worthless, but rather stay in between these two.

## THIRTY-NINE

The character kong (恐), repeated several times in chapter 39, translates as fear, and is written by combining the characters for heart (below) and binding (above), meaning that the heart is constricted with fear. Heshang Gong explains that the fears described in chapter 39 were a result of excessive desire. Though all was plentiful, a fear persisted that continuous accumulation was needed and this fear resulted in a loss of the very peace, unity, and contentment that made this plenitude possible. As with chapter 23, the teachings of chapter 39 may be rooted in the ancient Chinese science of *resonance response* (gan ying) – the same system of natural synchronicities that gave birth to the elemental phase correlations of Chinese medicine. Chapter 23 teaches that trust brings trust: by unifying with Dao, Dao will join with you. Chapter 39 teaches that if you do not allow yourself to unify with Dao, Dao will leave you.[82] Chapter 39 may also indicate that when chapter 23 refers to loss ("Those who are one with loss, loss is also happy to have them") it refers to this loss of Oneness described in chapter 39.

As in chapter 39, the *Dao De Jing* teaches that one of the greatest obstacles to unifying with Dao is the need for recognition. It is often difficult for people to accept that they cannot take credit for the comforts that they enjoy; as such, they cannot find humility, they cannot follow the teaching of chapter 28:

> Knowing glory, hold fast to humiliation
> And be a valley under Heaven
> Being a valley under Heaven
> Virtue will always fulfill you
>
> Return to your unaltered substance
> Unaltered wood is shaped into vessels
> Sages make use of this model
> When acting in positions of leadership
> Thereby, the greatest establishment is undivided

# ~ 40 ~

Returning! The movement of Dao
Gentle! The employment of Dao
Everything in the world is born from what is
What is, is born from what is not

---

[82] This may also explain what is meant by "(To be a person of) loss, be one with loss" in chapter 23.

# Chapter 40
## 去用 Abandoning and Using

反者道之動，反，本也。本者，道之所以動，動生萬物，背之則亡也。
"Returning! The movement of Dao"
"Returning" means returning to the root. From here, the Dao moves, and its movement gives birth to the myriad things. Refusing this brings death.

弱者道之用。柔弱者，道之所常用，故能常久。
"Gentle! The employment of Dao"
Adaptive and gentle: the Dao always operates in this way and thus always endures.

天下萬物生於有，天下萬物皆從天地生，天地有形位，故言生於有也。
"Everything in the world is born from what is"
Everything in the world is born from Heaven and Earth. Heaven and Earth are the seat of form. Therefore, Lao Zi says "born from what is."

有生於無。天地神明，蜎飛蠕動，皆從道生。道無形，故言生於無也。此言本勝於華，弱勝於強，謙虛勝盈滿也。
"What is, is born from what is not"
Heaven and Earth have spiritual intelligence (spiritual brilliance), as do even mosquitos, flies, and wasps. All things trace their birth back to Dao. Dao is without form. Therefore, Lao Zi says "born from what is not." This explains why the root overcomes the flower, the soft overcomes the hard, and the humble and empty overcome the full and satisfied.


FORTY
Returning to the formless, the mind returns to yi, the facet of mind that precedes will and thought – a pure openness, void of desire and naming, like and dislike, good and bad. From formlessness comes form. This openness is the crucible of internal cultivation, where acquired self is returned to original self of no-self – the formlessness from which all selves we create, in order to function in this world of selves, emerges. Emptiness, formlessness, One, Dao.

    Water has no shape and so it can take on all shapes. Reflecting this formlessness allows us to move through the world like water, slipping through every crack and wearing away every mountain before we can be defeated.[83]

---

[83] See also chapter 50:
"I have heard that those who are good at absorbing life
Travel the land without encountering rhinoceros or tigers
That they walk into groups of soldiers
Without requiring armour, or soldiers, for protection
The rhinoceros has no place to thrust its horn
The tiger has no place to grab with its claw
And the soldier has nowhere to place his weapon

# ~ 41 ~

When the highest student hears the Way
Diligently, he treads the path
When the mediocre student hears the Way
At first present, he falls back
When the lowest student hears the Way
He breaks into a great laugh
If he did not laugh
It wouldn't be the path

Thus, such sayings have been established:
The illuminated path appears dark
The path forward seems to go back
The level path appears uneven
The highest virtue, low as a valley
Great purity appears disgraced
Magnanimous virtue appears insufficient
Deep Virtue appears easily detached
True substance seems to change
Great squares are without corners
Great vessels develop slowly
Great voices rarely speak
Great images are without form

The Way is hidden and without name
Yet kindly lends itself
To our fruition

## Chapter 41
同異 Similarity and Difference

上士聞道，勤而行之。上士聞道，自勤苦竭力而行之。
"When the highest student hears the Way, diligently he treads the path"
When the highest student hears of the Dao, he gathers his resolve and expends every effort to persevere through the difficulties of practicing it.

---

Why is this so?
Because these people are without any death-traps"

中士聞道，若存若亡。中士聞道，治身以長存，治國以太平，欣然而存之，退見財色榮譽，惑於情慾，而復亡之也。
"When the mediocre student hears the Way, at first present, he falls back"
When the mediocre student hears of the Dao, he governs himself to live long; governs the nation to achieve great peace; and is naturally joyful in his life. Taking a step backwards in his cultivation, he looks at wealth and appearances, glory, and fame. His resolve becomes confused by desires and strong emotions, and he moves back again toward death.

下士聞道，大笑之。下士貪狠多欲，見道柔弱，謂之恐懼，見道質樸，謂之鄙陋，故大笑之。
"When the lowest student hears the Way, he breaks into a great laugh"
The lowest student is greedy, cruel, and lascivious. Seeing softness and flexibility as cowardice, and what is simple and natural as low and unattractive, he breaks into laughter.

不笑不足以為道。不為下士所笑，不足以名為道
"If he did not laugh, it wouldn't be the path"[84]
If they did not make the lowest student laugh, the names used to describe the Path would not be sufficient.

故建言有之：建，設也。設言以有道，當如下句
"Thus, such sayings have been established"
"Established," here, means well established – the well established sayings about Dao in the following sentences.

明道若昧，明道之人，若闇昧無所見。
"The illuminated path appears dark"
Enlightened men of Dao seem oblivious, in the dark, and without vision.

進道若退，進取道者，若退不及。
"The path forward seems to go back"
Advancing to attain Dao is like going backwards and not attaining it.

夷道若纇。夷，平也。大道之人不自別殊，若多比類也。
"The level path appears uneven"
"Level," here, means peaceful. The great man of Dao does not separate himself as being different or special, yet seems to be many different things.

上德若谷，上德之人若深谷，不恥垢濁也。
"The highest virtue, low as a valley"
A man of the highest virtue is like a deep valley. He is not ashamed of dirt and mud.

大白若辱，大潔白之人若汙辱，不自彰顯。

---

[84] There are conflicting theories as to why the lowest student laughs – that he is an unassuming sage, or that he is simply arrogant. On the other hand, the following descriptions of Dao are so seemingly topsy turvy that they will make the lowest student laugh; yet, if they were not like this, they would not describe Dao.

"Great purity appears disgraced"
A man of great cleanliness and purity seems as though filthy and ashamed. He does not make a clear display of himself.
廣德若不足，德行廣大之人，若愚頑不足也。
"Magnanimous virtue appears insufficient"
The man whose virtue is shown through acts of great magnanimity seems as though foolish, stubborn, and not satisfied.
建德若偷，建設道德之人，若可偷引使空虛也。
"Deep Virtue appears easily detached"
When Dao is well established in a man of virtue, it seems as though his virtue could be extracted or stolen, leaving him hollow and empty.
質真若渝，質樸之人，若五色有渝淺不明也。
"True substance seems to change"
A man of simplicity and naturalness appears to change colours on the surface, as though he does not have much depth, and is not enlightened.
大方無隅，大方正之人，無委屈廉隅。
"Great squares are without corners"
Great men who are square and true do not let an appointment to office bend them. They remain honourable in every corner of their being.
大器晚成，大器之人，若九鼎瑚璉，不可卒成也
"Great vessels develop slowly"
Men who are great vessels (of Virtue) are like tributary bronze cauldrons, or coral grain bowls. They never wear out.
大音希聲，大音猶雷霆待時而動，喻當愛氣希言也。
"Great voices rarely speak"
Great voices are like cracks of thunder. They wait for the right time and then act. This is a metaphor for cherishing energy-breath and thus speaking rarely.
大象無形，大法象之人，質樸無形容。
"Great images are without form"
Great men who model themselves in the image of Dao remain simple, natural, and without any apparent form.

道隱無名。道潛隱，使人無能指名也。
"The Way is hidden and without name"
The Dao is concealed and hidden. People are incapable of pointing to, or naming, it.
夫惟道，善貸且成。成，就也。言道善稟貸人精氣，且成就之也。
"Yet kindly lends itself to our fruition"
"Fruition," here, means "to be approached." This is to say that Dao kindly endows people with its own vital energy-breath, thereby bringing them toward completion.

FORTY-ONE

At the risk of ruining every joke ever told, European philosophers of the 17th and 18th century traced humour to a common event called "incongruous juxtaposition" – that is, the juxtaposition of circumstances into a category of which at least one of those circumstances does not fit. On realizing this incongruity, humour is the separation of the congruous and incongruous elements. This resolution is generally the impetus of all jokes (Lord help us).

In the case of chapter 41's contrasting opposites, the lowest student might laugh on hearing such things as "great squares are without corners, great images are without form," and to find out that the most noble of people, the Sage, is so seemingly simple, unrefined, and unimposing. The Sage is not likely to be hurt by the laughter of the low students, however, for he knows that life is made of the high and low, big and small, and that they do not all so easily fit together in the mind that is already full of names and categories. This is simply the way that people often are. They may stare, and they may gawk, but they will eventually move on to some other amusement, and the Sage will continue on his journey, knowing by now that this too is the Dao.

While chapter 41 depicts the unity of opposites in Dao, it can also be applied to Daoist cultivation of the heart-mind. This cultivation is based largely in turning the heart-mind back to the formlessness of intention (yi) – an awareness that precedes the formation of will and thought. Chapter 41 may also hint at this grasping of the subtlety and formlessness behind our will and thoughts, a note that may be more pronounced by contrasting chapter 41 with chapter 32, in which Lao Zi describes the formlessness preceding names:

> When the beginning was established, names came into being
> When this naming began, it was too late
> Even before things are known
> Know them
> Thereby, you will not be endangered
> Just as Dao exists in the world
> Valley streams flow into the ocean.

~ 42 ~

Dao gave birth to the One
The One gave birth to Two
Two gave birth to Three
Three gave birth to the myriad things

The myriad things carry the Yin principle (on their backs)

While embracing the Yang principle (in front of them)
They are infused with energy-breath
And made to be harmonious

People consider it terrible
To be orphaned, widowed, and outcast
Yet kings and elders refer to themselves in this way
This is because things sometimes diminish themselves
And then benefit
Sometimes benefit themselves
And are then diminished

When others teach
I also teach
Those who use brute force obtain only death
I take this as the father of my teaching

# Chapter 42
道化 The Transformations of Dao

道生一，道使所生者一也。
"Dao gave birth to the One"
Dao sent forth life, and there was Oneness.
一生二，一生陰與陽也。
"The One gave birth to Two"
The One gave birth to Yin and Yang.
二生三，陰陽生和清濁，三氣分為天地人也。
"Two gave birth to Three"
Yin and Yang gave birth to the harmony between clear and opaque. This separated into three energy-breaths, creating Heaven, Earth, and Humanity.
三生萬物。天地人共生萬物也，天施地化，人長養之也。
"Three gave birth to the myriad things"
Heaven, Earth, and Humanity gave life to the myriad things. Heaven bestows upon them and Earth transforms them. Humanity leads them and helps them grow.

萬物負陰而抱陽，萬物無不負陰而向陽，迴心而就日。
"The myriad things carry the Yin principle (on their backs), while embracing the Yang principle (in front of them)"
The myriad things always carry yin and face toward yang. Though they may turn around, their hearts and minds go toward the sun.
沖氣以為和。萬物中皆有元氣，得以和柔，若胸中有藏，骨中有髓，草木中有空虛與氣通，故得久生也。
"They are infused with energy-breath, and made to be harmonious"
Inside of all things is the original energy-breath (yuan qi), attained through harmony and softness. If it is concealed in the breast, it will also be within the bone marrow, just as it is in plants and trees in the empty hollows where energy-breath circulates. Thereby (do all things) obtain long life.

人之所惡，惟孤、寡、不穀，而王公以為稱。孤寡不穀者，不祥之名，而王公以為稱者，處謙卑，法空虛和柔。
"People consider it terrible to be orphaned, widowed, and outcast, yet kings and elders refer to themselves in this way"
"Orphan," "widow," and "outcast" are not auspicious names, yet kings and elders refer to themselves with them. By remaining humble and modest, this hollowness and emptiness allows them to be harmonious and flexible.
故物或損之而益，引之不得，推之必還。
"This is because things sometimes diminish themselves and then benefit"
Trying to extract may not obtain anything, but offering may result in a return.
或益之而損。夫增高者志崩，貪富者致患。
"Sometimes benefit themselves and are then diminished"
Those who increase their grandeur have an unstable will. Their greed for wealth makes them suffer worries.

人之所教，謂眾人所教，去弱為強，去柔為剛。
"When others teach"
The masses are taught to abandon flexibility and be inflexible – to abandon gentleness and be rigid.
我亦教之。言我教眾人，使去強為弱，去剛為柔
"I also teach"
Lao Zi is saying "I teach the masses to abandon inflexibility and be flexible – to abandon rigidity and be gentle.
強梁者不得其死，強梁者，謂不信玄妙，背叛道德，不從經教，尚勢任力也。不得其死者，為天命所絕，兵刃所伐，王法所殺，不得以壽命死。
"Those who use brute force obtain only death"
"Those who use brute force" refers to those who do not trust in the fathomless mystery – who turn their backs on, and rebel against, Dao and Virtue. They do not follow the teachings of the ancient classics, and so are compelled to rely on force.

They "obtain only death" because they cause Heaven to cut short their life and destiny. Soldiers attack them, and kings order their deaths. Without obtaining long life or destiny, they die.
吾將以為教父。父，使也。老子以強梁之人為教，誠之始也。
"I take this as the father of my teaching"

"Father," here, means "the cause." Lao Zi teaches those who use brute force by beginning with this warning.

## FORTY-TWO

While chapter 42 is commonly regarded as the principle revelation of Daoist cosmogony, Heshang Gong's commentary has served as its definitive explanation. Lao Zi hints at his intended meaning of the One, Two, and Three by referring to the polarities of yin and yang (the only use of these terms in the entire text), and referring to energy-breath (qi, mentioned only in chapters 10, 42, and 55). As yin and yang are evidently the branching off of the One into Two, we can understand that One holds the unity and non-differentiation of yin and yang. By this we can also understand that Dao is not simply yin and yang, for Dao contains the undifferentiated Oneness which expresses *both* yin and yang. Heshang Gong explains:

> Yin and Yang gave birth to the harmony between clear and opaque. This separated into three energy-breaths, creating Heaven, Earth, and Humanity.

The clear and opaque are expressed in Heaven and Earth, ethereal and condensed, with all things falling somewhere within the spectrum of the two. This polar spectrum expresses a middle ground: qi (energy-breath), with Humanity encompassing the broad middle ground of the spectrum between Heaven and Earth.[85]

As explained in my introduction, on "Dao, De, and Oneness in Heshang Gong's Commentary," Heshang Gong adds an essential detail to his use of the term Oneness when he states in chapter 51:

> *"Virtue takes care of them"*
> "Virtue," here, means "Oneness." Oneness is the host of all things. It surrounds them with energy-breath, and gathers and rears things into form. Oneness establishes the form and image of all things.

So, we may rightly infer from this that "the One" in chapter 42 also refers to De, Virtue. Such a reading is consistent with descriptions of De as a nurturing

---

[85] Reflecting Heshang Gong's explanation of the Three, Wang Ju Yi states in *Applied Channel Theory in Chinese Medicine* (Eastland Press, 2008): "So, in breaking yin and yang down into three parts, the ancient philosophers were not only accounting for the fact that yin and yang in combination create qi, but also that there is a pivot between yin and yang that is itself a state of being."

force in chapter 51, and the spontaneous process of nurturing life that follows from the One, to Two, to Three in chapter 42, arriving at all things being infused with qi:

> *"They are infused with energy-breath, and made to be harmonious"*
> Inside of all things is the original energy-breath (yuan qi), attained through harmony and softness. If it is concealed in the breast, it will also be within the bone marrow, just as it is in plants and trees in the empty hollows where energy-breath circulates. Thereby (do all things) obtain long life.

Heshang Gong also comments on chapter 42 as it deals with conduct when Lao Zi suggests that emptiness attracts fullness ("things sometimes diminish themselves and then benefit"). This translates into the cultivation of qi through behaviour: if one can abstain from the self-entitlement of greed and anger, they facilitate a clear and peaceful spirit, resulting in a clear and peaceful physiology where the internal organs are unburdened by stressful emotions. With the heart calmly housing the spirit and thereby facilitating a balanced function of the other organs, this harmonious internal environment helps to preserve both mind and body. With the internal kingdom peacefully governed by an enlightened spirit, intention, habit, decisions, and lifestyle all contribute to fulfilling the positive destiny of this kingdom. This is to nurture life (yang sheng)[86] through conduct by abstaining from greed and anger. Removing the urge to think we are special or better than the rest, we allow Oneness, Virtue, to bring us into alignment and balance. As in the quote above, Heshang Gong teaches that qi is cultivated though harmony ("Inside of all things is the original energy-breath (yuan qi), attained through harmony and softness"). With this understanding of cultivating Oneness, the elusive complementarity between the four paragraphs of chapter 42 can be found.

# ~ 43 ~

The softest thing in the world
Runs through the hardest thing in the world
That which is without form
Penetrates that which is without spaces or cracks
I thereby know that there is benefit in effortlessness

---

[86] Yang sheng is an ancient term which has largely been replaced in modern times by the term qi gong (energy-breath work), though it is still widely in use. Heshang Gong uses the term yang sheng in chapter 50, though it dates back to at least Xun Zi (c. 310-235 BC).

And in teaching without words

The benefit of effortlessness
Restores hope for the world

# Chapter 43
徧用 Pervasive and Useful

天下之至柔，馳騁天下之至堅。至柔者，水也。至堅者，金石也。水能貫堅入剛，無所不通。
*"The softest thing in the world runs through the hardest thing in the world"*
The softest thing is water. The hardest things are metal and stone. Water can go through what is tough and enter what is hard. There is nothing it cannot pass through.

無有入無間。無有謂道也。道無形質，故能出入無間，通神明濟群生也。
*"That which is without form penetrates that which is without spaces or cracks"*
"That which is without form" means Dao. Dao is without form or substance. Hence, it can leave and enter what is without spaces or cracks. When spiritual brilliance breaks through, the multitudes are born.

吾是以知無為之有益。吾見道無為而萬物自化成，是以知無為之有益於人也。
*"I thereby know that there is benefit in effortlessness"*
I see that Dao is effortless, yet the myriad things are naturally transformed and completed. Therefore, I know that effortlessness is beneficial to people.

不言之教，法道不言，師之以身。
*"And in teaching without words"*
The system of Dao is not spoken, but is learned through the body.

無為之益，法道無為，治身則有益於精神，治國則有益於萬民，不勞煩也。
*"The benefit of effortlessness"*
The system of Dao is effortless. By governing the body (with effortlessness), the spiritual vitality is benefited. By governing the nation (with effortlessness), things and people are benefited. Do not over-exert or agitate them.

天下希及之。天下，人主也。希能有及道無為之治身治國也。
*"Restores hope for the world"*
"The world," here, means people and rulers. There is hope for them to attain Dao by governing the body, and governing the nation, with effortlessness.

FORTY-THREE
Purifying the heart-mind allows the spirit to shine outward, to penetrate through dense emotional layers and illuminate our conscious mind with a higher percep-

tion of worldly circumstances. It breaks through the obstinate will fueled by anger, the urgencies of fear and elation, the habitual rumination of worry, and dense clouds of sorrow. Just as emotions are contagious, so too is spiritual brilliance. Thus, the Sage effortlessly connects with the spiritual intelligence of others, and rinses out the silt of their emotional habituation and thought patterns.

## ~ 44 ~

Reputation or yourself
Which do you hold most dear?
Yourself or your possessions
Which is of greater value?
To gain or to lose
Which does greater harm?
Strong craving assures great expense
Extensive hoarding assures substantial loss
Know what is sufficient, and you will not be disgraced
Know when to stop, and you will not be endangered
Thereby, you can endure

## Chapter 44
立戒 Established Warnings

名與身孰親。名遂則身退也。
"Reputation or yourself, which do you hold most dear?"
When reputation takes precedence, character loses priority.
身與貨孰多。財多則害身也。
"Yourself or your possessions, which is of greater value?"
Having too many possessions causes harm to the individual.
得與亡孰病。好得利則病於行也。
"To gain or to lose, which does greater harm?"
The wish to acquire and profit brings contamination to one's activities and behaviour.

甚愛必大費，甚愛色，費精神。甚愛財，遇禍患。所愛者少，所亡者多，故言大費。
"Strong craving assures great expense"
Strong cravings for beautiful appearances expend spiritual vitality. Strong cravings

for material wealth bring misfortune and worries. Though only a few things may be strongly craved, the losses will still be many. Hence the words "great expense."

多藏必厚亡。生多藏於府庫，死多藏於丘墓。生有攻劫之憂，死有掘塚探柩之患。

"Extensive hoarding assures substantial loss"
Those who are alive store many things in municipal storehouses. Those who are dead store many things in burial mounds. The living are saddened when they are robbed. The dead are worried when grave robbers search their tombs.

知足不辱，知足之人絕利去欲，不辱於身。

"Know what is sufficient and you will not be disgraced"
People who know what is sufficient will regulate profits and abandon desires. They will not disgrace themselves.

知止不殆，知可止，則財利不累於身，聲色不亂於耳目，則身不危殆也。

"Know when to stop and you will not be endangered"
By knowing how to stop, wealth and profits will not disturb one's character, sounds and appearances will not confuse the ears and eyes, and the body will not be endangered.

可以長久。人能知止足則福祿在己，治身者，神不勞；治國者，民不擾，故可長久。

"Thereby you can endure"
When people know how to stop at sufficiency, happiness and blessings will surround them. When governing the body, do not over-exert the spirit. In governing the nation, do not agitate the people. Thereby, these things may continue for a long time.

## FORTY-FOUR

In Chapter 44, Lao Zi demonstrates how the interchanges of passive and active, emptiness and fullness, yin and yang, relate to what is often at the root of desire – the strongest of all allures: status, wealth, and love (愛, also meaning craving/fondness). Lao Zi explains that the ardent pursuit of these goals tends to neglect one's most vital foundation – themselves. Thus, eradicating the pursuit of these ends is integral to the renunciant's pursuit of self-purification.

While self-cultivation implies self-preservation, Daoism differentiates between the self/individual/body (身, shen) and the "I/me" (我, wo). Cultivation of the self involves suspending the "I" while cultivating the self. The difference between the I and self could be understood as someone in a boat. Being on an ocean, we still need a boat (the sense of self), but the boat is not us, and so on getting to the shore we won't take it with us. We can realize that the boat is not us while still on the water, and even completely forget about it at times, but Daoism does not try to deny the existence of the boat. It accepts both boat and no-boat.

In the Daoist traditions that built their practices on Lao Zi's teachings, two interpretations of chapter 44 endure. On the one hand are those who have sworn off all worldly attachments, and on the other, those who have applied the last four lines to the chapter as a whole:

> Extensive hoarding assures substantial loss
> Know what is sufficient and you will not be disgraced
> Know when to stop and you will not be endangered
> Thereby you can endure

# ~ 45 ~

Great completion seems to be lacking
But when used, it is never depleted
Great fullness seems as though empty
But when used, it is never finished

Great straightness seems as though bent
Great skill seems as though clumsy
Great eloquence seems like mumbling

What is tense becomes cold
What is tranquil becomes warm
Clarity and tranquility
Can bring all under Heaven into alignment

## Chapter 45
### 洪德 Flooding with Virtue

大成若缺，謂道德大成之君也。若缺者，滅名藏譽，如毀缺不備也。
"Great completion seems to be lacking"
This means that when Dao and Virtue are greatly developed in the ruler, he seems as though deficient in them. Rejecting titles and hiding from fame, he seems as though injured, deficient, and not ready (to rule).
其用不弊，其用心如是，則無敝盡時也。
"But when used, it is never depleted"
When the heart-mind is used properly, it does not become broken or exhausted.
大盈若沖，謂道德大盈滿之君也。若沖者，貴不敢驕也，富不敢奢也。
"Great fullness seems as though empty"

This means that when Dao and Virtue are great and full in a ruler, he seems as though empty. Though praised, he does not dare to be arrogant. Though wealthy, he does not dare to be extravagant.

其用不窮。其用心如是，則無窮盡時也。
"But when used, it is never finished"
When the heart-mind is used properly, it does not become depleted or finished up.

大直若屈，大直，謂修道法度正直如一也。若屈者，不與俗人爭，若可屈折。
"Great straightness seems as though bent"
"Great straightness" means cultivating and following the natural principles of Dao as they accord with Oneness. Those who "seem as though bent" do not follow along with man's habitual combatitiveness and so appear flexible and bent.

大巧若拙，大巧謂多才術也。若拙者，亦不敢見其能。
"Great skill seems as though clumsy"
Great skill means abundantly talented and skilled. Those who "seem as though clumsy" simply do not show their abilities.

大辯若訥。大辯者，智無疑。若訥者，口無辟。
"Great eloquence seems like mumbling"
Those with great eloquence do not question their own wisdom. Those who seem to mumble use their mouths without restraint.

躁勝寒，勝，極也。春夏陽氣躁疾於上，萬物盛大，極則寒，寒則零落死亡也。言人不當剛躁也。
"What is tense becomes cold"
"Becomes," here, means "reaches to." In spring and summer, yang energy-breath is excitable and (related) illnesses increase while the myriad things multiply. At the extreme of yang, the cold seasons begin and coldness continues while things wither and die. (For these reasons) it is said that people should not be rigid and tense.[87]

靜勝熱，秋冬萬物靜於黃泉之下，極則熱，熱者生之源。
"What is tranquil becomes warm"
In autumn and winter, the myriad things are still, and yellow springs are in the earth. When cold arrives at its extreme, the warm seasons begin. This warmth activates the wellspring of life.

清靜能為天下正。能清靜則為天下之長，持身正則無終已時也。
"Clarity and tranquility can bring all under Heaven into alignment"
Clarity and tranquility can bring longevity to all under Heaven. By maintaining alignment in the body, it will not end before its time.

---

[87] Tensing the muscles in cold weather inhibits warmth from energy circulation, while deep relaxation increases it.

FORTY-FIVE

Seeing the larger picture, title and glory are illusory and meaningless. Knowing this, an enlightened leader does not cling to them. Though held in high honour, he or she does not lose humility, knowing that all the power in the world is of no real value on returning to the true essence of reality – Wu Ji: Ultimate Nothingness. This being the case, Lao Zi teaches to let go, for tension brings cold, while tranquility brings life-warmth. Clarity and tranquility bring all under heaven into alignment, just as they bring harmony to the heart-mind, spirit, and body. These patterns of Dao are expressed universally in the oneness of being and non-being.

## ~ 46 ~

When all under Heaven is in accord with Dao
People go back to leading their horses on foot
While (plowing and) fertilizing (their fields)
When all under Heaven is out of accord with Dao
War horses are bred in the countryside

There is no greater (cause for) weakness
Than what is desirable
There is no greater (cause for) misfortune
Than not recognizing sufficiency
There is no greater (cause for) error
Than the desire to obtain
Therefore, know how to be content with sufficiency
And you will have enduring satisfaction

## Chapter 46
儉欲 Economize Desires

天下有道，謂人主有道也。
"When all under Heaven is in accord with Dao"
This refers to when people and rulers are in accord with Dao.
卻走馬以糞，糞者，糞田也。兵甲不用，卻走馬治農田，治身者卻陽精以糞其身。
"People go back to leading their horses on foot, while (plowing and) fertilizing

(their fields)"
"Fertilizing," here, means fertilizing fields. Soldiers are not employed, and people go back to leading their horses on foot while managing and farming their fields. Those who govern the body lead yang essence to fertilize the body.

天下無道，謂人主無道也。
"When all under Heaven is out of accord with Dao"
This refers to when people and rulers are out of accord with Dao.

戎馬生於郊。戰伐不止，戎馬生於郊境之上，久不還也。
"War horses are bred in the countryside"
Military attacks do not stop, and war horses are bred in the upper regions and outer villages.

罪莫大於可欲。好淫色也。
"There is no greater (cause for) weakness than what is desirable"
Than being tempted by lewd appearances

禍莫大於不知足，富貴不能自禁止也。
"There is no greater (cause for) misfortune than not recognizing sufficiency"
Than possessing abundant wealth, and having no capacity for self-restraint

咎莫大於欲得。欲得人物，利且貪也。
"There is no greater (cause for) error than the desire to obtain"
Than the desire to obtain people and things for profit and greed

故知足之足，守真根也。
"Therefore, know how to be content with sufficiency"
Guard the root of reality within.

常足。無欲心也。
"And you will have enduring satisfaction"
You will have no desires in your heart.


## FORTY-SIX

Heshang Gong connects the metaphor of managing horses with internal cultivation, explaining that using horses to cultivate the fields is like cultivating the self, physically, energetically, and thus spiritually. His mention of leading yang essence (yang jing) to fertilize the body suggests yin and yang jing – the substantive (yin) and functional (yang) aspects of jing, with yin jing being the foundational side of jing and yang jing being the more expressed power of jing. This expressed power can be skillfully moderated and allowed to further nourish the foundational yin jing, though it is easily exhausted.[88]

The conservation of yang jing to nourish the foundational yin jing is akin to using horses to cultivate the fields, rather than gathering them to be mated and sent off to battle. This is to guard Dao within and use our powers to nourish the

---

[88] *Nei Jing Su Wen* chapter 3, and many commentaries pertaining to balancing yin and yang in the *Nei Jing*, support this understanding.

physical and spiritual self, rather than lose ourselves to anger and greed, squandering inner power and leaving us spiritually and physically depleted. Lao Zi explains that the base of misfortune, in taking the latter route, is not knowing when we have enough and letting this error in judgement bring about misguided desires. With cravings come all destabilizing emotions connected to that desire, leaving people feeling unsatisfied for not having things they never needed. It's not the lack of that thing that causes this unhappiness, but the initial acceptance of the desire for it in the first place. This falling out of accord with the way things are, and thereby falling out of accord with Dao, is to squander inner power on pursuits that only leave us more in need.

# ~ 47 ~

Without going out the door
Know all under Heaven
Without glancing out the window
See Heaven's Way
The further out one goes
The less they know

Therefore, the Sage does not move
Yet he knows
He describes and names (things)
Without seeing (them)
He brings about perfection
Without acting

## Chapter 47
鑒遠 Mirror the Distant

不出戶知天下，聖人不出戶以知天下者，以己身知人身，以己家知人家，所以見天下也。
"Without going out the door, know all under Heaven"
The Sage does not go out the door to know the world. By his own body, he knows the bodies of others. By his own house he knows the houses of others. This is seeing all under Heaven.
不窺牖見天道，天道與人道同，天人相通，精氣相貫。人君清淨，天氣自正，人君多欲，天氣煩濁。吉凶利害，皆由於己。

**"Without glancing out the window, see Heaven's Way"**

Heaven's Dao and man's Dao are united, for Heaven and man are in communication with each other. Vital energy-breaths pass between them. When the ruler is pure and peaceful, Heaven's energy-breath is aligned. When the ruler has many desires, Heaven's energy-breath is troubled and turbulent. Prosperity, terror, assistance, and harm, can all be brought about by oneself.

其出彌遠，其知彌少。謂去其家觀人家，去其身觀人身，所觀益遠，所見益少也。

**"The further out one goes, the less they know"**

This means that if you distance yourself from your house to observe others' houses, or distance yourself from your character to observe the character of others, then the benefit of observation will be distant, and the benefit of seeing will be small.

是以聖人不行而知，聖人不上天，不入淵，能知天下者，以心知之也。

**"Therefore, the Sage does not move, yet he knows"**

The Sage does not go up to Heaven, nor does he go into the ocean, but he can still understand the world. This is because he understands the heart and mind.

不見而名，上好道，下好德；上好武，下好力。聖人原小知大，察內知外。

**"He describes and names (things) without seeing (them)"**

When those above love Dao, those below love Virtue. When those above love military might, those below love power. The Sage begins with the small to know the large, examines the internal to know the external.

不為而成。上無所為，則下無事，家給人足，萬物自化就也。

**"He brings about perfection without acting"**

When those above are not impetuous, those below are not overworked. When people find satisfaction within their own houses, the myriad things are naturally drawn toward self-transformation.


## FORTY-SEVEN

Rather than seeking to change the behaviour of others, if we can settle the differences in ourselves we will find that many of our external problems no longer require resolution. Seeing the faults of others is quite simple, but self-awareness requires dedication and work. This inner work, however, is the master key to open every door that keeps us stuck in our ways, stuck in our path, and stuck in the revolving door of getting in our own way. As "the further out one goes, the less they know," an intent focus on others' failings only diverts this attention from our own. "Without glancing out the window, see Heaven's Way."

# ~ 48 ~

The pursuit of learning requires daily accumulation
The pursuit of Dao requires daily reduction
Reducing and reducing
Until arriving at effortlessness
Effortless, yet without inaction

Conquering all under Heaven
Is best done without the endeavour to do so
Perpetually, this endeavour will continue
Without satisfaction
Even when all under Heaven has been conquered

## Chapter 48
### 忘知 Forget Knowledge

為學日益，學謂政教禮樂之學也。日益者，情欲文飾日以益多。
"The pursuit of learning requires daily accumulation"
"Learning," here, means learning the proprieties of rites and music. For those who gain every day, strong emotions, desires, and sophistications, increase over time.

為道日損。道謂之自然之道也。日損者，情欲文飾日以消損。
"The pursuit of Dao requires daily reduction"
Dao means the Dao of natural spontaneity. For those who reduce each day, desires, strong emotions, and sophistications, eventually vanish.

損之又損，損情欲也。又損之，所以漸去。
"Reducing and reducing"
Reduce desires and strong emotions until they gradually disappear.

以至於無為，當恬淡如嬰兒，無所造為也。
"Until arriving at effortlessness"
Be quiet and unnoticeable like an infant, not taking on initiatives.

無為而無不為。情欲斷絕，德於道合，則無所不施，無所不為也。
"Effortless, yet without inaction"
When desires are completely removed, Virtue and Dao join together. Then there is nothing which is not taken care of, nothing which is not managed.

取天下常以無事，取，治也。治天下當以無事，不當以勞煩也。
"Conquering all under Heaven is best done without the endeavour to do so"
"Conquering," here, means governing. When governing all under Heaven, one should be without the endeavour to do so. It should not be done with over-exertion

and agitation.

及其有事，不足以取天下。及其好有事，則政教煩，民不安，故不足以治天下也。

"Perpetually, this endeavour will continue, without satisfaction, even when all under Heaven has been conquered"

By perpetuating the dream of this endeavour, the government teaches vexation and agitation, and the people are not at peace. As a result, even ruling the world will not bring satisfaction.


FORTY-EIGHT

When studying a skill or subject, new understandings and habits are forged with applied effort as we try to fix ideas and perceptions in the mind. Following Dao, however, requires that we shed acquired habits and presumptions. In doing so we remove our fixed ways of seeing things and allow for open perception – for circumstances to arrive and leave without emotion or intellect automatically labelling experience. Shedding habits and allowing for open perception, these two ways of cleansing the heart work like left and right feet continually moving us closer to Dao as we get less and less burdened by fixed perceptions and habitual emotions and desires.

Heshang Gong shows that this process of purification must take into account that hoarding knowledge often brings with it a sense of sophistication and superiority. Just as the pursuit of Dao requires that we reduce our attachment to "having all the answers," it also requires that we do away with this sense of superiority.

Giving up this attachment to having all the answers, we can also learn to have faith in Dao. As Lao Zi imparts in chapter 23, having faith that Dao will work things out only makes it easier for Dao to guide our lives in a propitious direction.


~ 49 ~


The Sage is without a fixed mind
Because he does not take his mind to be different
From that of the common people

To those who are excellent, I am excellent
To those who are not excellent, I am also excellent
This is the virtue of excellence

To those who are sincere, I am sincere

To those who are not sincere, I am also sincere
This is the virtue of sincerity

The Sage lives amongst the world with much timidity
Acting in the world as though clouded in his mind
The hundred families all focus their ears and eyes
And the Sage treats them all as his children

# Chapter 49
## 任德 Trust in Virtue

聖人無常心，聖人重改更，貴因循，若自無心。
"The Sage is without a fixed mind"
The Sage puts more importance on being able to change and improve. He places value on adjusting to a situation. This resembles having no mind of his own.
以百姓心為心。百姓心之所便，聖人因而從之。
"Because he does not take his mind to be different from that of the common people"
When the hundred families' minds are at ease – so too, then, is the Sage's.

善者吾善之，百姓為善，聖人因而善之。
"To those who are excellent, I am excellent"
When the hundred families act with excellence – so too, then, does the Sage.
不善者吾亦善之，百姓雖有不善者，聖人化之使善也。
"To those who are not excellent, I am also excellent"
When the hundred families do not act with excellence, the Sage reforms them by being excellent, himself.
德善。百姓德化，聖人為善。
"This is the virtue of excellence"
By acting with excellence, the Sage transforms the virtue of the hundred families.

信者吾信之，百姓為信，聖人因而信之。
"To those who are sincere, I am sincere"
When the hundred families are sincere, the Sage is also sincere.
不信者吾亦信之，百姓為不信，聖人化之為信者也。
"To those who are not sincere, I am also sincere"
When the hundred families are not sincere, the Sage reforms them by acting sincerely.
德信。百姓德化，聖人以為信。
"This is the virtue of sincerity"
By acting sincerely, the Sage transforms the virtue of the hundred families.

聖人在天下怵怵，聖人在天下怵怵常恐怖，富貴不敢驕奢。
*"The Sage lives amongst the world with much timidity"*
The Sage lives in the world with much timidity, always apprehensive and cautious, like a wealthy person hoping to maintain their wealth, and thus not daring to act arrogantly and ostentatiously.

為天下渾其心。言聖人為天下百姓混濁其心，若愚闇不通也。
*"Acting in the world as though clouded in his mind"*
The Sage goes about the world and the hundred families as though he were clouded in his mind, seeming as though stupid, deaf, and dumb.

百姓皆注其耳目，注，用也。百姓皆用其耳目為聖人視聽也。
*"The hundred families all focus their ears and eyes"*
"Focus," here, means "use." The hundred families all use their ears and eyes to observe and listen to the Sage.

聖人皆孩之。聖人愛念百姓如嬰孩赤子，長養之而不責望其報。
*"And the Sage treats them all as his children"*
The Sage loves and thinks of the hundred families as though they were children and infants, supporting them for a long time, yet not hoping to receive anything from them in the future.[89]

## FORTY-NINE

What is translated in the first line here as "fixed" (常, chang), and read as such by Heshang Gong, can also mean common and "ordinary," which would say that the Sage's mentality is not ordinary, but extraordinary. Ordinarily, people do not look inward to find the source of their emotions and reactions, but look externally at what triggered these emotions; they do not do their best for people who do not offer their own best; they are not sincere with those who are untrustworthy. The Sage, on the other hand, shows the same virtue to the scoundrel that he or she does to the saint, for they will not compromise their virtue in accordance with the virtue of others. This is not a form of martyrdom, but of self-cultivation.

Following this path, one will simply have to take the high road a disproportionate amount of the time. Such is the path of external-cultivation; that is, the method of purifying one's actions in the process of refining oneself.

---

[89] The term "the hundred families" is synonymous with "all people," while indicating clan divisions. Until approximately 500 BC, only people in the ruling and aristocratic classes held one of these family names.

# ~ 50 ~

To depart from life is to enter death
The companions of life are thirteen
The companions of death are thirteen
In their way of living, people approach death-traps
By way of (these) thirteen
Why is this so?
Because they seek a life of excess
I have heard that those who are good at absorbing life
Travel the land without encountering rhinoceros or tigers
They walk into groups of soldiers
Without requiring armour or soldiers for protection
The rhinoceros has no place to thrust its horn
The tiger has no place to grab with its claw
And the soldier has nowhere to place his weapon
Why is this so?
Because these people are without any death-traps

## Chapter 50
貴生 Treasuring Life

出生入死。出生,謂情欲出五內,魂靜魄定,故生。入死,謂情欲入於胸臆,精勞神惑,故死。

"To depart from life is to enter death"
When emotions and desires leave the five internal organs, the hun (yang spirits housed in the liver) become calm, and the po (yin spirits housed in the lungs) become settled. Vitality then flourishes.

When emotions and desires go deep into the consciousness of the heart, vital essence is over-exerted, and the spirit becomes confused. This causes death.

生之徒十有三,死之徒死十有三,言生死之類各有十三,謂九竅四關也。其生也目不妄視,耳不妄聽,鼻不妄嗅,口不妄言,味,手不妄持,足不妄行,精神不妄施。其死也反是也。

"The companions of life are thirteen, The companions of death are thirteen"
Lao Zi is saying that (the path to) life and death are both governed by thirteen things: the nine bodily apertures and four closures.[90] To nourish life, the eyes should not observe frantically, the ears should not listen frantically, the nose should not smell

---

[90] The nine apertures are the eyes (2), ears (2), nostrils (2), mouth, anus, and urethra. The four closures refer to the feet and hands.

frantically, the mouth should not speak or taste frantically, the hands should not grasp frantically, the feet should not walk frantically, and the spiritual vitality should not be frantically engrossed. For death, it is the opposite of this.

人之生，動之死地十有三。人知求生，動作反之十三死也。
"In their way of living, people approach death-traps by way of (these) thirteen"
People know to seek life; however, going against this, they bring about death by these thirteen things.

夫何故，問何故動之死地也。
"Why is this so?"
Asking why death arrives this way.

以其求生之厚。所以動之死地者，以其求生活之事太厚，違道忤天，妄行失紀。
"Because they seek a life of excess"
Those who die by seeking life try to make a living in order to support an excessive lifestyle. Defying Dao and disobeying Heaven, their frantic behaviour causes them to lose the true path.

蓋以聞善攝生者，攝，養也。
"I have heard that those who are good at absorbing life"
"Absorbing," here, means supporting.

路行不遇兕虎，自然遠離，害不干也。
"Travel the land without encountering rhinoceros' or tigers"
Natural spontaneity keeps them far away from harm, and also from going on the attack.

入軍不披甲兵，不好戰以殺人。
"They walk into groups of soldiers without requiring armour or soldiers for protection"
They do not approve of battle or killing.

兕無投其角，虎無所措爪，兵無所容其刃。養生之人，兕虎無由傷，兵刃無從加之也。
"The rhinoceros has no place to thrust its horn, the tiger has no place to grab with its claw, and the soldier has nowhere to place his weapon"
The rhinoceros and tiger have no reason to injure those who nurture life (yang sheng). The soldier has nothing to gain by doing so either.

夫何故，問兕虎兵甲何故不加害之。
"Why is this so?"
Why do the rhinoceros, tiger, and armed soldier have nothing to gain from hurting them?

以其無死地。以其不犯十三之死地也。言神明營護之，此物不敢害。
"Because these people are without any death-traps."
They do not violate the thirteen places of death. Lao Zi is saying that when spiritual lights fortify and protect (those who nurture life), these things will not dare to cause injury.

## FIFTY

When Classical Chinese Medicine explains mental disorders, it often refers to the hun-spirits (housed in the liver, yang and ethereal) and po-spirits (housed in the lungs, yin and earthly/bodily), as well as a pathological disconnection between the heart (which houses the shen-spirit) and kidneys (which house the yuan qi/source-energy and serve to ground and nourish the spiritual essence/jing-shen).[91]

Because the heart, housing the shen-spirit, acts as the emperor of the body, when the heart and spirit are in disorder, the health of the body no longer enjoys an easy balance and security. As this disorder worsens, prolonged frantic emotions stress the organs and cause a failure of communication between organ systems. Thus, the spirit is the "pivot" or "hinge" of an individual's health – perhaps why the second text of the *The Yellow Emperor's Classic of Internal Medicine (Huang Di Nei Jing)* is called *Classic of the Spritual Pivot (Ling Shu Jing)*.[92]

After touching briefly on the above medical points, Heshang Gong describes the path of cultivation in everyday life, where one guards the yuan-qi by not over-extending the senses and body in frantic response. From this, we may also understand why *"those who are good at absorbing life travel the land without encountering rhinoceros' or tigers; they walk into groups of soldiers without requiring armour or soldiers for protection."* If one encounters a wild animal and is shocked or panicked (frantic), the animal is more likely to attack them, just as soldiers are more likely to take notice of civilians who are startled by their presence. This practice, again, teaches us to look within for the path to balance and harmony, and not to be ensnared by diversions.

---

[91] Larre, Claude and Rochat de la Vallee, Elizabeth. *Rooted in Spirit: The Heart of Chinese Medicine*. New York: Station Hill Press, 1992.

[92] In their commentary on chapter eight of the *Ling Shu Jing*, Claude Larre and Elisabeth Rochat de la Vallée point out that, like chapter 50 of the *Dao De Jing*, the *Ling Shu Jing* also delineates 13 facets of life which develop in the process of forming a human life, the same facets which degenerate in the process of death. Those 13 facets in the *Ling Shu Jing* are: Virtue (from Heaven), qi (from Earth), life (生), jing (essence), shen (spirit), hun, po, the heart-mind, intention, will, thought, contemplation, and wisdom/competence (智).

A shared tradition behind DDJ50 and LSJ8 may be evidenced by the fact that DDJ50 is followed by DDJ51's description of De, a description which supports the *Ling Shu Jing*'s role for De in the creation of life.
See: Larre, Claude and Rochat de la Vallee, Elizabeth. *Rooted in Spirit: The Heart of Chinese Medicine*. New York: Station Hill Press, 1992. p. 152

# ~ 51 ~

Dao actuates them
Virtue takes care of them
Power completes them
This is why the myriad things
Cannot help but to respect Dao and cherish Virtue

Respecting Dao and cherishing Virtue
This is not commanded
Yet it has always been in their nature

Dao actuates them
Virtue takes care of them, extends their lifespans
Teaches them, completes them
Tests them, raises them
And brings them back (to their pure natures)

Actuates them but does not possess them
Sets them in motion but does not expect of them
Extends their lives without ruling and controlling
This is called Fathomless Virtue

## Chapter 51
養德 The Virtue of Nurturing

道生之，道生萬物。
"Dao actuates them"
Dao actuates the myriad things.
德畜之，德，一也。一主布氣而蓄養物形之，一為萬物設形像也。
"Virtue takes care of them"
"Virtue," here, means "Oneness." Oneness is the host of all things. It surrounds them with energy-breath, and gathers and rears things into form. Oneness establishes the form and image of all things.
勢成之。一為萬物作寒暑之勢以成之。
"Power completes them"
Oneness uses the power of hot and cold to complete all things.
是以萬物莫不尊道而貴德。道德所為，無不盡驚動，而尊敬之。
"This is why the myriad things cannot help but to respect Dao and cherish

Virtue"
Without Dao and Virtue, there would be no impetus for action. This is why they are venerated and respected.

道之尊，德之貴，夫莫之命而常自然。道一不命召萬物，而常自然應之如影響。
"Respecting Dao and cherishing Virtue. This is not commanded, yet it has always been in their nature to do so"
Dao and Oneness do not issue official commands to the myriad things, yet, they are naturally compelled to cherish that which resembles (Dao and Oneness) in image or sound.

故道生之，德畜之，長之育之，成之孰之，養之覆之。道之於萬物，非但生而已，乃復長養、成孰、覆育，全其性命。人君治國治身，亦當如是也。
"Dao actuates them; Virtue takes care of them, extends their lifespans, teaches them, completes them, tests them, raises them, and brings them back (to their pure natures)"
Dao does not simply stop at giving to the myriad things life, but also gives them longevity, supports them, completes them and tests them, brings them back (to their pure natures), and teaches them. It maintains the wholeness of their pure nature (xing), and destiny-life-force (ming). Rulers who govern a nation, or govern their own bodies, should also follow this.

生而不有，道生萬物，不有所取以為利也。
"Actuates them but does not possess them"
Dao gives life to the myriad things but does not take ownership of them or use them for profit.
為而不恃，道所施為，不恃望其報也。
"Sets them in motion but does not expect of them"
Dao puts things into action but does not expect any reward.
長而不宰，道長養萬物，不宰割以為利也。
"Extends their lives without ruling and controlling"
Dao rears and extends the lifespan of all things. It does not dominate them or separate them from their profits.
是謂玄德。道之所行恩德，玄闇不可得見。
"This is called Fathomless Virtue"
The Dao's mercy is carried out through Virtue. Fathomless and obscure, it cannot be seen.

## FIFTY-ONE

Like the followers of Abrahamic religions, the people of ancient China also worshipped a sole creator god, namely Shang Di (Highest Ruler), and the perhaps less anthropomorphised Tai Yi (Supreme One). Offering the relatively new cosmology of Dao and De, Lao Zi may suggest in chapter 51 that he regarded the worship of Shang Di and Tai Yi as an expression of the human impulse "to respect Dao and cherish De." As he explains in chapter four, "(Dao) precedes any concept of a sovereign."

Some parallels might be drawn from chapter 51 to traditional gender roles between mother and father, and De and Dao, with the father initiating conception (fertilization) and the mother bringing up the household. In the absence of any subjects before these verbs (teaching, completing, testing), Heshang Gong reads the nurturing roles as also attributed to Dao. This is likely because Dao and De are beyond this dichotomy of mother and father. All things came from Dao, including Oneness before it was separated into yin and yang (see DDJ42). They were not gestated in De. Further, it is the De of Heaven (yang) that mixes with the qi of Earth (yin) to gives rise to life, according to the Daoist cosmology in the *Huang Di Nei Jing*.[93] De may best be understood, then, not as Dao's counterpart, but as the effectiveness, expression, or essence of Dao.

Heshang Gong also clarifies in chapter 51 that Lao Zi speaks of Oneness and Virtue synonymously. To understand the connection or unity of De and Oneness, we can compare the nurturing quality of De in chapter 51 with the perfecting quality of Oneness in chapter 22:

> That which is flexible is preserved
> That which is bent is straightened
> That which is empty is filled
> That which is broken is repaired
> That which is lacking acquires
> That which is excessive becomes confused
> Therefore, the Sage embraces Oneness
> So as to bring the world into alignment

De is often said to be the power of Dao or the character of Dao, and could otherwise be understood as the *effect* of Dao. To understand this power and character as the aligning and harmonizing power of Oneness is also consistent with chapter 39:

> In the beginning was the attainment of Oneness
> Heaven attained Oneness
> And became clear

---

[93] See chapter 8 of the Ling Shu Jing, quoted above in chapter 21.

Earth attained Oneness
And became serene
…
The myriad things attained Oneness
And were born

# ~ 52 ~

The world has an origin
Known as the Mother of All Under Heaven

Having known the Mother, know the Son
Having known the Son, guard the Mother within
With no self, there is no danger

Seal the doors
Close the gate
By opening the doors
And increasing pursuits
There will be no help for you in later years

Seeing what is small is called "seeing clearly"
Maintaining suppleness is called "strengthening"
Use this light
Turn this clear vision back to its source
And you will not lose the body to illness
This is called "studying the Eternal"

## Chapter 52
歸元 Return to the Origin

天下有始，始有道也。
"The world has an origin"
This origin is Dao.
以為天下母。道為天下萬物之母。
"Which acts as the Mother of all under Heaven"
Dao acts in the world as the mother of all things.

既知其母，復知其子，子，一也。既知道己，當復知一也。
"Having known the Mother, know the Son"
"The Son," here, is Oneness. Having known the Dao for yourself, return to knowing Oneness.

既知其子，復守其母，己知一，當復守道反無為也。
"Having known the Son, guard the Mother within"
Having known Oneness for yourself, you should return to keeping Dao within and reverting to non-action.

沒身不殆。不危殆也。
"With no self, there is no danger"
It will not be in grave danger.[94]

塞其兌，兌，目也。目不妄視也。
"Seal the doors"
"The doors" refer to the eyes. The eyes should not make frivolous observations.

閉其門，門，口也。使口不妄言終身不勤。人當塞目不妄視，閉口不妄言，則終生不勤苦。
"Close the gate"
"The gate" refers to the mouth. If the mouth does not speak frantically, then the body will not be over-exerted. When people seal their eyes, not making frantic observations, and close their mouths, not making frantic speech, this results in a life without strain or hardship.

開其兌，開目視情欲也。
"By opening the doors"
By opening the eyes to observe what one craves.

濟其事，濟，益也。益情欲之事。
"And increasing pursuits"
"Increasing," here, means "advancing" – advancing in the pursuits of your cravings.

終身不救。禍亂成也。
"There will be no help for you in later years"
This is to pursue misfortune and chaos.

見小曰明，萌芽未動，禍亂未見為小，昭然獨見為明。
"Seeing what is small is called 'seeing clearly'"
A sprouting shoot which has not yet moved is like misfortune and chaos not seen while they were small. Only by seeing with enlightened clarity does the present become illuminated.

守柔曰強。守柔弱，日以強大也。
"Maintaining suppleness is called strengthening"

---

[94] See chapter 13 for a similar comment.

Maintaining suppleness and flexibility makes one stronger day by day.

用其光，用其目光於外，視時世之利害。
"Use this light"
Using the eyes externalizes the light. Chasing the world with your eyes can cause you harm.

復歸其明。復當返其光明於內，無使精神泄也。
"Turn this clear vision back to its source"
Return it by sending this light and clear vision back inside of you so that your spiritual vitality will not leak out.

無遺身殃，內視存神，不為漏失。
"And you will not lose the body to illness"
Direct your gaze to the spirit within so that it is not neglected or lost.

是謂習常。人能行此，是謂修習常道。
"This is called 'studying the Eternal'"
All people can practice this. This is called "studying and practicing the Eternal Dao."


FIFTY-TWO
Having found the source of life within ourselves, we can look upon the outer world with a new appreciation and perspective. Looking upon life with this new appreciation and perspective, we can again look within ourselves to find that source of life, cherishing it and not letting it scatter through our obsessions with externals. Rather than giving that intense focus to things outside of ourselves, we can turn that focus inwards to our internal reservoirs, reconnecting with the source of life, and guarding our senses from obsession with externals. Over time, this will give rise to spiritual intelligence/spiritual brilliance (shen ming).

The technique of meditation described in chapter 52 later became known as "turning the light around (回光)," and was greatly expanded upon in Lu Dongbin's *Secret of the Golden Flower*.[95]

See, also, my comments in chapter one for its correlations with chapter 52.


# ~ 53 ~

If I were steadfast in understanding
I would simply walk the Great Path
Having only one rightful fear

---

[95] Carl Jung famously wrote a commentary for the Wilhelm/Baynes translation of *Secret of the Golden Flower* and credited it with influencing his understanding of consciousness.

The Great Way is like cleared land
Yet the people love narrow tracks

The court is kept immaculate
Yet the fields are overgrown with weeds
The granaries are so empty
Yet their clothes so full of colour
In their belts are sharp swords
While they waste food and drink
Hoarding treasures to rival a mint

This is called thieving and boasting
It is surely not the Way!

# Chapter 53
## 益證 Evidence of Profiteering

使我介然有知，行於大道。介，大也。老子疾時王不行大道，故設此言。使我介然有知於政事，我則行於大道，躬行無為之化。
*"If I were steadfast in understanding, I would simply walk the Great Path"*
"Steadfast," here, means "great." Lao Zi was sickened by the kings of his day who did not walk the Great Path. Thus, he wrote: "If I were steadfast in understanding political affairs, I would simply walk the Great Path. I would practice it in myself, and reform without effort."

唯施是畏。唯，獨也。獨畏有所施為，恐失道意。欲賞善，恐偽善生；欲信忠恐詐忠起。
*"Having only one rightful fear"*
"Only," here, means "single." The only fear that could be had is the fear of forgetting the Dao. If you desire to be rewarded for excellence, beware the emergence of false excellence. If you desire sincerity and selflessness, beware the emergence of false selflessness.

大道甚夷，而民好徑。夷，平易也。徑，邪、不平正也。大道甚平易，而民好從邪徑也。
*"The Great Way is like cleared land, yet the people love narrow tracks"*
"Cleared land," here, means flat and easy. "Narrow paths" refer to wickedness, which is not flat and straightforward. The Great Dao is flat and easy, yet people prefer to follow the wicked and narrow paths.

朝甚除，高台榭，宮室修。
*"The court is kept immaculate"*

Old towering pavilions and palatial study halls.
田甚蕪，農事廢，不耕治。
"Yet the fields are overgrown with weeds"
Agricultural professions are discarded and ploughing times are poorly managed.
倉甚虛，五穀傷害，國無儲也。
"The granaries are so empty"
The five grains becomes diseased and the nation has no reserves.
服文綵，好飾偽，貴外華。
"Yet their clothes so full of colour"
Their illustrious appearances are deceptive. Their honour is but an external decoration.
帶利劍，尚剛強，武且奢。
"In their belts are sharp swords"
Their rigid and unyielding strength is wasteful and exaggerated.
厭飲食，財貨有餘，多嗜欲，無足時。
"While they waste food and drink, and hoard treasures (to rival a mint)"
Having many desirous weaknesses, one is never satisfied.

是謂盜誇。百姓而君有餘者，是由劫盜以為服飾，持行誇人，不知身死家破，親戚並隨也。
"This is called thieving and boasting"
When the hundred families and elites have excessive possessions, thieves and robbers wear fancy clothes, and boastfulness is encouraged. Not realizing that their bodies will die and their houses will rot – so do their parents and relatives.
非道哉。人君所行如是，此非道也。復言也哉者，痛傷之辭。
"It is surely not the Way!"
Rulers who act like this are on the wrong path. As though repeating the sentence, he follows this with an exclamation. It is an impassioned lament.


FIFTY-THREE
The path of righteousness and goodness is not hard to find, though it is easily confused by rationales such as "the law said I could; the government ordered it; it was common practice." Looking to law, government, religion, or culture for one's moral compass is unnecessary. We know what we do not want imposed upon ourselves, and so we know that we should not impose the same on others. Further, by not wishing anyone to sacrifice their well-being for our own, we will not be in danger of following this golden rule to a fault.

Daoists and Buddhists both share the same five precepts that help remind a person of the basics for doing right by others: No killing, no stealing, no lying, no sexual impropriety, and no intoxication. Exploring these five precepts reveals a greater magnitude than may appear on the surface. For example, no killing also relates to not wasting, as waste requires unnecessary consumption; no stealing also relates to consideration of others, as to disrespect someone is to steal their dignity; no lying also relates to being genuine and pure – to not falsifying your persona; no sexual impropriety also relates to excessive desires, as excessive desires can become like an intoxicant and cause us to act against our own good judgement; no intoxication is not simply a matter of prudishness, but of appreciating, using, and cultivating our own power, our own consciousness. The directions to this Great Path are always the same: the path is within you, and that is where you walk it; however, we can know that we have strayed from it when cultivating ourselves leads to the depletion of others.

# ~ 54 ~

If well established it is not uprooted
If well embraced it is not torn away
Children and grandchildren
Will then make sacrificial offerings without end

Cultivate this in the body
And its Virtue will be true
Cultivate this in the home
And its Virtue will be overabundant
Cultivate this in the village
And its Virtue will be long lasting
Cultivate this in the nation
And its Virtue will be plentiful
Cultivate this in the world
And its Virtue will be widespread

Thus, it is by the body that the body is observed
It is by the home that the home is observed
It is by the village that the village is observed
It is by the nation that the nation is observed
And it is by the world that the world is observed
How do I know the world to be this way?
By this

# Chapter 54
## 修觀 Cultivating Observation

善建者不拔，建，立也。善以道立身立國者，不可得引而拔之。
"If well established, it is not uprooted"
"Established" means fixed in place. When Dao is firmly fixed in place within the body, or within the nation, it cannot be pulled out and uprooted.

善抱者不脫，善以道抱精神者，終不可拔引解脫
"If well embraced, it is not torn away"
This excellence is obtained by those who embrace the spiritual vitality with Dao. They can never be uprooted. They cannot be pulled out by loosening this embrace and removing them.

子孫祭祀不輟。為人子孫能修道如是，長生不死，世世以久，祭祀先祖，宗廟無絕時。
"Children and grandchildren will then make sacrificial offerings without end"
When people have children and grandchildren who can cultivate Dao like this, they have long life and do not die. From generation to generation, they continue to worship and sacrifice to the original ancestor, and the ancestral shrines are well kept.

修之於身，其德乃真，修道於身愛氣養神，益壽延年。其德如是，乃為真人。
"Cultivate this in the body and its Virtue will be true"
Cultivate Dao in the body by cherishing the energy-breath and nurturing the spirit. This will benefit you by prolonging the aging process. With such Virtue you will become a Genuine Person (zhen ren).[96]

修之於家，其德乃餘，修道於家，父慈子孝，兄友弟順，夫信妻貞。其德如是，乃有餘慶及於來世子孫。
"Cultivate this in the home and its Virtue will be overabundant"
Cultivate Dao in the home and fathers will be kind, children will be filial, older brothers will be friendly, younger sibling will be obedient, and wives will be trustworthy and virtuous. With such Virtue, you will have an overabundance of celebrations, and many generations of children and grandchildren.

修之於鄉，其德乃長，修道於鄉，尊敬長老，愛養幼少，教誨愚鄙。其德如是，乃無不覆及也。
"Cultivate this in the village and its Virtue will be long lasting"
Cultivate Dao in the village and elders will be respected and honoured, infants and children will be loved and supported, and the uneducated will be taught and encouraged. With such Virtue, there will be no one who is not protected and supported.

修之於國，其德乃豐，修道於國，則君信臣忠，仁義自生，禮樂自興，政平無私。其德如是，乃為豐厚也。

---

[96] The term "Genuien Person" (zhen ren) appears numerous times in the *Zhuang Zi*, and refers to those whose simplicity and purity have reached a state of perfection.

*"Cultivate this in the nation and its Virtue will be plentiful"*
When Dao is cultivated in the nation, rulers are trustworthy, and ministers are loyal. Benevolence and righteousness naturally arise, and courtesy and joy naturally follow. Political affairs are also peaceful and not affected by self-interest. When virtue is like this, it brings substantial abundance.

修之於天下，其德乃普。人主修道於天下，不言而化，不教而治，下之應上，信如影響。其德如是，乃為普博。

*"Cultivate this in the world and its Virtue will be widespread"*
Leaders who cultivate Dao in the world do not speak, yet there is reform. They do not teach, yet there is order. Humble duties are respected, and their sincerity leaves a lasting impression. When virtue is like this, it expands into all areas.

故以身觀身，以修道之身，觀不修道之身，孰亡孰存也。

*"Thus, it is by the body that the body is observed"*
To cultivate Dao in the body, observe what happens when one does not cultivate Dao in the body. To learn what causes the loss of life, learn what preserves life.

以家觀家，以修道之家，觀不修道之家。

*"It is by the home that the home is observed"*
To cultivate Dao in the home, observe what happens when Dao is not cultivated in the home.

以鄉觀鄉，以修道之鄉，觀不修道之鄉也。

*"It is by the village that the village is observed"*
To cultivate Dao in the village, observe what happens when Dao is not cultivated in the village.

以國觀國，以修道之國，觀不修道之國也。

*"It is by the nation that the nation is observed"*
To cultivate Dao in the nation, observe what happens when Dao is not cultivated in the nation.

以天下觀天下。以修道之主，觀不修道之主也。

*"And it is by the world that the world is observed"*
To cultivate Dao in the ruler, observe what happens when Dao is not cultivated in the ruler.

吾何以知天下之然哉，以此。老子言，吾何知天下修道者昌，背道者亡。以此五事觀而知之也。

*"How do I know the world to be this way? By this."*
Lao Zi says "How do I know that those who cultivate Dao, prosper, and those who oppose Dao, die? It is by these five observations that I know this."

## FIFTY-FOUR
Just as molecules make up cells, cells make up tissues, tissues make up organs, organs make up organ systems, and organ systems make up a body, human life

exists in numerous levels of interdependence with our natural and social environments. Chapter 54 reflects ancient Chinese medicine's primary focus on nourishing health so as to avoid any need for corrective therapies. Along with Daoists' strategies for understanding and facilitating natural harmony, so as to avoid any need for forced behaviours, was the aim of establishing this natural harmony, Dao, in themselves, in their households, villages, nations, and in the world.

Establishing natural harmony in oneself, a spontaneous desire arises to help one's family. This is not a desire born of socialization or fear, but an impulse to protect others as we would protect ourselves. Having established harmony within, we are able to expand this healing intention to the next level of our network – family, which may include teachers and close friends. When harmony is established in the family network, this family can expand its harmony to the community. When harmony is established in a community, it can have profound influences on cities and even nations, locally and internationally.

A technique to begin cultivating this harmony is to first find it within during meditation by feeling the life force and harmony within after some time and experience with qi cultivation (qi gong). Feeling this life force and harmony as love, love yourself and establish this Virtue. Once you have established this Virtue in yourself, think of a parent, older sibling, or teacher and expand it out to them (traditionally, teachers are thought of at this second phase of the meditation). When you have established it with them, think of a friend and expand it out to them. When you have established it with them, think of a "neutral" person, for example the clerk at your local convenience store, and expand it out to them. When you have well established it with a neutral person, think of an antagonist or enemy in your life and expand it out to them. Once you have established it with them, think of all beings (material, spiritual, plant, animal, etc.) and expand it out to them.

I have adapted this meditation from the common Buddhist "maitri (loving-kindness) meditation" to Daoist principles as they have resonated for me during qi gong practice. It is commonly recommended for maitri meditation that one generally thinks of people opposite to the gender to which they are attracted, so as to avoid potentially confused feelings of romantic attachment. On the other hand, this meditation can be helpful to overcome turbulence between romantic partners by thinking of one's partner during the third phase – extending out to friends. In this instance, however, one should close the meditation at the end of this phase, rather than extend this feeling out to neutrals, enemies/antagonists, and all beings. They should also be careful not to let the feeling of love become submerged in feelings of attachment, as attachment often turns one to think of their own needs, rather than the wellbeing of others.

A good posture to take during this meditation is that of embracing a tree trunk in front of you, with the tips of your left and right fingers about 10 inches apart, at chest level, feeling the energy described above within this embrace as you go through this meditation. The posture should be straight and the shoulders released of tension for this position.[97] An intention or focus for this meditation can be drawn from the last section of chapter 13 in the Dao De Jing:

> Those who make the world to be their own self
> And care for it as such
> To them the world can be entrusted

Another way to translate this is "When he loves himself as he loves the world, the world can be entrusted to him." Feeling this life force and harmony as love, love yourself as the world and the world as yourself, for the world is in you just as you are in the world.[98]

# ~ 55 ~

He who embraces abundant Virtue
Is like an infant

Poisonous snakes do not sting him
Ferocious beasts will not steal him
Birds of prey will not take him away
His bones are flexible and tendons pliant
Yet his grasp is firm
He does not yet know
About the joining of male and female
Yet becomes aroused
He is full of vitality
He can scream all day long
And his voice does not become hoarse
He is full of calmness

To know calm is called "endurance"
To know endurance is called "illumination"
Nourishing life is called "predicting the future"
When the mind is attuned to the breath
This is called "powerful"

---

[97] See "Zhan Zhuang" for more on this meditation posture.
[98] See, also, the reference to chapter 54 in my comments on chapter 74.

When things have grown and become old
We call this "not Dao"
What is "not Dao," finishes early

# Chapter 55
玄符 Mysterious Signs

含德之厚，謂含懷道德之厚也。
"He who embraces abundant Virtue"
This means that when you embrace Dao in your heart, Virtue is abundant (in you).
比於赤子。神明保佑含德之人，若父母之於赤子也。
"Is like an infant"
Spiritual lights protect Virtuous people as a father and mother protect their infant.

毒蟲不螫，蜂蠆蛇虺不螫。
"Poisonous snakes do not sting him"
Wasps and poisonous snakes do not bite him.
猛獸不據，攫鳥不搏。赤子不害於物，物亦不害之。故太平之世，人無貴賤，仁心，有刺之物，還返其本，有毒之蟲，不傷於人。
"Ferocious beasts will not steal him. Birds of prey will not take him away"
Infants do not harm creatures, so creatures do not harm them. In eras of supreme peace, people do not distinguish between rich and poor, but hold benevolence in their hearts; stinging creatures go underground, and poisonous creatures do no harm.
骨弱筋柔而握固。赤子筋骨柔弱而持物堅固，以其意心不移也。
"His bones are flexible and tendons pliant, yet his grasp is firm"
The infant's tendons and bones are pliant and weak, yet he can hold things firmly in his grasp. This is because his will and heart do not waver.
未知牝牡之合而峻作精之至也。赤子未知男女會合而陰陽作怒者，由精氣多之所致也。
"He does not yet know about the joining of male and female, yet becomes aroused. He is full of vitality."
The infant does not know about male, female, or copulation, yet yin and yang arouse his passions. His vital energy-breaths are abundant.
終日號而不啞，和之至也。赤子從朝至暮啼號聲不變易者，和氣多之所至也。
"He can scream all day long and his voice does not become hoarse. He is full of calmness."
An infant can easily scream, cry, and talk from morning until night, yet his harmonious energy-breath remains abundant.
知和曰常，人能和氣柔弱有益於人者，則為知道之常也。
"To know calm is called 'endurance'"

People can harmonize the energy-breath and obtain the benefits of softness and flexibility within the body. This will teach them the endurance of Dao.

知常曰明，人能知道之常行，則日以明達於玄妙也。
*"To know endurance is called 'illumination'"*
Knowing and practicing the endurance of Dao, day by day, one becomes clear-sighted, and sacred mysteries are revealed.

益生曰祥，祥，長也。言益生欲自生，日以長大
*"Nourishing life is called 'predicting the future'"*
"Predicting the future," here, means longevity. This is to say that nourishing life brings the desire to live out one's days, while also greatly extending them.

心使氣曰強。心當專一和柔而神氣實內，故形柔。而反使妄有所為，和氣去於中，故形體日以剛強也。
*"When the mind is attuned to the breath, this is called 'powerful'"*
When the mind unifies in harmony and softness, spirit-energy flourishes within. The body then becomes pliant. Reverting to reckless actions, the harmonized energy-breath abandons equilibrium, and the body gradually becomes unyielding.

物壯則老，萬物壯極則枯老也。
*"When things have grown and become old"*
When fully grown, things become dry and old.

謂之不道，枯老則不得道矣。
*"We call this 'not Dao'"*
Drying out and aging is not the way to attain Dao!

不道早已。不得道者早死。
*"What is 'not Dao,' finishes early"*
Not obtaining Dao, they die early.

FIFTY-FIVE

In relaxation and fully embraced De, the essences of the body circulate and make one more physically and spiritually robust, relaxing the mind and nourishing the body. Western science might describe this as the circulation of hormones, such as serotonin, participating in the complex processes of homeostasis. Daoists, however, find their traditional understandings and terminologies far more effective for learning how to bring these effects about, with practices that have proven effective for more than 2000 years.

   From this robust yet relaxed state, the mind can access information, and the body can stay in motion, for far longer than when they are stressed. Observing an infant when they are relaxed, we can see pure awareness, free of preconception, free of worry. This state of mind is not so uncommon for adults, but the over-processed awareness of a mind obsessed with desire, good and bad, right and wrong, tends to interrupt it. The infant is still keenly aware of his internal energy and feels it grow in his fist as he grips something, almost as though absorbing it into his own energy. His will and mind are undivided by doubt.

The way to cultivate this "genuine will" is described by Guigu Zi (Ghost Valley Master, c. 250 BC) in his "Seven Techniques of Yin Talisman":

> Develop the will when heart-mind-energy and thoughts do not reach (their goal). When you have a desire, the will appears as you think about it. Will is the envoy of desire. When there are many desires, the heart-mind is scattered. When the heart-mind is scattered, the will falters. When the will falters, thinking does not reach (the objective)…
>
> To begin cultivating the will, try to stabilize yourself in peacefulness. Stabilizing yourself in peacefulness, the will and intention will be genuine and firm. When the will and intention are genuine and firm, power and influence will not be separated. If spiritual intelligence is always firmly protected, you will be able to separate (others' power and influence over you).[99]

# ~ 56 ~

Those who know, do not speak
Those who speak, do not know

Close your ports
Shut your gates
Dull your points
Separate your tangles
Soften your glare
Be like ashes
This is to say
"Be one with the sacred"

(Such a state) cannot be attained by affection
It cannot be attained by neglect
It cannot be attained by profiting
It cannot be attained by harming

---

[99] Translation by Dan G. Reid, found in: "*The Thread of Dao: Unraveling Early Daoist Oral Traditions…*" (2017).

It cannot be attained by importance
And it cannot be attained by worthlessness
Thus, it is the most valuable thing under Heaven

# Chapter 56
玄德 Sacred Virtue

知者不言，知者貴行不貴言也。
"Those who know do not speak"
Those who know, value practice rather than words.
言者不知。駟不及舌，多言多患。
"Those who speak do not know"
A team of four horses could not catch up to the tongue. Many words – many worries.

塞其兌，閉其門，塞閉之者，欲絕其源。
"Close your ports, shut your gates"
Block and shut them, for desires separate you from the root.
挫其銳，情欲有所銳為，當念道無為以挫止之。
"Dull your points"
When desires and strong emotions push for action, you should effortlessly dull and stop them by giving your thoughts over to Dao.
解其紛，紛，結恨不休也。當念道恬怕以解釋之
"Separate your tangles"
The tangles are knots of hatred which do not stop (becoming entangled). You should give your thoughts over to Dao while quietly and carefully untying and releasing them.
和其光，雖有獨見之明，當和之使闇昧，不使曜亂。
"Soften your glare"
If you are the only one who sees clearly, you should calmly allow yourself to be closed and obscured. Do not dazzle and confuse others.
同其塵，不當自別殊也。
"Be like ashes"
You should not distinguish yourself as separate and special.
是謂玄同。玄，天也。人能行此上事，是謂與天同道也。
"This is to say: Be one with the sacred"
Sacred, here, means Heaven. For all people, to practice this is the highest pursuit. This requires following the same way by which Heaven is one with Dao.

故不可得而親，不以榮譽為樂，獨立為哀。
"(Such a state) cannot be attained by affection"
Do not be delighted by honour and glory. The one who stands alone is sad.

亦不可得而踈；志靜無欲，故與人無怨。
"It cannot be attained by neglect"
With a tranquil will, free of desires, one associates with others without resentment.
不可得而利，身不欲富貴，口不欲五味。
"It cannot be attained by profiting"
Let the self not desire riches and honour. Let the mouth not desire the five flavours.
亦不可得而害，不與貪爭利，不與勇爭氣。
"It cannot be attained by harming"
Do not follow others in their greed and competition for profit; do not follow others in striving and competing for air.
不可得而貴，不為亂世主，不處暗君位。
"It cannot be attained by importance"
Do not take on the chaos of being master of the world. Do not sit in the darkness of the ruler's throne.
亦不可得而賤，不以乘權故驕，不以失志故屈。
"And it cannot be attained by worthlessness"
Do not charge after power like a team of horses, nor lose your determination and become resigned.
故為天下貴。其德如此，天子不得臣，諸侯不得屈，與世沉浮容身避害，故天下貴也。
"Thus, it is the most valuable thing under Heaven"
When your virtue is like this, the Son of Heaven will not force you to be one of his ministers, and the marquis and lords will not seek to subdue you. Being in accord with the time, you can sink and float (with the waves), and avoid bringing harm to yourself. Thus, (being one with the sacred) is the most valuable thing in the world.

## FIFTY-SIX

While *"those who know, do not speak; those who speak, do not know"* may reflect the teachings on humility in chapter 41,[100] or on being aware of our ignorance as in chapter 71,[101] the rest of chapter 56 places these words in a context closer to the practice of internal observation described in chapter 52. Thus, a closer parallel is found at the end of chapter 5: "To speak countless words is worthless. This is not as good as guarding balance within."

Guarding balance within or "guarding the center" can also be understood as guarding Oneness – holding Virtue within. Doing so, natural harmony and balance are spontaneously restored. This practice begins with silence – closing the mouth, looking inward, and allowing Oneness to spontaneously balance your

---

[100] Chapter 41 includes the line "When the lowest student hears the Way, he breaks into a great laugh."
[101] Chapter 71 includes the line "Not knowing, but thinking you know, is illness."

body, emotions, and mind – to separate your tangles (ch. 56) and untie the the knots (ch. 4) – until you become like dust blowing in the wind of Dao. As such, "there is nowhere for the tiger to place his claw" (ch. 49).

# ~ 57 ~

When aligned, the nation is well governed
When aberrant, the military is effective

It is by having no endeavour to do so
That the world is conquered
How do I know this to be the case?
By this

When taboos are abundant in the world
The people are extremely poor
When the people have an abundance of sharp weapons
The nation grows dark
When people have an abundance of skill and ingenuity
Irregular things flourish
When standards are increasingly publicized
Thieves and robbers abound

Thus the Sage says:
I do nothing, and the people reform themselves
I love stillness, and the people regulate themselves
I do not endeavour, and the people enrich themselves
I am without desires, and the people are natural

## Chapter 57
淳風 In a Simple Manner

以正治國，以，至也。天使正身之人，使有國也
"When aligned, a nation is well governed"
"When," here, means "by arriving at." Heaven brings alignment to the body, and also to the nation.
以奇用兵，奇，詐也。天使詐偽之人，使用兵也

"When aberrant, the military is effective"[102]

Aberrant, here, means "deceptive." Heaven causes the deceitful to be cheated, and for the military to be used against them.

以無事取天下。以無事無為之人，使取天下為之主。
"It is by having no endeavour to do so, that the world is conquered"

While being without such endeavours, the man of non-action causes the world to be conquered by a king's actions.

吾何以知其然哉，以此。此，今也。老子言，我何以知天意然哉，以今日所見知。
"How do I know this to be the case? By this"

"By this," means, "by present circumstances." Lao Zi says "How do I know that things are like this? By observing present circumstances."

天下多忌諱而民彌貧。天下謂人主也。忌諱者防禁也。今煩則姦生，禁多則下詐，相殆故貧。
"When taboos are abundant in the world, the people are extremely poor"

"The world," here, refers to the king. Those who fear taboos defend their restrictions. Today's troubles result from a debaucherous lifestyle. When restrictions are many, those below become dishonest. This puts them in danger, and thus, in poverty.

民多利器，國家滋昏。利器者，權也。民多權則視者眩於目，聽者惑於耳，上下不親，故國家昏亂。
"When the people have an abundance of sharp weapons, the nation grows dark"

Sharp weapons signify authoritative power. When the people have excessive power, what they see dazzles the eyes, what they hear baffles the ears, high and low status are not treated as one family, and the nation then falls into darkness and confusion.

人多伎巧，奇物滋起。人謂人君、百里諸侯也。多技巧，謂刻畫宮觀，雕琢章服，奇物滋起，下則化上，飾金鏤玉，文繡彩色日以滋甚。
"When people have an abundance of skill and ingenuity, irregular things flourish"

By "people," here is meant the lords and marquis connected to rulers of 100 villages. When there is an abundance of skill and ingenuity in carving, painting, architecture, decoration, inlaying, cutting jade, and fashion, strange things begin to multiply. Those below can join the elite ranks by making decorative gold inlays and jade carvings. Decorative embroidery of varied hues and colours multiply day by day.

法物滋彰，盜賊多有。法物，好物也。珍好之物滋生彰著，則農事廢，飢寒

---

[102] A similar phrase appears in The Art of War (500BC), 以正合，以奇勝 "Use alignment to unite. Use the unexpected/unusual to conquer." Apparently a common turn of phrase, it appears here to show this effect in society as well.

並至，而盜賊多有也
"When standards are increasingly publicized, thieves and robbers abound"
"Standards," here, refer to the love of material things. When the love of material things is held in high esteem, and becomes a part of everyday life, the farming professions are no longer valued, and people on all sides become hungry and cold. Thieves and robbers then multiply.

故聖人云：謂下事也。
"Thus the Sage says"
Speaking from a humble position

我無為而民自化，聖人言：我修道承天，無所改作，而民自化成也。
"I do nothing, and the people reform themselves"
The Sage says "I cultivate Dao and receive from Heaven. Without being made anew, the people transform and perfect themselves.

我好靜而民自正，聖人言：我好靜，不言不教，而民自忠正也。
"I love stillness, and the people regulate themselves"
The Sage says "I love stillness, and do not speak or teach, yet the people are, of themselves, loyal and honourable."

我無事而民自富，我無徭役徵召之事，民安其業故皆自富也。
"I do not endeavour, and the people enrich themselves"
I do not enslave people or use the law to put them to work, yet the people are peaceful and professional, all enriching themselves.

我無欲而民自朴。我常無欲，去華文，微服飾，民則隨我為質樸也。聖人言：我修道守真，絕去六情，民自隨我而清也。
"I am without desires, and the people are natural"
I am always without desires, abandoning flowery decorations and wearing only simple clothing and ornaments. The people then follow me in being simple and natural.
 The Sage says "I cultivate Dao and hold onto reality (by) cutting off and discarding the six emotions. The people then follow me of their own accord and become pure.


## FIFTY-SEVEN

Though our minds are capable of incredible ingenuity, they can also overcome us like a poorly trained horse disregarding its rider. Relying too much on the power of our intellect can easily devolve into obsession, worry, and an incapacity for raw, true, experience. When the mind-horse begins to overpower oneself, a common mistake is to further employ mental activity in trying to calm the mind – to give the mind what it wants: to know more, to understand more, to think more, to dominate. Like giving candy to a petulant child, this will never train the mind.

 In Daoist and Classical Chinese medicine, the mind is made up of inner spirits, housed in the body as intention in the spleen, earthly yin spirits in the lungs, will and competence in the kidneys, ethereal yang spirits in the liver, and spiritual-brilliance in the heart. To see how the Sage's way of government can equally be applied to self-government, simply replace "the people" with "inner spirits" in Heshang Gong's commentary on the last few lines of this chapter:

> The Sage says "I love stillness, and do not speak or teach, yet the [inner spirits] are, of themselves, loyal and honourable... I do not enslave [the inner spirits] or use the law to put them to work, yet the [inner spirits] are peaceful and professional, all enriching themselves... I cultivate Dao and hold onto reality (by) cutting off and discarding the six emotions. The [inner spirits] then follow me of their own accord and become pure."

It is important to recognize the consistent abstention from force in the Sage's method of government: Finding inner stillness, the ruler naturally summons his inner Sage – his spiritual-brilliance (spiritual intelligence) – and is enlightened as to the right course, so long as he can accept the Sage's urging toward kindness, frugality, and modesty. Bringing order to the nation by clarity and stillness is analogous to the method of stilling the body until inner clarity and stillness arrive. This method is described in Guan Zi's *Art of the Heart-Mind* (c.350 BC),[103] the second volume of which commences by describing the technique of stilling the body in order to still the mind.

> When the bodily form is not aligned, Virtue does not approach;
> When the center is not pure and clear, the heart-mind is not stable.
> An aligned bodily form is adorned with Virtue;
> The myriad things (thereby) attain completion.
> When these wings (of Virtue and the heart-mind)[104] naturally come together,
> The spirit knows no limits.
> Illuminated, it's comprehension of the world
> Spans throughout the four directions.
> Therefore it is said: "When things do not confuse the senses,
> And the senses do not confuse the heart-mind –
> This is called 'inner Virtue'."
> Thereby, the energy of intention is settled;
> Having (settled), it returns to alignment.
> Energy-breath then fills the body,
> And one's conduct is righteous and upright.

---

[103] The *Art of the Heart-Mind (Xin Shu)* is said by both tradition and modern re-dating to have preceded Lao Zi's *Dao De Jing*. It also likely preceded the *Nei Ye*, which appears to have been a redacted synthesis of the *Xin Shu* and similar teachings (see *The Thread of Dao: Unraveling Early Daoist Oral Traditions*, by D.G. Reid)

[104] "These wings" may otherwise refer to spirit and qi, said by Ma Danyang to be the underlying meaning of pure nature (xing) and destiny-life-force (ming), the combination of which is central to the Daoist Nei Dan (internal elixer) tradition. See Komjathy, Luis. *The Way of Complete Perfection: A Quanzhen Daoist Anthology*. Albany: State University of New York Press, 2013.

If this fullness (of energy-breath) is not pleasant, the heart-mind does not benefit.
If one's conduct is not upright, the people will not be provided for.
Therefore, Sages resemble Heaven during such times: They are without thought of self when sitting above all.
They resemble Earth during such times: They are without thought of self when supporting all.
As for thought of self, it puts the world in chaos.[105]

## ~ 58 ~

When the government is dull and confused
The people are unadulterated
When the government is discriminating and analytical
The people are lacking

Misfortune! Good fortune relies on it
Good fortune! Misfortune is concealed within it
Who knows where the limits lie?
When there is no alignment
Proper alignment reverts to aberrance
Excellence reverts to divergence
While the people are transfixed, days become years
Therefore, the Sage keeps things square
And doesn't make alterations
(He is) honourable, yet not injurious
Upright, yet not excessive
Shining, yet not dazzling

## Chapter 58
順化 Following and Transforming

其政悶悶，其政教寬大，悶悶昧昧，似若不明也
"When the government is dull and confused"

---

[105] Reid, Dan G. *The Thread of Dao: Unraveling Early Daoist Oral Traditions in Guan Zi's Purifying the Heart-Mind (Bai Xin), Art of the Heart-Mind (Xin Shu), and Internal Cultivation (Nei Ye)*. Montreal: Center Ring Publications, 2017.

When the government teaches people to be open-minded and generous, the people know that there is much they do not know and seem almost unintelligent.
其民醇醇，政教寬大，故民醇醇富厚，相親睦也
"The people are unadulterated"
When the government teaches people to be open-minded and generous, the people are pure, wealthy, and kind, treating everyone like family and friends.
其政察察，其政教急疾，言決於口，聽決於耳也
"When the government is discriminating and analytical"
When the government only quickly teaches people what they need to know in emergencies, people speak only from their mouths, and hear only with their ears.
其民缺缺。政教急疾。民不聊生。故缺缺日以踈薄。
"The people are lacking"
When the government only quickly teaches people what they need to know in emergencies, the people do not appreciate the small things in life. The people then act as though there are not enough days in the year, and neglect those in need.

禍兮福所倚，倚，因也。夫福因禍而生，人遭禍而能悔過責己，修道行善，則禍去福來。
"Misfortune! Good fortune relies on it"
"Relies on it," here, means "is the reason for it." So, good fortune relies on the misfortune from which it arose. When people come across misfortune yet are able to repent for ignoring their responsibilities, they cultivate Dao and walk the good road. Then misfortune leaves them and good fortune arrives.
福兮禍所伏。禍伏匿於福中，人得福而為驕恣，則福去禍來。
"Good fortune! Misfortune is concealed within it"
Misfortune creeps into good fortune when people obtain good fortune and then act haughty and unrestrained in their self-indulgence. Good fortune then leaves them and misfortune arrives.
孰知其極，禍福更相生，誰能知其窮極時。
"Who knows where the limits lie?"
In alterations of misfortune and fortune, who can know when destitution may reach its limit and swing in the other direction?
其無正，無，不也。謂人君不正其身，其無國也
"When there is no alignment"
"Is not," here, means "does not." So, when the ruler does not properly align his person, there will be no proper alignment (with Dao) in the nation.
正復為奇，奇，詐也。人君不正，下雖正，復化上為詐也。
"Proper alignment reverts to aberrance"
Aberrance, here, means dishonesty. When the ruler is not properly aligned, those below, even though upright, are changed by the dishonesty of those above them.
善復為訞。善人皆復化上為訞祥也。
"Excellence reverts to divergence"

People of excellence are all changed by the strange ways of those above them.
人之迷，其日固久。言人君迷惑失正以來，其日已固久。
"While the people are transfixed, days become years"
While the ruler is charmed and mislead, the loss of his proper alignment approaches. Then days disappear into years.

是以聖人方而不割，聖人行方正者，欲以率下，不以割截人也。
"Therefore, the Sage keeps things square and doesn't make alterations"
The Sage acts upright and true, wishing to set a good example for those below. He does not divide and obstruct the people.
廉而不害，聖人廉清，欲以化民，不以傷害人也。今則不然，正己以害人也。
"(He is) honourable, yet not injurious"
The Sage's honour is pure, hoping to thereby reform the people, and not harm or injure them. The tendency today is not like this, where people align themselves only to harm others.
直而不肆，肆，申也。聖人雖直，曲己從人，不自申也。
"Upright, yet not excessive"
Excessive, here, means extending upwards. Sages, though upright, will bend themselves to assist others. They do not continue extending upwards in spite of others needs.
光而不曜。聖人雖有獨見之明，當如闇昧，不以曜亂人也。
"Shining, yet not dazzling"
The Sage, though he may be the only one to see clearly, seems as though in the dark. He does not try to dazzle and confuse people.


FIFTY-EIGHT
If one tries hard enough, they can quite skilfully create rationales to excuse abuses and distort facts. This gives rise to profoundly disordered situations where basic definitions and accounts of events are twisted beyond any hope of determining reality. Inevitably, communication breakdown follows (perhaps intentionally), and this disorder remains so long as the distortions are not rectified and true accounts restored and accepted.

The Huainan Zi states:

> Sages use a single measurement, complying with what has been well established. They do not alter its acceptability; they do not change its regularity. Thus, they can determine what accords to the level, knowing what is crooked by what is just.[106]

---

[106] From the *Huainan Zi* (edited by Liu An, 139 BC), chapter one. Translated by Dan G. Reid.

This translates into internal cultivation by suggesting the "level and just" of inner stability, where attaining one's desires ("good fortune") may end in great dissatisfaction ("misfortune"), and an addiction to distractions ("while the people are transfixed") can cart us through a life of second-hand experiences. Remaining upright yet considerate, without being taken in by a sense of superiority ("shining yet not dazzling"), one may hold fast to the level and not try to "change its regularity."

# ~ 59 ~

In governing people
And serving Heaven
There is nothing like forbearance

Only through forbearance
Can one say they have prepared early
To be prepared early
Means resolving to accumulate Virtue
By resolving to accumulate Virtue
Nothing is insurmountable
When nothing is insurmountable
Limits are unknown
When limits are unknown
There can be a nation

Possessing the Mother of the nation
One's rule will have longevity
This is called deepening the roots
And strengthening the stalk
Long life endures by observing the Dao

## Chapter 59
守道 Guarding Dao Within

治人，謂人君治理人民。
"In governing people"
This refers to (using) logic and reason when ruling and governing people of all classes.
事天，事，用也。當用天道，順四時。
"And serving Heaven"

Serving, here, means applying. To apply Heaven's Way is to obey the four seasons.
莫若嗇。嗇，愛惜也。治國者當愛民財，不為奢泰。治身者當愛精氣，不為放逸。
"There is nothing like forbearance"
Forbearance, here, means caring and regretting (waste). Those who govern the nation must cherish the people as the wealth (of the nation), and not be wasteful and extravagant. Those who govern the body must cherish their vital energy-breaths, and not cause them to flee.

夫為嗇，是謂早服。早，先也。服，得也。夫獨愛民財，愛精氣，則能先得天道也。
"Only through forbearance can one say they have prepared early"
Early, here, refers to prioritizing. Prepared, here, refers to obtaining. So, it is only by cherishing the people as the wealth (of the nation), and by cherishing the vital energy-breaths, that one can prioritize obtaining the Way of Heaven.
早服謂之重積德。先得天道，是謂重積得於己也
"To be prepared early means resolving to accumulate Virtue"
The first priority should be to obtain the Way of Heaven. This means appreciating the gravity of obtaining it in oneself.
重積德則無不剋，剋，勝也。重積德於己，則無不勝。
"By placing importance on accumulating Virtue, nothing is insurmountable"
To overcome means victory. By appreciating the gravity of accumulating Virtue, one will never be defeated.
無不剋則莫知其極，無不剋勝，則莫知有知己德之窮極也。
"When nothing is insurmountable, limits are unknown"
When nothing is insurmountable, nobody thinks about what they have, or whether their Virtue is destitute or limitless.
莫知其極可以有國。莫知己德者有極，則可以有社稷，為民致福。
"When limits are unknown, there can be a nation"
When nobody presumes to know the limits of Virtue, the provinces and their people can be blessed.

有國之母，可以長久。國身同也。母，道也。人能保身中之道，使精氣不勞，五神不苦，則可以長久。
"Possessing the mother of the nation, one's rule will have longevity"
For the nation and the body, this is the same. The mother means "Dao." People can protect the body and keep Dao within when the vital energy-breaths are not overexerted. Then the five spirits[107] will not suffer, and longevity will continue.
是謂深根固蒂，人能以氣為根，以精為蒂，如樹根不深則拔，蒂不堅則落。言當深藏其氣，固守其精，使無漏泄。

---

[107] The five spirits are discussed in chapter six

*"This is called deepening the roots and strengthening the stalk"*
People can use energy-breath to work the root, and use vital essence to work the stalk. Similarly, if a tree's roots are not deep, it will be uprooted, and a stalk that is not firm will fall. This suggests deepening and accumulating energy-breath, while strengthening vital essence. Then there will be no leaking or flowing out.[108]
長生久視之道。深根固蒂者,乃長生久視之道。
*"Long life endures by observing the Dao"*
By deepening the roots and solidifying the stalk, you will lengthen your life and continue to observe Dao.


## FIFTY-NINE

The idea of forbearance appears prominently in the Dao De Jing, most notably in Lao Zi's three treasures—kindness, foregoing, and humility—found in chapter 67. Lao Zi also counsels forbearance in chapter 59 where he speaks to the necessity of preparing early. In preparing early, Lao Zi says, one must accumulate Virtue (積德). Heshang Gong comments on chapter 59, "The first priority should be to obtain the Dao of Heaven. This means appreciating the gravity of obtaining [the Dao of Heaven] in oneself. (先得天道,是謂重積得於己也)"

Terms like foregoing, thrift, and forbearance all imply self-control, refraining from something, and patient endurance. These meanings can be variously understood when applied to living in the world, governing a nation, or governing the self embodiment (身), but in all cases forbearance is an investment that begins from within, with benefits both internally and externally. In the outside world, we govern our time and finances to fit the reality of our situation. In running a nation or a business, one must take care to work within an organization's capacity. In governing our body and self, we must recognize that as human beings we live within the structure of nature reflected throughout our embodied selves, as detailed in the Yellow Emperor's Internal Medicine Classic (Huang Di Nei Jing). In living according to this natural structure, we accord with Heshang Gong's advice that, "The first priority should be to obtain the Dao of Heaven... in oneself." In forbearance we can synchronously accumulate Virtue, observe Dao, and "deepen the roots and strengthen the stalk."

---

[108] The root should be understood here as one's spiritual connection to Dao through true nature (xing) and destined life-force (ming), as explained in chapter 16. The stalk should be understood as the physical body. Leaking and flowing out can be understood as the energy-breath and spiritual vitality escaping for various reasons mentioned throughout Heshang Gong's commentary (see also, the commentary on chapter 52).

Some Daoist texts, (for example, the scrolls mentioned in footnote #2) also say that the retention and transmutation of sexual fluids is required for physical, energetic, and spiritual cultivation. It is likely that Heshang Gong was aware of these practices, given his knowledge of ancient Chinese medical theory, and is referring to such retention as well.

# ~ 60 ~

Govern a large state as though boiling a small fish

When Dao reaches all under Heaven
Ghosts will not take over the spirit
It is not that ghosts will not take over the spirit
But that the spirit will not injure the person
It is not that the spirit will not injure the person
But that the Sage also will not injure people
So both of them will not bring injury
Thus, Virtue will intermingle and return

## Chapter 60
居位 Inhabiting the Throne

治大國者若烹小鮮。鮮，魚。烹小魚不去腸、不去鱗、不敢撓，恐其糜也。治國煩則下亂，治身煩則精散。
"Govern a large state as though boiling a small fish"
When boiling a small fish, the intestines are not removed, the scales are not removed, and you shouldn't dare touch it for fear that it will become mashed. Governing the state with vexation brings chaos to those below. Governing the body with vexation causes the spiritual vitality to scatter.

以道蒞天下，其鬼不神。以道德居位治天下，則鬼不敢以其精神犯人也。
"When Dao reaches all under Heaven, ghosts will not take over the spirit"
When Virtue inhabits the throne[109] and governs the nation according to Dao, ghosts do not dare violate the spiritual vitality in human beings.
非其鬼不神，其神不傷人。其鬼非無精神也，非不入正，不能傷自然之人。
"It is not that ghosts will not take over the spirit, but that the spirit will not injure the person."
Ghosts are not without spiritual vitality. It is not that they are unable to enter morally strong people, but that they are unable to injure those who follow the simplicity of nature (zi ran).
非其神不傷人，聖人亦不傷。非鬼神不能傷害人。以聖人在位不傷害人，故鬼不敢干之也。
"It is not that the spirit will not injure the person, but that the Sage also will not injure people"

---

[109] The heart-mind is also considered the throne of the body.

It is not that ghosts and spirits are unable to injure and kill people, but that a Sage in the throne will not injure and kill people. Thus, ghosts will not dare to oppose them.
夫兩不相傷，鬼與聖人俱兩不相傷也。
*"So both of them will not bring injury"*
Ghosts obey the Sage and so neither will injure the other.
故德交歸焉。夫兩不相傷，則人得治於陽，鬼神得治於陰，人得保全其性命，鬼得保其精神，故德交歸焉。
*"Thus, Virtue will intermingle and return"*
These two do not injure each other. People obtain order through yang, while ghosts and spirits obtain order through yin. People obtain the protection and health of their pure nature (xing) and destiny-life-force (ming). Ghosts obtain the protection of their spiritual vitality. As a result, Virtue intermingles and returns.

## SIXTY

Lao Zi explains that one must be careful not to injure their spiritual energies, and so should consider the method of cooking a small fish, taking great care not to upset the impurities within and cause them to spread throughout. Heshang Gong explains that, when cooking a small fish, neither the scales nor the intestines are removed, and so care is taken not to let impurities contaminate it. In governing a nation, the potential for anger, resentment, violence, and revolt is always present. In self-cultivation, the potential for distraction, desire, frustration, and discouragement are always present. The more force and effort one applies, in either case, the more likely they are to set these forces loose. Trying to contain them once set loose is like trying to cage an army of ghosts. They cannot be forced and they cannot be contained – the only way to bring them back to a peaceful state is by cultivating Virtue.[110]

When the heart-mind (the throne) is occupied by spiritual intelligence (the Sage), it is also more difficult to be overthrown by the negativity of others. As Heshang Gong states, *"It is not that (spirits) are unable to enter morally strong people, but that they are unable to injure those who follow the simplicity of nature (zi ran)."* Those submerged in negativity or overwhelmed by emotions will have difficulty not expressing their negativity, and may need to get others emotional so that they can communicate with them on a lower frequency. To defend against this, one may need to employ all of the sagely strategies for responding to aggressors laid out in chapters 66-79.

---

[110] See the *Xin Shu* on cultivating Virtue, in my comments on chapter 57.

# ~ 61 ~

The greatness of a great state lies in it being beneath the current

It is the junction of the world
It is the female of the world

The female always uses gentleness to overcome the male
And by gentleness puts herself underneath him

Thus, the greatness of a state
Lies in being below the small state
So that it can absorb the small state
The small state is then brought under the large state
So that it can absorb from the large state
Then again, the low absorbs
And again, the low becomes absorbed

The large state limits its desires
To uniting the efforts of farmers
The small state limits its desires
To the profitability of professions
These two both attain to their desires
When the large properly puts itself below

## Chapter 61
謙德 The Virtue of Humility

大國者下流,治大國,當如居下流,不逆細微。
"The greatness of a great state lies in it being beneath the current"
To govern a large state requires residing below the current, and not rejecting all that is small.
天下之交,大國,天下士民之所交會。
"It is the junction of the world"
The large state is where the world's scholars meet and collaborate.
天下之牝。牝者,陰類也。柔謙和而不昌也。
"It is the female of the world"
Female is of the yin category: Soft and pliant, modest, harmonious, and not flashy.

牝常以靜勝牡,女所以能屈男,陰勝陽,以,安靜不先求之也。

"The female always uses gentleness to overcome the male"
A woman can bend a man's will. Yin conquers yang. A woman does this by being calm and gentle, and not putting her demands first.
以靜為下。陰道以安靜為謙下。
"And, by gentleness, puts herself underneath him"
The yin of Dao, through tranquility and gentleness, humbles and lowers (all things.)
故大國以下小國，則取小國，能謙下之，則常有之。
"Thus, the greatness of a state lies in being below the small state, so that it can absorb the small state"
By being humbly beneath (the small state), (the large state) can always possess it.
小國以下大國，則取大國。此言國無大小，能持謙畜人，則無過失也。
"The small state is then brought under the large state so that it can absorb from the large state"
This says that when a nation no longer distinguishes the large from the small, it can support humble farmers, and so not have too many losses.
故或下以取，或下而取。下者謂大國以下小國，小國以下大國，更以義相取。
"Then again, the low absorbs, and again the low becomes absorbed"
"The low," here, refers to the large state because the large state has put itself below the small state. The small state, having the large state below it, enjoys righteousness and mutual benefit.

大國不過欲兼畜人，大國不失下，則兼併小國而牧畜之。
"The large state limits its desires to uniting the efforts of farmers"
The large state does not lose its position underneath, and so combines the small states' farmers and livestock.
小國不過欲入事人。使為臣僕。
"The small state limits its desires to the profitability of professions"
It allocates the use of ministers and servants.
夫兩者各得其所欲，大者宜為下。大國小國各欲得其所，大國又宜為謙下。
"These two both attain to their desires when the large properly puts itself below"
With the large state and small states each desiring to profit their people, the large state returns appropriately to humbly putting itself below.


SIXTY-ONE
The great state putting itself below the small state could be understood as a method of emptying, or humbling, the heart-mind (considered the emperor of the body and house of the spirit) so as to cultivate qi. As qi supports the spirit, and spirit supports the good harmony of elements in the body or nation, the spirit secures life in the body and allows qi to also reside there. Guan Zi's *Purifying the Heart-Mind (Bai Xin)* describes this method as it pertains to internal cultivation (see especially the first line in the excerpt below). Note that in "Discourse Record

of Perfected Danyang," xing (pure nature) and ming (destiny-life-force) are shown to be some of the various terms for spirit and qi, respectively.[111]

> Holding to a ceremonious outward appearance, respectfully welcome that which approaches.
> Those today who seek its approach require this method to (invite) Dao.
> Without soaring (into the sky), without spilling over, the destiny-life-force (ming) will be extended.
> Harmonize by returning to the center, where both body and pure nature (xing) are preserved.
> Be unified and without division. This is called "knowing Dao."
> Wishing to be enveloped by it, you must unify to the furthest extent, and solidify that which is protected within.[112]

# ~ 62 ~

Dao is the mystery of all things
It is the excellent man's treasure
It is the bad man's refuge

Pleasant words can be used for currency
Acts of reverence can be used for social advancement
Why, then, would bad men be rejected?
When the Son of Heaven is enthroned
Three ministers are appointed
He is given the jade seal
And preceded by four cavalrymen
This, however, is not as good
As sitting down and moving forward in this Dao

Why did the ancients treasure Dao?
Was it not said: "By it, those who seek, shall obtain
And the guilty will be liberated?"
Thus, the whole world treasures it

---

[111] Komjathy, Luis. *The Way of Complete Perfection: A Quanzhen Daoist Anthology*. Albany: State University of New York Press, 2013.
[112] Reid, Dan G. *The Thread of Dao: Unraveling Early Daoist Oral Traditions in Guan Zi's Purifying the Heart-Mind (Bai Xin), Art of the Heart-Mind (Xin Shu), and Internal Cultivation (Nei Ye)*. Montreal: Center Ring Publications, 2017.

# Chapter 62
## 為道 Acting With Dao

道者萬物之奧，奧，藏也。道為萬物之藏，無所不容也。
"Dao is the mystery of all things"
Mystery, here, means hidden. Dao is hidden in all things. It has no appearance of its own.

善人之寶，善人以道為身寶，不敢違也。
"It is the excellent man's treasure"
Men of excellence treasure Dao in their bodies and do not dare to be apart from it.

不善人之所保。道者，不善人之保倚也。遭患逢急，猶知自悔卑下。
"It is the bad man's refuge"
Dao is relied on by bad men to protect them. When they come across suffering and urgent situations, they know to repent and humble themselves below it.

美言可以市，美言者獨可於市耳。夫市交易而退，不相宜善言美語，求者欲疾得，賣者欲疾售也
"Pleasant words can be used for currency"
Pleasant words alone can be used for trade. This exchange makes for ease, and retirement. Beautiful language is not the same as appropriate and good speech. Demanding such words from people is to have a desire for illness; those who sell these words hope to sell such an illness.

尊行可以加入。加，別也。人有尊貴之行，可以別異於凡人，未足以尊道。
"Acts of reverence can be used for social advancement"
Improve, here, means "to distinguish." Men praise lofty activities which will help them to distinguish themselves as different from ordinary people. Some attain this by praising Dao.

人之不善，何棄之有。人雖不善，當以道化之。蓋三皇之前，無有棄民，德化淳也。
"Why, then, would bad men be rejected?"
Bad men can be reformed by Dao. Under the protection of the Three Sovereigns,[113] people were never rejected. They were reformed by Virtue and became honest and simple.

故立天子，置三公，欲使教化不善之人。
"When the Son of Heaven is enthroned, three ministers are appointed"
In hopes of teaching and reforming bad men.

雖有拱璧以先駟馬，不如坐進此道。雖有美璧先駟馬而至，故不如坐進此道。
"He is given the jade seal, and preceded by four cavalrymen. This, however, is not as good as sitting down and moving forward in this Dao"

---

[113] See footnote in chapter 19 about the Three Sovereigns

Having the jade seal and being preceded by four cavalrymen is not as good as sitting down and moving forward in this Dao.

古之所以貴此道者，何不日以求得？古之所以貴此道者，不日日遠行求索，近得之於身。
"Why did the ancients treasure Dao? Was it not said: 'By it, those who seek, shall obtain?'"
The ancients treasured the Dao. They did not seek for it day after day, far and wide, but rather obtained it from nearby, within themselves.

有罪以免耶，有罪謂遭亂世，闇君妄行形誅，修道則可以解死，免於眾也。
"'And the guilty will be liberated?'"
To be guilty means to be caught up in the chaos of the world where foolish rulers act recklessly in sentencing people to execution. Those who study Dao may, thereby, escape death. It liberates the masses.

故為天下貴。道德洞遠，無不覆濟，全身治國，恬然無為，故可為天下貴也。
"Thus, the whole world treasures it"
Dao and Virtue are like an endless treasure house, where nothing that goes in is not returned. The body can be maintained and the nation governed by this natural calm and effortlessness. For this reason, the whole world treasures (Dao and Virtue).

SIXTY-TWO
While flattery, promotion, and awesome displays of power might win people over to gain position, sell goods, or encourage allegiance, the ultimate treasure, Dao, can only be won by a sincere heart and mind. Lao Zi explains that the bad man must repent so as to find his way into Dao's favour, while the good man treasures Dao within himself so as to never let it escape his embrace. Both the good and bad must forget any sense that they can convince Dao of their internal merits – they must be pure within in order to secure Dao's protection.

~ 63 ~

Act without acting
Work without working
Taste without tasting
Treat the great as small
And the many as few
Respond to hatred with virtue

In this world, difficult endeavours
Must be approached through what is easy
Deal with what is wide through what is thin

In this world, all great endeavours
Must be approached through what is easy
Therefore sages, with their focus on the end
Do not attack what is great
Thus, they can complete great things

So, frivolous promises surely lack sincerity
Abundant ease ensures abundant difficulty
Therefore, sages prepare for difficulty to arise
And thus finish without difficulty

# Chapter 63
恩始 The Gift of Beginning Early

為無為，因成循故，無所造作。
"Act without acting"
Things can be completed by following the state of events and not creating additional tasks.
事無事，預有備，除煩省事也。
"Work without working"
Prepare in advance in order to eliminate worries and minimize tasks.
味無味。深思遠慮，味道意也。
"Taste without tasting"
Deeply consider issues that are far off. Have the intention to taste Dao.
大小多少，陳其戒令也。欲大反小，欲多反少，自然之道也。
"Treat the great as small and the many as few"
By fixing your resolution at the first appearance of a warning, your desire for the great to become small or the many to become few (will be aided by) the spontaneous nature of Dao.
報怨以德。脩道行善，絕禍於未生也。
"Respond to hatred with virtue"
When seeking Dao and practicing excellence, stop calamities before they arise.

圖難於其易，欲圖難事，當於易時，未及成也。
"In this world, difficult endeavours must be approached through what is easy"
Desiring to plan for difficult tasks, take charge of them while they are easy, rather

than catching up at the end.
為大於其細。欲為大事，必作於小，禍亂從小來也。
"Deal with what is wide through what is thin"
Wishing to manage great tasks, it is important to work on what is small. Misfortune and chaos can arise from what is small.

天下難事必作於易，天下大事必作於細。從易生難，從細生著。
"In this world, all great endeavours must be approached through what is easy"
In this world, great endeavours must be approached through what is tiny. What is easy gives birth to what is difficult; what is tiny gives birth to what is fully developed.
是以聖人終不為大，故能成其大。處謙虛，天下共歸之也。
"Therefore sages, with their focus on the end, do not attack what is great. Thus, they can complete great things"
Staying humble and empty, the whole world returns to them.

夫輕諾必寡信，不重言也。
"So, frivolous promises surely lack sincerity"
Do not take words too seriously.
多易必多難。不慎患也。
"Abundant ease ensures abundant difficulty"
Without caution, there will be suffering.
是以聖人猶難之，聖人動作舉事，猶進退，重難之，欲塞其源也。
"Therefore, sages prepare for difficulty to arise"
Sages move into action when issues arise. Whether issues are advancing or retreating, heavy or light, they want to stop them at the source.
故終無難矣。聖人終生無患難之事，猶避害深也
"And thus finish without difficulty"
Sages finish life without worry or difficult tasks by staying far away from harm.


## SIXTY-THREE

As shown in chapter 62, the greatest loss is the loss of Dao. To prepare early in this matter is to keep watch over the heart and mind for sprouts of resentment,[114] arrogance, selfishness, hatred, entitlement, inauthenticity, inconsideration, and any other tendencies that can easily grow in the shadows and spread like a dangerous mold. Deep attention to internal hygiene is an indispensible exercise for those who wish to refine their character.

---

[114] See: Feng Yi, Wang; Hausen, Johan, *Discourse on Transforming Inner Nature*, Purple Cloud Press, 2018

# ~ 64 ~

That which is stable is easy to hold
That which has not yet shown a sign is easy to plan for
That which is brittle is easy to crumble
That which is small is easy to scatter

Act on what has not yet come into existence
Bring order to what has not yet gone into chaos

A tree trunk which you can barely wrap your arms around
Began as insignificant, and thin as a hair
A nine story tower began with the movement of dirt
The journey of 1000 li began with a single step
Those who take control are defeated
Those who cling will lose
Therefore, sages do not take control and so are not defeated
They do not take hold and so do not lose

When people pursue endeavours
They are usually a short distance from finishing
When defeated
By being as cautious in the end as you are in the beginning
You will not be defeated in your endeavours

Therefore, sages desire what is not desired
They do not exalt goods that are difficult to obtain
And they teach what is not taught

Returning to what the masses have disregarded
They protect the spontaneous nature of all things
And do not dare try to control them

## Chapter 64
守微 Preserving the Small

其安易持，治身治國安靜者，易守持也。
"That which is stable is easy to hold"
When governing the body, or governing a nation, that which is calm and stable is easy to protect and hold onto.

其未兆易謀，情欲禍患未有形兆時，易謀止也。
"That which has not yet shown a sign is easy to plan for"
When strong emotions, desires, disasters, and worries, have not yet shown any portent, they are easy to plan for and stop.
其脆易破，禍亂未動於朝，情欲未見於色，如脆弱易破除。
"That which is brittle is easy to crumble"
Misfortune and chaos which have not yet begun, and desires and strong emotions which have not yet appeared, all resemble what is brittle and weak. Thus, they are easy to destroy and eliminate.
其微易散。其未彰著，微小易散去也。
"That which is small is easy to scatter"
That which is minutely small, and not yet clearly manifest, is easy to scatter and eliminate.

為之於未有，欲有所為，當於未有萌芽之時塞其端也。
"Act on what has not yet come into existence"
The desire to act is like a sprout which has not yet pushed through the soil, yet is not blocked from above.
治之於未亂。治身治國於未亂之時，當豫閉其門也。
"Bring order to what has not yet gone into chaos"
To govern the body, or state, which has not yet become chaotic, is as easy as closing the gates.

合抱之木生於毫末；從小成大。
"A tree trunk which you can barely wrap your arms around began as insignificant, and thin as a hair"
This refers to moving from small to large.
九層之臺起於累土；從卑立高。
"A nine storey tower began with the movement of dirt"
This refers to moving from a humble status to being established in a high position.
千里之行始於足下。從近至遠。
"The journey of 1000 li[115] began with a single step"
This refers to moving from near to distant.
為者敗之，有為於事，廢於自然；有為於義，廢於仁；有為於色，廢於精神也。
"Those who take control are defeated"
Trying to control and interfere abandons the simplicity of nature. Trying to force righteousness discards humanity. Trying to control appearances abandons the spiritual vitality.
執者失之。執利遇患，執道全身，堅持不得，推讓反還。
"Those who cling will lose"

---

[115] 1000 li = 500 kilometers

Clinging to profit brings about worry. Clinging to Dao maintains the body. Clenching the hand does not allow one to obtain anything, while opening it and giving something may bring more in return.

是以聖人無為故無敗，聖人不為華文，不為色利，不為殘賊，故無敗壞。
"Therefore, sages do not take control, and so are not defeated"
Sages do not partake in flowery sophistication. They do not try to make things appear of more worth than they are, and they do not get involved in punishing traitors. As a result, they are not defeated or ruined.

無執故無失。聖人有德以教愚，有財以與貧，無所執藏，故無所失於人也。
"They do not take hold and so do not lose"
Sages posses Virtue and use it to teach simplicity. They possess wealth and use it to share with the poor. They do not clench and hoard these things, and so are without any place to lose them.

民之從事，常於幾成而敗之。從，為也。民之為事，常於功德幾成，而貪位好名，奢泰盈滿而自敗之也。
"When people pursue endeavours, they are usually a short distance from finishing when defeated"
The people, in trying to accomplish their goals, are often far closer than they realize to perfecting their Virtue when greed for position, and love of reputation, cause them to exaggerate and exalt themselves, to overflow with self-satisfaction, and thereby cause their own defeat.

慎終如始，則無敗事。終當如始，不當懈怠。
"By being as cautious in the end as you are in the beginning, you will not be defeated in your endeavours"
Treat the end the same as the beginning – do not become idle and negligent.

是以聖人欲不欲，聖人欲人所不欲。人欲彰顯，聖人欲伏光；人欲文飾，聖人欲質朴；人欲色，聖人欲於德。
"Therefore, sages desire what is not desired"
Sages desire what others do not desire. Others desire to be noticed. The Sage desires to conceal his light. Others desire ornamentation. Sages desire what is simple and natural. Others desire appearances. Sages desire to be Virtuous.

不貴難得之貨；聖人不眩為服，不賤石而貴玉。
"They do not exalt goods that are difficult to obtain"
Sages do not get excited over fashionable clothes, cheap stones, or valuable jade.

學不學，聖人學人所不能學。人學智詐，聖人學自然；人學治世，聖人學治身；守道真也。
"And they teach what is not taught"
Sages teach what others cannot teach. Others teach how to be clever and deceptive. Sages teach the simplicity of nature. Others teach about governing the world. Sages teach about governing the self and holding the true Dao within.

復眾人之所過；眾人學問反，過本為末，過實為華。復之者：使反本也。
*"Returning to what the masses have disregarded"*
The masses learn through questions and answers, and disregard the root as though it were insignificant. They disregard what is most valuable and pursue flowery outward appearances. The Sage brings them back to the root.

以輔萬物之自然。教人反本實者，欲以輔助萬物自然之性也。
*"They protect the spontaneous nature of all things"*
In teaching people to return to the root[116] and appreciate its supreme value, their desire is to foster the intrinsic simplicity of nature in all things.

而不敢為。聖人動作因循，不敢有所造為，恐遠本也。
*"And do not dare try to control them"*
Sages are aroused to action in accordance with events. They do not dare to use superfluous effort for fear of straying from the root.

## SIXTY-FOUR

If people took times of health as the opportune moment to exercise and eat more healthily, illness and physical disabilities would be far less common in the world. As Qi Bo explains to the Yellow Emperor in the *Nei Jing, Su Wen*, chapter two:

> As for Dao, the sages practice it; the foolish decorate themselves with it. To accord with yin and yang leads to life; to oppose them leads to death. To accord with yin and yang leads to order; to oppose them leads to chaos… Therefore, sages did not establish order to stop illness, they established order before illness arose. They did not establish order to stop chaos, they established order before chaos arose. To provide medicine after illness is already affixed, or instill order after chaos has already ensued, this is like digging a well after one is already thirsty, or fashioning weapons after war has already begun.[117]

While chapters 63 and 64 caution wariness, they also teach the importance of planting seeds, of making the small efforts that eventually bring great results. For example, Heshang Gong says, "Clenching the hand does not allow one to obtain anything, while opening it and giving something may bring more in return." Small generosities may build unforeseen relationships and connections. Small kindnesses and acts of virtue foster harmony and plant the seeds that grow into fields of social collaboration, giving vitality and purpose to communities and the people within them.

---

[116] "The root" is discussed in chapter 16
[117] Translated by Dan G. Reid

# ~ 65 ~

The ancient masters who aligned society with Dao
Did not do so by enlightening the people
But rather, fostered their simplicity

Difficulty in governing people
Comes from a wealth of wisdom
Hence, when knowledge is used to govern the nation
This results in thievery from the nation
Not using knowledge to govern the nation
Blesses the nation

Understand the broader application of these two principles
There is an infinite understanding
Which can be found in these principles
This is called Fathomless Virtue
Fathomless Virtue, profound and far-reaching
Following it, things return back to their nature
Arriving at great submission

## Chapter 65
淳德 The Virtue of Simplicity

古之善為道者，非以明民，將以愚之。說古之善以道治身及治國者，不以道教民明智巧詐也，將以道德教民，使質朴不詐偽。

"The ancient masters who aligned society with Dao, did not do so by enlightening the people, but rather fostered their simplicity"
The ancient masters employed Dao to govern the body, and applied this same skill to governing the state. They did not teach Dao to the people as intellectual knowledge that would help them to be clever and deceitful. To transmit Dao and Virtue to the people is to teach them to be simple and natural, rather than artificial and deceitful.

民之難治，以其智多。民之所以難治者，以其智多而為巧偽。
"Difficulty in governing people comes from a wealth of wisdom"
People are difficult to govern because they use their abundant knowledge to be clever and deceitful.

故以智治國，國之賊；使智慧之人治國之政事，必遠道德，妄作威福，為國之賊也。

"Hence, when knowledge is used to govern the nation, this results in thievery from the nation"

When people of knowledge and intelligence govern the affairs of the nation, they are sure to go far from Dao and Virtue. In their foolishness, they act pompously when the nation receives blessings and become thieves of the nation.

不以智治國，國之福。不使智慧之人治國之政事，則民守正直，不為邪飾，上下相親，君臣同力，故為國之福也。

"Not using knowledge to govern the nation, blesses the nation"

When people of shrewd intelligence are not involved in governing the affairs of the nation, the people embrace correctness and uprightness. They do not do evil things or act deceptively. The upper and lower classes treat each other like one family, and the emperor unifies their strength. This causes a nation to be blessed.

知此兩者亦稽式。兩者謂智與不智也。常能智者為賊，不智者為福，是治身治國之法式也。

"Understand the broader application of these two principles"

"These two" means using knowledge, and not using knowledge. It is common for learnedness to create thieves, and for un-learnedness to create good fortune. This same pattern applies to both governing the body, and governing the nation.

常知稽式，是謂玄德。玄，天也。能知治身及治國之法式，是謂與天同德也。

"There is an infinite understanding which can be found in these principles. This is called Fathomless Virtue"

Fathomless, here, means Heavenly. If one understands the principles of governing the body, they will understand the principles of governing the nation. Of this, it is said "to follow Heaven is to unite with Virtue."

玄德深矣，遠矣，玄德之人深不可測，遠不可及也。

"Fathomless Virtue, profound and far-reaching"

The person of fathomless Virtue is immeasurably deep. Their depth cannot be fully reached.

與物反矣！玄德之人與萬物反異，萬物欲益己，玄德施與人也。

"Following it, things return"

The person of fathomless Virtue helps all things to reverse abberations. The myriad things desire to profit themselves, while (the person of) fathomless Virtue brings assistance to others.

然後乃至於大順。玄德與萬物反異，故能至大順。順天理也。

"Back to their nature, arriving at great submission"

Fathomless Virtue helps the myriad things to reverse abberations. Thus, they can arrive at great submission. This means submitting to Heaven's intrinsic order.

SIXTY-FIVE

Though many businesses suffer for not listening to the experiences of those in lower ranks, much like diseases often develop from persistently ignored discomforts, organized structures can also fail from "too many cooks in the kitchen" syndrome. Where organized leadership is necessary, for example in an army, a large kitchen staff, or the human body, too many "better ideas" may result in analysis-paralysis – hesitation leading to ineffectiveness, or even incompetence and inefficiency.

In the body, the brain is the hub of the nervous system where orders are received and sent out, but it is not the very top of the chain of command. The heart processes emotions and stress, as well as a sense of balance and well being. If the heart-mind/emperor is lost, the brain can do little to change this, and the orders sent out by the brain will reflect this confusion, resulting in disorder elsewhere in the body. Thus, the intellectual mind must serve the spirit, housed in the heart-mind, and allow the spirit to guide the body's affairs with its intrinsic harmony and balance. This, in turn, strengthens intelligence by allowing the heart-mind to perceive clearly, without excessive thought processes blocking what appears plainly in front of it. This is to absorb through the shen ming (神明),[118] the "spiritual intelligence or spiritual illumination" that is reached through the "art of the heart-mind (xin shu/xin fa)" described throughout Daoist meditation texts.[119]

## ~ 66 ~

The rivers and oceans
Can be the kings to so many valley streams
Because they are good at being below them
Thus, they can be the kings to so many valley streams

Therefore, if you want to be above people
You must speak as though below them
Desiring to lead the people
You must put yourself behind them

Therefore, the Sage resides above
And the people do not feel his weight
He resides in front
And the people do not feel mistreated

---

[118] Ming (明), often translated as "enlightenment," means "to see clearly," with its character denoting light by combining the radicals for the sun and moon.
[119] See: Reid, Dan G. *The Thread of Dao: Unraveling Early Daoist Oral Traditions in Guan Zi's Purifying the Heart-Mind (Bai Xin), Art of the Heart-Mind (Xin Shu), and Internal Cultivation (Nei Ye)*. Montreal: Center Ring Publications, 2017.

As a result, all under Heaven advance happily
And are not embittered
It is because he does not force anyone
That the world cannot respond to his force

# Chapter 66
後己 Leaving Oneself Behind

江海所以能為百谷王者，以其善下之，故能為百谷王。江海以卑，故眾流歸之，若民歸就王。以卑下，故能為百谷王也。
"The rivers and oceans can be the kings to so many valley streams because they are good at being below them. Thus, they can be the kings to so many valley streams."
It is because the large oceans are humble and low that the currents all flow toward them. In the same way, the people are drawn toward the king. It is by being low and humble that the king can rule the hundred families.

是以欲上民，欲在民之上也。
"Therefore, if you want to be above people"
Desiring to be the people's superior
必以言下之；法江海處謙虛。
"You must speak as though below them"
You must follow the oceans, making yourself humble and empty.
欲先民，欲在民之前也。
"Desiring to lead the people"
Desiring to be in front of the people
必以身後之。先人而後己也。
"You must put yourself behind them"
Lead others by putting yourself behind them

是以聖人處上而民不重，聖人在民上為主，不以尊貴虐下，故民戴而不為重。
"Therefore, the Sage resides above and the people do not feel his weight"
The Sage places the people in the position of honour, of the host. He does not perpetuate any reverence of the wealthy, or oppression of the poor. Thus, the people are supportive of him and do not feel weighed down.
處前而民不害。聖人在民前，不以光明蔽後，民親之若父母，無有欲害之心也。
"He resides in front, and the people do not feel mistreated"
The Sage stands in front of the people, but does not block the light of truth from shining behind him. Like the peoples' fathers and mothers, he has no wish to injure

their minds.

是以天下樂推而不厭。聖人恩深愛厚，視民如赤子，故天下樂推進以為主，無有厭也。

*"As a result, all under Heaven advance happily, and are not embittered"*

The Sage's kindness is profound and his affectionate love is plentiful. He looks after the people as though they were infants. Thus, the whole world pushes forward happily, treating the Sage as their chief and not holding onto any bitterness.

以其不爭，天下無厭聖人時，是由聖人不與人爭先後也。

*"It is because he does not force anyone"*

No one in the world dislikes the Sage's rule, so all unite under the Sage and do not fall into man's contentious ways of fighting with those ahead or behind them.

故天下莫能與之爭。言人皆有為，無有與吾爭無為。

*"That the world cannot respond to his force"*

This is to say that all people use force, but there is no way to resist what does not use any force.

## SIXTY-SIX

Though a leadership role suggests the highest position with many people serving underneath, leadership is best viewed as the most humble position. While those of lower rank serve one leader, the leader must serve everyone – they are ultimately responsible for the outcome of everyone's job, for the effectiveness and coordination of everyone on their team, and so are in fact the lowest servant of that team.

An ancient metaphor for good leadership, appearing in chapters 11 and 39 of the *Dao De Jing*, is "the hub of the wheel" – the emptiness at the center which unites all spokes and allows for them to turn in unison. This, of course, represents the ultimate leader – Dao, the empty, fathomless principle upon which all things are based – but also describes the importance of selflessness in a leader. If the leader is not empty of the selfish desire to dominate, the wheel cannot turn smoothly and will not last. Thus, he or she must take the role of the lowest servant, serving all for the good function of the unit, allowing it to turn effortlessly and without bearing the resistance of a center that cannot go unnoticed.

## ~ 67 ~

Everyone says my way is vast
And yet, it appears to be foolish
Because it is great

It appears foolish
As though reflecting a time long since past
It is delicate

I have three treasures
Which I hold close and protect
The first is kindness
The second is economy
The third is not brazenly taking precedence over the world

Through kindness, there can be courage
Through economy, there can be generosity
Through not brazenly taking precedence over the world
I can fashion vessels of longevity

Now, if one neglects kindness in courage
Neglects economy in generosity
Neglects humility in being at the forefront
They will die.

So, kindness in times of war brings victory
And protecting it brings strength and stability
Heaven will bring its aid
And kindness will be protected

# Chapter 67
三寶 Three Treasures

天下皆謂我道大，似不肖。老子言：天下謂我德大，我則佯愚似不肖。
"Everyone says my way is vast. And yet, it appears to be foolish"
Lao Zi says: "When the world declares my Virtue to be vast, I feign stupidity and appear to be foolish."
夫唯大，故似不肖，唯獨名德大者為身害，故佯愚似若不肖。無所分別，無所割截，不賤人而自貴。
"Because it is great, it appears foolish"
Those who hold a reputation for great virtue bring trouble to themselves. Hence, Lao Zi feigns stupidity and appears foolish. By not distinguishing, separating, categorizing, or alienating, he does not demean people or exalt himself.
若肖久矣。肖，善也。謂辨惠也。若大辨惠之人，身高自貴行察察之政所從來久矣。

*"As though reflecting a time long since past"*

"Reflecting" here, means appearing to be excellent. People who distinguish and exalt themselves are scrutinized and compared against the kingdoms of the past.

其細也夫。言辨惠者唯如小人，非長者。

*"It is delicate"*

In seeking recognition and favour, only petty men exalt themselves. They will not last.

我有三寶，持而保之。老子言：我有三寶，抱持而保倚。

*"I have three treasures, which I hold close and protect"*

Lao Zi says "I have three treasures which I hold, defend, and rely on."

一曰慈，愛百姓若赤子。

*"The first is kindness"*

To love all people as though they were infants[120]

二曰儉，賦斂若取之於己也。

*"The second is economy"*

To reduce taxes as though I were taking them from myself.

三曰不敢為天下先。執謙退，不為倡始也。

*"The third is not brazenly taking precedence over the world"*

Holding firmly onto humility, standing back, and not initiating with force.

慈故能勇，以慈仁，故能勇於忠孝也。

*"Through kindness, there can be courage"*

Because of their kindness and consideration of others, people can be courageous and devoted to filial duties.

儉故能廣，天子身能節儉，故民日用廣矣。

*"Through economy, there can be generosity"*

When the Son of Heaven is frugal toward himself, the people can be generous in their daily affairs.

不敢為天下先，不為天下首先。

*"Through not brazenly taking precedence over the world"*

By not pretending to be the chief leader

故能成器長。成器長，謂得道人也。我能為得道人之長也。

*"I can fashion vessels of longevity"*

---

[120] Ci 慈 is most often translated as compassion, love, or charity. It can be understood here as kindness, encompassing both the practice of charity, and the feeling of compassion. Charity is advocated in chapter 81, chapter seven, and in numerous comments by Heshang Gong.

This stanza has been a source of interest and debate for both its simplified focus of practice, and its apparent similarity to the Christian doctrine of love. Heshang Gong clarifies the meaning of ci by using another word, ai 愛, which refers to affectionate love. That Lao Zi follows his value for kindness/charity with his value for forgoing, while Heshang Gong depicts acts of charity so frequently, also suggests this meaning.

A strong connection exists between the three treasures of "kindness, forgoing, and putting the world first" and the selflessness illustrated in chapter seven.

Fashioning vessels of longevity means helping people to attain Dao. "I can help bring about the longevity of those who attain Dao."

今舍慈且勇，今世人舍慈仁，但為勇武。
*"Now, if one neglects kindness in courage"*
If someone neglects kindness and consideration of others, while acting courageously and aggressively;
舍儉且廣，舍其儉約，但為奢泰。
*"Neglects economy in generosity"*
If they neglect their budget, and act wastefully and debaucherously;
舍後且先，舍其後己，但為人先。
*"Neglects humility in being at the forefront"*
If they neglect to humble themselves, and put themselves at the forefront,
死矣！所行如此，動入死地。
*"They will die."*
Such behaviour is like walking into a deathtrap.

夫慈以戰則勝，以守則固。夫慈仁者，百姓親附，并心一意，故以戰則勝敵，以守衛則堅固。
*"So, kindness in times of war brings victory, and protecting it brings strength and stability"*
Having kindness and consideration of others brings the hundred families to care for both their own families and those of others with the unified focus of their hearts. This results in a resolute and stable defense, and thus, if there is war, victory over enemies.
天將救之，以慈衛之。天將救助善人，必與慈仁之性，使能自營助也。
*"Heaven will bring its aid, and kindness will be protected"*
Heaven gives assistance to people of excellence. It is imperative that all abide by their intrinsically kind and considerate natures, so that they too may be assisted and protected.


## SIXTY-SEVEN
Chapter 67 begins by demonstrating the importance of being comfortable out of the spotlight. Heshang Gong comments:

> Those who hold a reputation for great virtue bring trouble to themselves. Hence, Lao Zi feigns stupidity and appears foolish. By not distinguishing, separating, categorizing, or alienating, he does not demean people or exalt himself.

In today's world, with so many ways to bask in the digital spotlight, it is easy to think of ourselves as special or better than others and then become confused and depressed when we fall out of that spotlight and feel insignificant. Worries, sadness, fear, and anger can all crop up from our sense of acceptance or lack thereof. Thus, it is necessary not to rely or prop ourselves up on renown, fame, and reputation – "name" (名, ming), as it is often referred to in the *Dao De Jing*. Consider chapter one – "the name that can be named is not the eternal name." This "name" of ours is ultimately meaningless. In the Eternal, glory, renown, and reputation are illusions. The value we give to them is merely an illusory construct of the mind.

In the temporal world, however, Lao Zi practices "three treasures":

Cí (慈): love, charity, mercy – kindness
Jiǎn (儉): forgoing, moderation, simplicity – economy
bù gǎn wéi tiānxià xiān (不敢為天下先): not brazenly taking precedence over the world

While these "three treasures" are three, they are also one. For example, not putting oneself first requires forgoing, and practices kindness; forgoing requires not putting oneself first, and allows for generosity and kindness; kindness requires moderating one's own desires, while putting others first. This is the external practice of the three treasures. Aside from practicing these as compassion, frugality, and humility, another way to engage all three of these treasures is active empathy – listening to others to understand how they experience the world, speaking less, and putting your own feelings, opinions, or ideas aside as you focus on discovering how that person experiences, and feels about, what it is they're talking about.

What is often missed in reading chapter 67 is that the three treasures of kindness, economy, and humility are presented as the yin counterparts of the chapter's other, more yang, values: courage, generosity, and fostering longevity in others.

Just as someone who amasses physical power can neglect their character and become imbalanced, ultimately weakening themselves in the process, excessive yang (function) can often weaken yin (substance) and so in turn weaken the whole. Thus, to be truly strong, yin and yang must be balanced – the seeds or roots (yin) must be watered in order to support the fruit (yang). Wishing to be courageous, one must first hold and protect kindness; wishing to be generous, one must first not be extravagant toward themselves; wishing to foster longevity in others, one must be careful not to put themselves first. Given this pairing with "not putting oneself first," vessels of longevity (器長) may also carry a pun referring to the fostering of leadership (長) by not putting oneself first. Thus, these three treasures, while ultimately effective in themselves, are also keys for unlocking the success of courage,[121] generosity,[122] and fostering others.[123]

---

[121] See chapter 73, which is dedicated to noble courage with a nuance of balance and kindness that can be more easily discerned by studying chapter 67.

As with most elements in the *Dao De Jing,* the three treasures can apply to internal practice. As such, kindness is nurturing qi and bringing harmony to the spirit; forgoing is removing thoughts and not indulging in sights, sounds, and activities around oneself; not putting oneself first is transcending the self through the internal practice of the first two treasures.[124]

# ~ 68 ~

Those who are good at managing armies
Do not encourage warfare
Those who are skilled at warfare
Do not become angry
Those who are skilled at overpowering enemies
Do not clash with them
Those who are skilled at employing people
Put themselves in service to them

This is called the power and virtue of non-combatitiveness
This is called directing people's skills
This is called reflecting Heaven
As it was at the beginning of time

## Chapter 68
配天 Reflecting Heaven

善為士者不武，言貴道德，不好武力也。
"Those who are good at managing armies do not encourage warfare"
This is a counsel to value Dao and De, and not dream of military power.
善戰者不怒，善以道戰者，禁邪於胸心，絕禍於未萌，無所誅怒也。
"Those who are skilled at warfare do not become angry"
Those who are skilled in the ways of war do not allow wickedness to enter their hearts, but cut off this source of misfortune before it sprouts. This way, they do not kill in anger.
善勝敵者不與，善以道勝敵者，附近以仁，來遠以德，不與敵爭，而敵自服也。
"Those who are skilled at overpowering enemies do not clash with them"

---

[122] See also chapter 81
[123] See also chapters 7, 51, and 66
[124] Given the importance of these three treasures to Daoism, I feel I should point out that these interpretations are my own, and not, to my knowledge, those of any Daoist organizations.

Those who are skilled in the ways of overpowering enemies remain altruistic with those near them, and draw people from afar by Virtue. They do not fight with enemies but rather dress them in their own uniforms.

善用人者為之下。善用人自輔佐者，常為人執謙下也。
"Those who are skilled at employing people put themselves in service to them"
Those who are skilled at employing people protect themselves by acting subordinate, and always maintaining a position of humility when engaging with others.

是謂不爭之德，謂上為之下也。是乃不與人爭之道德也。
"This is called the power and virtue of non-combatitiveness"
This means that the superior acts as though inferior. In this way, they do not follow along with man's contentious ways, but adhere to Virtue.

是謂用人之力，能身為人下，是謂用人臣之力也
"This is called directing people's skills"
The ability of an individual depends on those beneath him. This means that to direct people is to minister their skills.

是謂配天古之極。能行此者，德配天也。是乃古之極要道也。
"This is called reflecting Heaven as it was at the beginning of time"
The ability to act in this way reflects the Virtue of Heaven. It is the most ancient characteristic of Dao.


SIXTY-EIGHT
To fully grasp Lao Zi's strategy in chapter 68, and understand how "Those who are skilled at overpowering enemies do not clash with them," it may help to look at chapter 63 in which Lao Zi says:

> Treat the great as small
> And the many as few
> Respond to hatred with virtue

Rather than pushing back hatred with hatred, war may be avoided by responding with kindness. If someone is angry and insulting, by disregarding their aggression, seeking the reason for their pain, and responding to their aggression with kindness, love, and compassion, seeking to help them however you can, you employ the virtue of water – the power and technique of the Sage. As Lao Zi illustrates:

> Those who are skilled at warfare
> Do not become angry
> Those who are skilled at overpowering enemies
> Do not clash with them
> Those who are skilled at employing people

Put themselves in service to them
This is called the power and virtue of non-combatitiveness

This "technique" is further explained in the following chapter – chapter 69.

# ~ 69 ~

In the employment of an army, there is a saying:
"I dare not be the host, but I will be a guest
I dare not advance an inch, but will step back a foot"

This is called advancing without advancing
Embracing without arms
Attacking without an enemy
Guarding without militant force

Misfortune has no greater cause
Than not respecting an enemy
By not respecting an enemy
How much do we risk destroying what is precious?

Hence, armies standing in opposition
Could benefit by standing together
Those who are saddened (by this destruction)
Will be victorious!

## Chapter 69
玄用 Utilizing the Fathomless

用兵有言：陳用兵之道。老子疾時用兵，故託己設其義也。
"In the employment of an army, there is a saying"
This is advice for employing military strategy. Lao Zi was troubled by the prevalence of military force during his time. Thus, he tried to transmit a basis of righteousness.
吾不敢為主而為客，主，先也。不敢先舉兵。客者，和而不倡。用兵當承天而後動。
"I dare not be the host, but I will be a guest"
To be "the host" means to be "the first." Do not be the first to initiate military ac-

tion. Being the guest is to remain peaceful, and not introduce battle. Use of military force will then accord with Heaven and receive support and momentum.

不敢進寸而退尺。侵人境界，利人財寶，為進；閉門守城，為退。
"I dare not advance an inch, but will step back a foot"
Crossing others' borders to take their treasures and money is advancing an inch. Closing the gates to protect the municipality is stepping back a foot.

是謂行無行，彼遂不止，為天下賊，雖行誅之，不成行列也。
"This is called advancing without advancing"
Advancement without cease is the thief of all under Heaven. Only by terminating this does it not cross every line.

攘無臂，雖欲大怒，若無臂可攘也。
"Embracing without arms"
When desire turns into great anger, it is without arms yet takes possession.

扔無敵，雖欲仍引之，若無敵可仍也。
"Attacking without an enemy"
When desires are continually pursued, they have no enemy but continue to pursue.

執無兵。雖欲執持之，若無兵刃可持用也。何者？傷彼之民懼罪於天，遭不道之君，慇忍喪之痛也。
"Guarding without militant force"
When desires are held onto and protected, this is like not having an army but still putting it to use. How is this so? Injuring others and causing them sorrow is a crime against Heaven. When a ruler who does not follow Dao is encountered, mercy, remorse, and sympathy will accompany the funeral rites.

禍莫大於輕敵。夫禍亂之害，莫大於欺輕敵家，侵取不休，輕戰貪財也。
"Misfortune has no greater cause than not respecting an enemy"
The great turmoil of social upheaval has no greater cause than crossing, and not respecting, an enemy and his territory. Invasions and conquests continue without rest when war is considered to be less significant than one's own greed for wealth.

輕敵，幾喪吾寶。幾，近也。寶，身也。欺輕敵者，近喪身也。
"By not respecting an enemy, how much do we risk destroying what is precious?"
By "how much" is meant "how close." By "what is precious" is meant "the body." By cheating and not respecting an enemy, one comes close to losing their body.

故抗兵相加，兩敵戰也。
"Hence, armies standing in opposition could benefit by standing together"
This refers to two armies at war.

哀者勝矣。哀者慈仁，士卒不遠於死。
"Those who are saddened (by this destruction) will be victorious!"
Those who are saddened are merciful (ci), and considerate of others (ren). They will

not have their soldiers sent off to die in foreign lands.

SIXTY-NINE
"Stepping back a foot" appears to suggest the strategy of responding with virtue and winning over an opponent by absorbing them.[125] This is to win without fighting ("advancing without advancing"), to bring them in by their own volition ("embracing without arms"), not treating the other side as an enemy yet resolving the conflict ("attacking without an enemy"), and bringing security and prosperity with this neutralization of conflict ("guarding without militant force"). To achieve this, one accepts the invitation to engage, but does not vie for dominance: "I dare not be a host, but will be a guest; I dare not advance an inch, but will step back a foot."

# ~ 70 ~

My words are very easy to understand, very easy to follow
Yet none in the world are able to understand them
None are able to put them into practice
Words have a lineage, actions have a ruler
It is because there is no knowledge (of these things)
That I am not known
Those who understand me are rare
And so, those few I treasure
It is for these reasons
That the Sage wraps himself in coarse cloth
While concealing jade in his heart

## Chapter 70
知難 The Difficulty of Knowing

章吾言甚易知，甚易行。老子言：吾所言省而易知，約而易行。
"My words are very easy to understand, very easy to follow"
Lao Zi says, "My speech is concise and easy to understand. These precepts are easy to follow."
天下莫能知，莫能行。人惡柔弱，好剛強也

---

[125] See my comments on chapter 68.

"Yet none in the world are able to understand them, none are able to put them into practice"
People hate the soft and pliant, but like the hard and tough.
言有宗，事有君。我所言有宗祖根本，事有君臣上下，世人不知者，非我之無德，心與我之反也
"Words have a lineage, actions have a ruler"
(In other words) "My words come from a lineage of ancestors connected to the root. My actions have a ruler who ministers over what is above and below. The people of today's generations do not know of these. Were I without Virtue, my mind would have also led me away from them."
夫唯無知，是以不我知。夫唯世人之無知者，是我德之暗，不見於外，窮微極妙，故無知也。
"It is because there is no knowledge (of these things), that I am not known"
It is because people today do not know of these things that my secret virtue is not seen on the surface. Infinitesimal, immeasurably mysterious, it is therefore unknown.
知我者希，則我者貴。希，少也。唯達道者乃能知我，故為貴也。
"Those who understand me are rare, and so, those few I treasure"
Rare, here, means few. Only those who arrive at Dao are able to understand me. For this reason, they are treasured.
是以聖人被褐懷玉。被褐者薄外，懷玉者厚內，匿寶藏德，不以示人也。
"It is for these reasons that the Sage wraps himself in coarse cloth while concealing jade in his heart"
Those who wear coarse cloth appear poor, externally. Those who conceal jade in their hearts have great wealth, internally. By hiding treasure, and concealing Virtue, they are not put on display for others.

## SEVENTY

Studying, chanting, memorizing, theorizing, and sharing Lao Zi's words may only be filling one's yard with bags of seed, fertilizer, garden tools, and sprinkler systems without ever planting a garden. Dao is the root of Lao Zi's words. If we can find and follow Dao within ourselves, his words will seem very simple and easy to follow.

# ~ 71 ~

To know that you do not know is best
Not knowing, but thinking you know, is illness

*Only being sickened by their sickness*
*Does one not become ill*
*Sages are not ill because they are sickened by their sickness*

# Chapter 71
知病 Knowledge and Illness

知不知上，知道言不知，是乃德之上。
*"To know that you do not know is best"*
Those who know Dao say that they do not know, yet their Virtue is superior.
不知知病。不知道言知，是乃德之病。
*"Not knowing, but thinking you know, is illness"*
Those who do not know Dao, yet say that they know – their virtue is ill.
夫唯病病，是以不病。夫唯能病苦眾人有強知之病，是以不自病也。
*"Only being sickened by their sickness does one not become ill."*[126]
Only if one can feel the suffering of this illness when everyone else feels powerful in their knowledge will they themselves not succumb to it.

聖人不病，以其病病，是以不病。聖人無此強知之病者，以其常苦眾人有此病，以此非人，故不自病。夫聖人懷通達之知，託於不知者，欲使天下質朴忠正，各守純性。小人不知道意，而妄行強知之事以自顯著，內傷精神，減壽消年也。

*"Sages are not ill because they are sickened by their sickness."*
The Sage is without the illness of trying to appear clever. Because, ordinarily, people all suffer from this illness, he is not like other people – he does not suffer from this. For the Sage to be intelligent, he must allow knowledge to pass through him. This requires that he maintain a position of uncertainty.

Desiring that all under Heaven be plain in substance, loyal, and honourable, he protects the purity of their true nature (xing). Petty men do not know the Dao other than in their own minds, and so absurdly follow their stubborn beliefs and act in ways that reveal their ignorance. Internally, this injures the spiritual vitality and decreases the lifespan by many years.

SEVENTY-ONE
It is better to think you may be wrong and find out you were right, than to think you're right and find out you were wrong.

Quite appropriately, this chapter leaves few translators without a degree of uncertainty as to the meaning of (literally) "so, only sick sick, therefore not sick.

---

[126] Reading the repetition of bing (illness) as an adjective: "Therefore, only the sickly are not ill."

Sages not sick, therefore they sick sick." This might say "so, only (through being) sick of (this) sickness is one not sick. Sages are not sick; therefore, they (are certainly) sick of (this) sickness." Many words in Classical Chinese can be either nouns, verbs, adverbs, or adjectives depending on context. The repetition of a word can emphasize it or turn it into an adjective, and so *sick sick* could also mean *sickly*: "so, only the sickly are not ill" – only those who feel that they have this illness are not ill. This reading would suggest mindfulness, and an attitude similar to the common advice from Zen teachers on quiet sitting: the problem is not that thoughts [feelings, emotions, ignorance] arise; the problem is not being aware of thoughts [feelings, emotions, ignorance] when they arise.

# ~ 72 ~

When the people do not fear displays of power
Greater displays of power will follow
Let their homes not be disrespected
Let their lives not be tiresome
If they are not tiresome
They will not grow tired of them
Therefore the Sage knows himself
But does not display himself
Loves and cares for himself
But does not overestimate himself
He abandons that and chooses this

## Chapter 72
愛己 Cherishing Oneself

民不畏威，則大威至。威，害也。人不畏小害則大害至。大害者，謂死亡也。畏之者當愛精神，承天順地也。
"When the people do not fear displays of power, greater displays of power will follow"
Displays of power, here, refer to injuries. When people do not fear small injuries, greater injuries follow. By greater injuries is meant "death and destruction." Those who fear these things should cherish their spiritual vitality, receive from Heaven, and submit to Earth.
無狎其所居，謂心居神，當寬柔，不當急狹也。

"Let their homes not be disrespected"
This means that for the heart-mind to house the spirit, it is important to be broad and flexible, not urgent and tight.

無厭其所生，人所以生者，以有精神。託空虛，喜清靜，飲食不節，忽道念色，邪僻滿腹，為伐本厭神也。

"Let their lives not be tiresome"
Man's place of life contains his spiritual vitality. When clear and empty, when enjoying clarity and tranquility, and when drink and food are not stagnating, revelations of Dao spontaneously come to mind. When filling the belly with foul things, you effectively attack the root and exhaust the spirit.

夫唯不厭，是以不厭。夫唯獨不厭精神之人，洗心濯垢，恬泊無欲，則精神居之不厭也。

"If they are not tiresome, they will not grow tired of them."
This refers to not exhausting people's spiritual vitality. Cleanse the heart-mind, wash away the stains; anchor yourself in tranquility, and be without desires. Then spiritual vitality will not grow tired of its house.

是以聖人自知，不自見，自知己之得失，不自顯見德美於外，藏之於內。

"Therefore the Sage knows himself but does not display himself"
He knows himself and his inner gains and losses. He does not show his virtue and beauty externally, but conceals them within.

自愛不自貴。自愛其身以保精氣，不自貴高榮名於世。

"Loves and cares for himself but does not overestimate himself"
He cares for himself and his body by securing his vital energy-breaths.[127] He neither appraises himself nor puts value on worldly glory and renown.

故去彼取此。去彼自見、自貴，取此自知、自愛

"Abandons that and chooses this"
He abandons displaying himself and overestimating himself while choosing to know himself and care for himself.

SEVENTY-TWO
To rule by force requires the continued application of force to maintain this rule. As Lao Zi explains, simply not overburdening the people will keep them from growing tired of this burden and striking back. The Sage rules with kindness and humility, imposing as little as possible while fostering vitality and harmony.

The opening line of chapter 72 may not refer to the ruler's power but to Dao's power. If we go against Dao by living an imbalanced lifestyle, we reject the balance of yin and yang in which we reside.

The latter part of this chapter suggests that one is endangered by putting

---

[127] See footnote in chapter 10 for an explanation of the vital energy-breaths (jing-qi).

themselves above the greater good, above righteousness. The saying "abandons that and chooses this" also appears in chapter 12 (containing the line "the five tones deafen the ears") where it refers to choosing contentment over craving and seeking, being mindful that desires will lead us away from Dao and cause us to be met by its fierceness (see chapter 73). The second paragraph of chapter 72 is also complemented by chapter 13, which warns against looking to others for our self-acceptance.

Heshang Gong points out that just as the people will grow tired of a nation full of strife and anxiety – where they are presumably unable to safely roam, express themselves, or abide peacefully and happily – the inner spirits will tire of living in a body that is constantly oppressed by tension and anxiety, or polluted by unhealthy foods. Thus, the Sage does not allow his spirit and body to be depleted by the demands of seeking glory and renown. He takes what he has, and leaves unnecessary temptations. He cherishes spiritual vitality within and does not imperil it with a lifestyle that abuses his inner treasures.

# ~ 73 ~

Courage that is reckless brings death
Courage that is not reckless brings life
Of these two
One is useful, the other is harmful

Heaven's lurking ferocity
Who has ever known its extent?
Therefore the Sage also endures this circumstance

Heaven's Dao does not contend
Yet is excellent at overcoming
Does not speak
Yet is excellent at accomplishing what is necessary
Does not give summons
Yet is excellent at drawing toward itself
Remains uncontrived
Yet is excellent at organizing

Heaven's net is immense
It is loose
Yet loses nothing

# Chapter 73
## 任為 Relying on Force

勇於敢則殺，勇敢有為，則殺其身。
"Courage that is reckless brings death"
Courage that is reckless is forceful – wei. This brings death to the body.
勇於不敢則活。勇於不敢有為，則活其身。
"Courage that is not reckless brings life"
Courage that is neither reckless, nor forceful, brings life to the body.[128]
此兩者，謂敢與不敢也。
"Of these two,"
Meaning not reckless, and reckless.
或利或害，活身為利，殺身為害。
"One is useful, the other is harmful"
Bringing life to the body is useful, bringing death to the body is harmful.

天之所惡。惡有為也。
"Heaven's lurking ferocity"
This ferocity is forceful.
孰知其故？誰能知天意之故而不犯？
"Who has ever known its extent?"
Who can know Heaven's plan and not disobey it?
是以聖人猶難之。言聖人之明德猶難於勇敢，況無聖人之德而欲行之乎？
"Therefore the Sage also endures this circumstance"
This means that the Sage's enlightened virtue does not exempt him from difficulty were he to be recklessly courageous. Imagine then, being without the Sage's virtue and wishing to act this way!

天之道，不爭而善勝，天不與人爭貴賤，而人自畏之。
"Heaven's Dao does not contend yet is excellent at overcoming"
Heaven does not abide by men's class struggles, yet men are naturally afraid of it.
不言而善應，天不言，萬物自動以應時。
"Does not speak yet is excellent at accomplishing what is necessary"
Heaven does not speak, yet all things naturally move in accord with its timing.
不召而自來，天不呼召，萬物皆負陰而向陽。
"Does not give summons yet is excellent at drawing toward itself"

---

[128] Courage is associated with the rising wood-energy of the liver and gallbladder (also associated with decision making), and with the free-flowing water-energy of the kidneys. The courage of water is exhibited in its natural spontaneity (zi ran). The courage of wood is exhibited in its determined expansion.

Heaven does not shout commands, yet the myriad things all carry yin and follow yang.

繹然而善謀。繹，寬也。天道雖寬博，善謀慮人事，修善行惡，各蒙其報也。

"Remains uncontrived yet is excellent at organizing"

Chan (繹) means open-minded, and spontaneous. Heaven's way, though it acts spontaneously and takes chances, is good at organizing. In looking after one's own affairs, cultivate excellence and shun evil, for each will suffer their own fate.

天網恢恢，疏而不失。天所網羅恢恢甚大，雖疏遠，司察人善惡，無有所失。

"Heaven's net is immense. It is loose, but loses nothing"

Heaven's net, like those used for catching birds, is immense. Though loose and spanning a great distance, it is capable of noticing men's goodness and wickedness, with no place going unnoticed.

SEVENTY-THREE

Understanding Lao Zi's power and virtue of kindness, compassion, and love as applied to overcoming adversity,[129] we may better understand how "Heaven's Dao does not contend, yet is excellent at overcoming; does not speak, yet is excellent at accomplishing what is necessary; does not give summons, yet is excellent at drawing toward itself; remains uncontrived, yet is excellent at organizing. Heaven's net is immense. It is loose, yet loses nothing." We can also better understand why "courage that is reckless brings death" by looking to chapter 67, in which he states, "if one neglects kindness in courage, they will die."

# ~ 74 ~

If the people do not fear death
Of what use is threatening them with death?
By ordering that people stay under the constant threat of death
Those who are unusual
Will be seized and killed by their leaders
Who dares (to do such a thing)?

The Eternal is in charge of executions
To replace this executioner
This is called "making the cuts of a master craftsman"

---

[129] See chapter 67, 68, 69

When making these cuts in place of a master craftsman
It is incredibly rare that there is no injury
To one's own hand

# Chapter 74
## 制惑 A System in Confusion

民不畏死，治國者刑罰酷深，民不聊生，故不畏死也。治身者嗜欲傷神，貪財殺身，民不知畏之也。
*"If the people do not fear death"*
If those who rule a nation go too far in the severity of their punishments, the people will neither value life, nor fear death. If those who govern their bodies are weakened by desires, they will injure their spirit. Greed for wealth kills the body. People do not know to fear these things.

奈何以死懼之？人君不寬刑罰，教民去情欲，奈何設刑法以死懼之？
*"Of what use is threatening them with death?"*
If the rulers do not carefully consider punishments and penalties, nor teach the people to abandon their desires and strong emotions, how can the establishment of punishments and laws cause them to fear death?

若使民常畏死，當除己之所殘剋，教民去利欲也
*"By ordering that people stay under the constant threat of death"*
They should rid themselves of cruelty and domineering, and teach the people to abandon avarice.

而為奇者，吾得執而殺之。孰敢？以道教化而民不從，反為奇巧，乃應王法執而殺之，誰敢有犯者？老子疾時王不先道德化之，而先刑罰也。
*"Those who are unusual will be seized and killed by their leaders. Who dares (to do such a thing)?"*
Though Dao shows the way, people do not follow it. They practice unusual skills and then the king declares it a crime and executes them. Who dares to commit such a violation? It was troubling to Lao Zi that the kings of his day did not first reform themselves by Dao and Virtue before they started punishing and penalizing others.

常有司殺者。司殺者，謂天居高臨下，司察人過。天網恢恢，疏而不失也。
*"The Eternal is in charge of executions"*
What is in charge of executions is Heaven. It resides above, and descends to the bottom. It is in charge of examining people's crimes. Heaven's net is immense, loose, yet nothing is lost.

夫代司殺者，是謂代大匠斲。天道至明，司殺有常，猶春生夏長，秋收冬藏，斗杓運移，以節度行之。人君欲代殺之，是猶拙夫代大匠斲木，勞而無功也。

*"To replace the executioner – this is called "making the cuts of a master craftsman"*

Heaven's Way is enlightened. In taking charge of killing, this is also the case. The same goes for sprouting in spring, growing in summer, harvesting in autumn, and storing in winter. The handle of the big dipper in the sky changes fortune as it moves, each section moving in precise measurement. When rulers desire to replace this in matters of killing, this is akin to a clumsy man trying to do the carving of a highly skilled craftsman and doing the work without any skill.

夫代大匠斲者，希有不傷手矣。人君行刑罰，猶拙夫代大匠斲，則方圓不得其理，還自傷。代天殺者，失紀綱，不得其紀綱還受其殃也。

*"When making these cuts in place of a master craftsman, it is incredibly rare that there is no injury to one's own hand"*

When rulers take control of executions and punishments, it is akin to a clumsy man trying to do the carving of a highly skilled craftsman. In this case, the square and the round will not be true, and he will injure himself. Replacing Heaven in deciding on executions, one will miss the guidelines. They will not obtain their objectives and, missing the guidelines, misfortune will fall on them as well.

SEVENTY-FOUR

Chapter 74 can be read as a warning against refusing to adapt to change. If one tries to eliminate all forces of change and reject the alternations of Dao, they only diminish their ability to influence change in the long run as they will be in a constant battle against the natural rebounds of yin and yang. In martial arts, a common phrase is "learning through loss" – learning how to defend by observing how our defenses were broken, gaining balance by experiencing imbalance. Rather than trying to deny failures, it is better to sit with those failures and observe them. As Heshang Gong states in chapter 54:

> To cultivate Dao in the body, observe what happens when one does not cultivate Dao in the body. To learn what causes the loss of life, learn what preserves life. To cultivate Dao in the home, observe what happens when Dao is not cultivated in the home…

# ~ 75 ~

The people are starving
Because those above them indulge in over-taxation
This causes starvation
The people are difficult to govern

Because those above them are meddlesome
This causes difficulty in governing

The people are careless towards death
Because they seek fullness of life
This causes carelessness towards death
So then, only those without regard for their lives
Will strive for fullness of life
Therein resides the virtue of valuing life

# Chapter 75
貪損 The Consequences of Greed

民之饑，以其上食稅之多，是以飢。人民所以饑寒者，以其君上稅食下太多，民皆化上為貪，叛道違德，故饑。
"The people are starving because those above them indulge in over-taxation. This causes starvation."
The people starve in the cold when rulers increase taxes until there is no longer enough food to go around. The people then become greedy, rebel against Dao, and disobey Virtue. This causes starvation.

民之難治，以其上之有為，是以難治。民之不可治者，以其君上多欲，好有為也。是以其民化上有為，情偽難治。
"The people are difficult to govern because those above them are meddlesome. This causes difficulty in governing."
Rulers who perpetuate their many desires and wish to be in control, are unable to govern the people. The people, influenced by those above them, become false in their sentiments and difficult to govern.

民之輕死，以其上求生之厚，人民所以侵犯死者，以其求生活之道太厚，貪利以自危。
"The people are careless towards death because they seek fullness of life."
The people will invade homes, rob, and murder, when they seek to live a lifestyle of excess. Their greed becomes a danger to themselves.

是以輕死。以求生太厚之故，輕入死地也。
"This causes carelessness towards death."
By seeking a life of excess, people's recklessness leads them into perilous traps.

夫為無以生為者，是賢於貴生。夫唯獨無以生為務者，爵祿不干於意，財利不入於身，天子不得臣，諸侯不得使，則賢於貴生也。
"So then, only those without regard for their lives will strive for fullness of life. Therein resides the virtue of valuing life."

It is only the solitary man without concern for life who truly strives for life, and does not think about being blessed with rank and title. When valuables and favours do not take precedence over the concern for one's own body and character, ministers will not try to overtake the emperor, and lords will not be betrayed by their messengers. This follows the virtue of valuing life.


## SEVENTY-FIVE

Though Daoist philosophy is often thought to be apolitical, and a Daoist's involvement in politics to be a breach of the Daoist way of life, this common view somehow misses the fact that the *Dao De Jing* is as much a political treatise as it is a manual for self-cultivation. As Heshang Gong points out in chapters 13 and 66, this political philosophy favours acting toward the citizens as a mother and father love their children: do not oppress them, do not abuse them, and do not punish them excessively. The ruling class should not live opulently at the expense of the people, for the poverty and competition created by this will only diminish the people's loyalties as they fight to survive amongst scarcity. Just as a ruler should not oppress its people, the body functions best when the heart-mind is not overactive and interfering, extending the above remediations to the internal power dynamics of the body.

As a political theory, this may say seem akin to libertarianism, though likely not the type of libertarian-capitalism found in neoliberalism, which affords corporations the liberty to dominate, tyrannize, and exploit, regardless of the effects this has on the societies and ecologies in which they operate. Lao Zi's libertarianism appears to be something more akin to the cooperative libertarian-socialism of William Godwin (d. 1836), Charles Fourier (d. 1837), and Mikhail Bakunin (d. 1876), if not also the "social ecology" of Murray Bookchin (d. 2006). Evidence of this can be seen in chapter 80 where Lao Zi advocates small cooperative and voluntary (liberated) groups, similar to Fourier's "phalanges" (see chapter 80). While very similar to anarchism, libertarian-socialism may also accept a degree of federalism and state, so long as state involvement is minimal and supportive, like the wu wei approach to government that Lao Zi advocates for the emperor, as modeled on Dao and De (see chapter 51).

This lesson of minimizing taxes follows the cultivation of life in that if someone gorges themselves on delicacies or other pleasures, they do so at the expense of themselves. Even intense elation has a gradual weakening effect, much as any other extreme emotion. Thus, Lao Zi points out that the Dao of enjoying the pleasures of life lies in enjoying simple pleasures, where the pendulum does not swing so wide as to exhaust the person when it swings back the other way ("only those without regard for their lives will strive for fullness of life. Therein lies the virtue of valuing life."). Most of these hazardous activities involve excessive consumption, perhaps as a way to escape a sense of lack somewhere in one's life. Rather than focus on filling the senses, it would be better to fill one's life with whatever is missing – community, fulfilling employment, fulfillment of talents, exercise, outdoor activity, healthy eating, healthy environment, or perhaps simply self-confidence. Rather than tax your body, it's better to just, as James Brown said, "get up off'a that thing!"

## ~ 76 ~

When born, people are soft and pliant
At death, they become hard and inflexible
As with all things
When plants and trees begin to grow
They are flexible and pliant
Yet, when dying
They become dry and rotten
Thus, hardness and inflexibility are the approach of death
While softness and pliancy are the approach of life
Therefore armies that are rigid will not be victorious

When the tree is strong
It encompasses both (rigidity and suppleness)
The rigid and large reside at the bottom
While the soft and delicate reside at the top

## Chapter 76
戒強 Admonishing Rigidity

人之生也柔弱，人生含和氣，抱精神。故柔弱也
"When born, people are soft and pliant"
When people are born, they are filled with a harmonious energy-breath. They embrace the spiritual vitality and are thus soft and pliant.
其死也堅強。人死和氣竭，精神亡，故堅強也。
"At death, they become hard and inflexible"
When people die, the harmonious energy-breath is exhausted and the spiritual vitality perishes, resulting in hardness and inflexibility.
萬物草木之生也柔脆，和氣存也。
"As with all things, when plants and trees begin to grow, they are flexible and pliant"

Their harmonious energy-breath remains.
其死也枯槁。和氣去也。
"Yet, when dying, they become dry and rotten"
Their harmonious energy-breath departs.
故堅強者死之徒，柔弱者生之徒。以上二事觀之，知堅強者死，柔弱者生也。
"Thus, hardness and inflexibility are the approach of death, while softness and pliancy are the approach of life"
These two functions can now be observed, knowing that hardness and inflexibility bring death, and that softness and pliancy bring life.
是以兵強則不勝，強大之兵輕戰樂殺，毒流怨結，眾弱為一強，故不勝。
"Therefore armies that are rigid will not be victorious"
Strong and large armies take war lightly and take pleasure in murder. This spreads like a poison and congeals the hatred of the formerly acquiescent masses, making them united and powerful. This does not lead to victory.

木強則共。本強大則枝葉共生其上。
"When the tree is strong, it encompasses both (rigidity and suppleness)"
When the roots are strong and large, branches and leaves will grow above them.
強大處下，柔弱處上。興物造功，大木處下，小物處上。天道抑強扶弱，自然之效。
"The rigid and large reside at the bottom, while the soft and delicate reside at the top"
By rising up, things develop their abilities. The large part of a tree resides at the bottom, while the small parts reside at the top. Heaven's Dao presses down the strong, and lifts up the weak. This is the result of natural spontaneity (zi ran).


SEVENTY-SIX
Daoist and Shaolin martial arts train the body to become like a young tree, with limbs strong and flexible, circulating qi and blood like a well hydrated tree-branch coursing with sap, nearly unbreakable due to the flexibility and density of its fibres. Tendons are strengthened and power is condensed into the muscles (considered wood element/phase) so that even a seventy-year-old master can strike with the force of an iron bar and gracefully glide around his opponent like water flowing through a channel. While the martial applications of these arts are many, perhaps their greatest gift is the longevity they instill in teaching centeredness within chaos. If we can learn to naturally adapt, "learn to unlearn," and not attach our past to our present experiences, we will defeat far more adversaries than in any external battles.

In consideration of the previous ten chapters' elucidation of resistance to change and the superior efficacy of love, compassion, and kindness for neutralizing conflict, we might read chapter 76 as admonishing rigid combativeness when faced with opposition. Like the roots and branches of a tree, we can remain centered and grounded while swaying with the winds of circumstance and environment, yielding to change without letting it uproot us. Much as a tree is a constant source of oxygen, being deeply rooted in Dao while natural and simply *as oneself* (zi ran) allows an interplay with the positive energy around us. *"When the tree is strong, it encompasses both (rigidity and suppleness). The rigid and large reside at the bottom; the soft and delicate reside at the top."*

# ~ 77 ~

The Way of Heaven
Is it not like the stretching of a bow?
What is high, it causes to be pulled low
What is low, it causes to be uplifted
What has excess, it causes to be diminished
What lacks sufficiency it causes to be restored

Heaven's Way diminishes what has excess
And restores what lacks sufficiency
The way of man, however, is not this way
Diminishing what suffers lack
And assisting where there is excess
Who can have in excess, and care for all under Heaven?
Only those who have Dao

Therefore, sages act but do not expect anything in return
They achieve their ends without lingering
And have no desire to exhibit inner worth

## Chapter 77
天道 Heaven's Dao

天之道，其猶張弓與，天道暗昧，舉物類以為喻也。
"The Way of Heaven – is it not like the stretching of a bow?"
Heaven's Way is dark and obscure. Various categories of things are used to describe it metaphorically.
高者抑之，下者舉之，有餘者損之，不足者補之。言張弓和調之，如是乃可用耳，夫抑高舉下，損強益弱，天之道也。
"What is high, it causes to be pulled low. What is low, it causes to be uplifted. What has excess, it causes to be diminished. What lacks sufficiency it causes to be restored."
This describes the stretching of a bow and its harmonizing movement. The ears can also be attuned in the same way by pressing down what is high and raising what is low. Impairing the powerful and assisting the gentle is Heaven's Way.

天之道，損有餘而補不足。天道損有餘而益謙，常以中和為上。
"Heaven's Way diminishes what has excess, and restores what lacks sufficiency"
By always upholding balance and harmony, Heaven's Way diminishes what has excess and benefits the humble.
人之道則不然，損不足以奉有餘。人道則與天道反，世俗之人損貧以奉富，奪弱以益強也。
"The way of man, however, is not this way – diminishing what suffers lack, and assisting where there is excess"
Man's way goes in the opposite direction of Heaven's way. Today it is customary to hinder the poor and serve the rich; to rob the weak and profit the strong.
孰能有餘以奉天下？唯有道者。言誰能居有餘之位，自省爵祿以奉天下不足者乎？唯有道之君能行也。
"Who can have in excess, and care for all under Heaven? Only those who have Dao"
Lao Zi asks "who can maintain their inner peace while in possession of the royal surplus?" Originally, during times of prosperity, the provincial lords would make donations to the population rather than satiating themselves. Only rulers who have Dao can practice this.

是以聖人為而不恃，聖人為德施，不恃其報也。
"Therefore, sages act but do not expect anything in return"
Sages act virtuously and generously, without requiring acknowledgement.
功成而不處，功成事就，不處其位。
"They achieve their ends without lingering"
They achieve what needs to be done without lingering in positions of authority.
其不欲見賢。不欲使人知己之賢，匿功不居榮，畏天損有餘也。
"And have no desire to exhibit inner worth"
They have no desire to make grand statements and have their worthiness known to others. Hiding their achievements, they do not bask in glory, fearing that Heaven will diminish what is excessive.

## SEVENTY-SEVEN

Chapter 77 also dismisses misinterpretations of chapter 75, which assert that Lao Zi advocated for an entirely non-intervening government. While Lao Zi does advocate for a leadership that is not over-meddling or burdensome to its people, he also advocates for leadership that facilitates balance and harmony in society by governing in accordance with "the Way of Heaven." If the ruler "has Dao," if they can recognize and appreciate sufficiency, they can abstain from excessive expenditures and use surplus to care for the people. This is simply the Way of Heaven and the Dao of virtuous government; as such, the Sage does not expect praise for acting accordingly.

Though internal meanings can be found in chapter 77, for example, the mixing of yin and yang, of Heavenly and Earthly essences, of the spiritual vitality of the heart and kidneys, and of spirit and qi, its overt and external (political/worldly) reference to social and economic balance is in no way negated by its internal meanings. Thus, this blatant social role of government should not be dismissed by looking only at these internal meanings. As chapter 65 explains, "when knowledge is used to govern the nation, this results in thievery from the nation. Not using knowledge to govern the nation blesses the nation."

## ~ 78 ~

In all under Heaven
Nothing is softer or more adaptable than water
Yet, for attacking that which is hard and strong
Nothing is more capable of victory
There is nothing which does so with such ease
Weakness overcomes strength
Softness overcomes rigidity
In all under Heaven, nothing is ignorant of this
Yet nothing puts it into practice
Therefore the Sage says:
Receiving (responsibility for) the state's foulness
For this, one is called Governor of the Province (Host of the Gods of Soil and Grain)
Receiving (responsibility for) the state's bad omens
For this, one is called Emperor of All Under Heaven
Though correct, such words seem reversed

# Chapter 78
## 任信 Relying on Sincerity

天下莫柔弱於水，圓中則圓，方中則方，壅之則止，決之則行。
"In all under Heaven, nothing is softer or more adaptable than water"
When inside a circle it fits the circle. When inside a boat it fits the boat. When obstructed it halts; when the decision is made, it follows through.[130]

而攻堅強者莫之能勝，水能懷山襄陵，磨鐵消銅，莫能勝水而成功也。
"Yet, for attacking that which is hard and strong, nothing is more capable of victory"
Water is able to embrace a mountain, nourish a mound, wear down iron, and disintegrate copper. Nothing is more capable of victory than water when it comes to completing these tasks.

以其無以易之。夫攻堅強者，無以易於水。
"There is nothing which does so with such ease"
When attacking the hard and strong, nothing does this as easily as water.

弱之勝強，水能滅火，陰能消陽。
"Weakness overcomes strength"
Water can extinguish fire. Yin can disintegrate yang.

柔之勝剛，舌柔齒剛，齒先舌亡。
"Softness overcomes rigidity"
The tongue is soft and the teeth are hard, but the teeth die before the tongue.

天下莫不知，知柔弱者久長，剛強者折傷。
"In all under Heaven, nothing is ignorant of this"
All know that the soft and pliant endure a long time, while the hard and strong break and get injured.

莫能行。恥謙卑，好強梁。
"Yet nothing puts it into practice"
Ashamed of a humble position, they dream of being powerful and immovable.

是以聖人云：謂下事也。
"Therefore the Sage says:"
In reference to the following positions

受國之垢，是謂社稷主；人君能受國之垢濁者，若江海不逆小流，則能長保其社稷，為一國之君主也。
"Receiving (responsibility for) the state's foulness – for this, one is called Governor of the Province (Host of the Gods of Soil and Grain)"
Rulers who can take on the foulness of a state are like large rivers and seas which do not reject the water from smaller channels. In this way, they can long protect the province and create one nation for the emperor.

---

[130] Jue, 決, "decide," is written as 氵 water + 夬 fork. The decision is followed at a fork in the river.

受國不祥，是為天下王。人君能引過自與，代民受不祥之殃，則可以王天下。
"Receiving (responsibility for) the state's bad omens – for this, one is called Emperor of All Under Heaven"
If a ruler can go beyond serving himself, and put himself in front of the people while dealing with disasters and bad omens, he may become emperor of all under Heaven.

正言若反。此乃正直之言，世人不知，以為反言
"Though correct, such words seem reversed"
These correct and proper words are unknown today, which causes the reverse to be spoken.

## SEVENTY-EIGHT

Water is the most humble substance. It adapts to everything, never asserting its own will, and yet over time all things succumb to it. Like water, emperors and states should also adapt to the people and serve them. Though they have power, they are in fact the ultimate servants, ensuring the basic rights and needs of even the lowest beggar and criminal. Though water adapts, becoming solid in winter, evaporating in heat, and consolidating into rain, it never changes its basic nature and never refuses the myriad living things. It is the epitome of virtue and the epitome of love, kindness, and compassion.

# ~ 79 ~

When pacifying a great rivalry
Some hatred surely remains
How can this be considered excellent?
Therefore, the Sage holds the left side of the contract
And does not oblige the other party
Those with virtue take initiative in fulfilling the treaty
Those without virtue take initiative in mounting invasions
The way of Heaven has no partiality
It always serves to further excellence amongst people

## Chapter 79
任契 Relying on Contracts

和大怨，殺人者死，傷人者刑，以相和報。
"When pacifying a great rivalry"
Those who murder people are killed and those who injure people are punished.

("Pacifying a great rivalry") refers to bringing calm to these situations.

必有餘怨，任刑者失人情，必有餘怨及於良人也
"Some hatred surely remains"

Those who rely on punishments lose the faith of the people. Some hatred is then certain to remain and catch up even to the virtuous.

安可以為善？言一人，則先天心，安可以和怨為善？
"How can this be considered excellent?"

The words of this one man echo the original mind of Heaven. In the pursuit of peace, how can quiet hatred be considered excellent?

是以聖人執左契而不責於人。古者聖人執左契，合符信也。無文書法律，刻契合符以為信也。但刻契為信，不責人以他事也。
"Therefore, the Sage holds the left side of the contract, and does not oblige the other party"

In the past, when sages held the left side of the contract, this meant that they united the tally with honesty. They did not embellish the books, standards, or laws, but tallied and inscribed the contract with honesty. They did not oblige the other party with new affairs.

有德司契，有德之君，司察契信而已。
"Those with virtue take initiative in fulfilling the treaty"

When an emperor is virtuous, initiative is taken to examine a contract, ensuring that it is fair and complete.

無德司徹。無德之君，背其契信，司人所失。
"Those without virtue take initiative in mounting invasions"

When an emperor is without virtue, he betrays the agreements of the contract, and forces people from their homes.

天道無親，常與善人。天道無有親疏，唯與善人，則與司契同也。
"The way of Heaven has no partiality. It always serves to further excellence amongst people."

The way of Heaven does not have any familial loyalties. It only helps people of excellence. Therefore, those who take initiative in adhering to the contract will receive its assistance.


SEVENTY-NINE

In resolving a great dispute, some offenses are sure to go unaddressed, and so no great dispute can be fully resolved until these offenses can be disregarded.

    Regarding self-cultivation, this chapter suggests learning to quiet that part of the mind that seeks every detail to be explained. The understanding offered by a bit more knowledge will not bring peace to the mind – the resolute intention to bring clarity to the mind is what will clear it of wandering thoughts and give rise to peacefulness. In the process of clearing the mind, many issues, items, and details will present themselves, and they must all be forgotten, much as the innumerable debts forgiven so as to resolve an old dispute.

# ~ 80 ~

(Govern the nation like) a small state with few people
Furnished with a file of ten equipped soldiers
But not employing them
(Where) its people respect the seriousness of death
And never migrate
Though having boats and carriages
They are without any reason to ride in them
Though having a military and weapons
There is no reason to display them

Have the people return to the simple notation system
Of knotting ropes
If their food is tasty
If their clothing is beautiful
If their homes are tranquil
And their customs are joyous
The neighbouring states could be close enough to see
Their chickens and dogs heard on each side
Yet the people will grow old and pass away
Without ever going to visit those places

## Chapter 80
獨立  Standing Alone

小國寡民，聖人雖治大國，猶以為小，儉約不奢泰。民雖眾，猶若寡少，不敢勞之也。
"(Govern the nation like) a small state with few people"
The Sage govern the large nation as though it were small, and is minimalistic when drawing a constitution rather than extravagant with his authority. The people, though very many, are treated as though very few so that he does not dare over-exert them.
使有什伯之器而不用，使民各有部曲什伯，貴賤不相犯也。器謂農人之器。而不用，不徵召奪民良時也。
"Furnished with a file of ten equipped soldiers, but not employing them"
When every person has a family member in their local military, neither rich nor poor will commit crimes against each other. "Equipped" means equipped with farming tools. "Not employing them" means that the people are not drafted into the army during peace time.

使民重死而不遠徙。君能為民興利除害，各得其所，則民重死而貪生也。政令不煩則民安其業，故不遠遷徙離其常處也。

"(Where) its people respect the seriousness of death, and never migrate"
The Son of Heaven can influence the people to live an active lifestyle, to be skilful and effective, to remove dangers and obstacles, and to each obtain their place in the world. As a result, the people will respect the seriousness of death and have a powerful desire for life. Governmental decrees should not cause difficulty. Then the people will stabilize their professions and not migrate away to establish themselves somewhere else.

雖有舟輿，無所乘之；清靜無為，不作煩華，不好出入遊娛也。

"Though having boats and carriages, they are without any reason to ride in them"
Clear, tranquil, and effortless, they will not trouble themselves with gross luxuries, nor yearn to travel around for pleasure.

雖有甲兵，無所陳之。無怨惡於天下。

"Though having a military and weapons, there is no reason to display them"
There will be no hatred or evil in the world.

使民復結繩而用之，去文反質，信無欺也。

"Have the people return to the simple notation system of knotting ropes"
Leaving embellishments and returning to the basics, their words will be sincere and without deception.

甘其食，甘其蔬食，不漁食百姓也。

"If their food is tasty"
If they enjoy sweet vegetables, they will not seek food from others.

美其服，美其惡衣，不貴五色。安其居，安其茅茨，不好文飾之屋。

"If their clothing is beautiful"
If it is beautiful enough that they do not hate their clothes, they will not prize many-coloured garments.

安其居，安其茅茨，不好文飾之屋。

"If their homes are tranquil"
If they have tranquil straw thatched homes, they will not wish to adorn their rooms with decorations.

樂其俗。樂其質朴之俗，不轉移也。

"And their customs are joyous"
If they enjoy the basic substance of the customs, and do not alter them.

鄰國相望，雞犬之聲相聞，相去近也。

"The neighbouring states could be close enough to see, their chickens and dogs heard on each side"
Meaning that they are separated by very little distance.

民至老死不相往來。其無情欲。

"Yet the people will grow old and pass away without ever going to visit those

places"
They will be free from desires and strong emotions.

## EIGHTY

From an internal perspective, chapter 80 speaks to contentment during silent sitting – learning to find peace where one sits, without seeking distractions or external aids – simply finding peace with oneself and one's place.

Taking Lao Zi's recommendation for independent communities as a genuine goal, and seeking a reference point for Lao Zi's political theories in those known in the Western world, it may help to look at the communities, similar to those proposed here by Lao Zi, which began to pop up in the mid-1800s under the influence of Charles Fourier. Fourier developed an early form of libertarian-socialism based on small cooperative and voluntary (liberated) groups called "phalanges" (phalanxes), as described in his *Theory of the Four Movements and the General Destinies* (1808).

> The phalange, in Fourier's conception was to be a cooperative agricultural community bearing responsibility for the social welfare of the individual, characterized by continual shifting of roles among its members. He felt that phalanges would distribute wealth more equitably than under capitalism and that they could be introduced into any political system, including a monarchy.[131]

In contrast to later Marxist ideologies, Fourier also advocated:

> That every laborer be a partner, remunerated by dividends and not by wages. That every one, man, woman, or child, be remunerated in proportion to the three faculties, *capital, labor, and talent*.[132]

These "phalanges" were not entirely successful, however, lasting only a few years on average, perhaps because they did not adhere to Lao Zi's oft repeated call to cultivate oneself by finding contentment in sufficiency and reducing desires. Likely in reaction to the institutionalized repression of his day, Fourier advocated libertine sexuality and a reawakening of passions that were violently suppressed in the Victorian era. Had he learned and taught the tranquil transcendence of desires through Daoist self-cultivation, these phalanges may have attained greater longevity. As stated in chapter 37, "when the tranquility of desirelessness is established, all under heaven stabilizes itself."

Similar to the work model of the "phalange" are co-op businesses where all

---
[131] https://www.britannica.com/biography/Charles-Fourier
[132] Albert Fried and Ronald Sanders, ed., *Socialist Thought: A Documentary History*. New York: Columbia University Press, 1964.

who work in the business own an equal share of it, and duties may be more varied and dynamic. As the co-op business model continues to gain in popularity, Lao Zi's advice will also benefit the longevity of these businesses as it reflects Fourier's slightly more extravagant recommendation:

> That the workshops and husbandry offer the laborer the allurements of elegance and cleanliness... In order to attain happiness, it is necessary to introduce it [happiness] into the labors which engage the greater part of our lives. Life is a long torment to one who pursues occupations without attraction. Morality teaches us to love work: let it know, then, how to render work lovable, and, first of all, let it introduce luxury into, husbandry and the workshop. If the arrangements are poor, repulsive, how arouse industrial attraction?[133]

## ~ 81 ~

True words are not beautified
Beautified words are not true words
The skilled are not argumentative
The argumentative are not skilled
Those who (presume to) know do not remain open-minded
The open-minded do not (presume to) know

Sages do not hoard
Having helped others
Oneself gains more
Having given to others
Oneself continues to gain
The Dao of Heaven is effective
And does no harm
The Dao of the Sage is to actuate
And not oppose

---

[133]Ibid.

# Chapter 81
## 顯質 Appearance and Substance

信言不美，信者，如其實也。不美者，朴且質也
"True words are not beautified"
True words are like authentic treasures. "Not beautified" means that they are of true substance.

美言不信。美言者，滋美之華辭。不信者，飾偽多空虛也。
"Beautified words are not true words"
By "beautified words" is meant long winded and flowery speech. "Not true words" means that these ornate fabrications are just hollow and empty.

善者不辯，善者，以道修身也。不綵文也。
"The skilled are not argumentative"
"The skilled" refers to those who practice Dao and self-cultivation. They do not use dazzling rhetoric.

辯者不善。辯者，謂巧言也。不善者，舌致患也。山有玉，掘其山；水有珠，濁其淵；辯口多言，亡其身。
"The argumentative are not skilled"
"Argumentative" means skilled in debate. "Not skilled" means that their tongues bring worry and suffering. Mountains containing jade are excavated. Water containing jewels is turned into a muddy abyss. An argumentative mouth with many words destroys the body.

知者不博，知者，謂知道之士。不博者，守一元也。
"Those who (presume to) know do not remain open-minded"
"Knowledgeable" refers to the academic's way of knowing. This is not open-minded. Embrace the origin of Oneness.

博者不知。博者，多見聞也。不知者，失要真也
"The open-minded do not (presume to) know"
"Open-minded" means seeing and hearing much. This is not "knowing," (because knowledge) misses the vital truth.

聖人不積，聖人積德不積財，有德以教愚，有財以與貧也。
"Sages do not hoard"
Sages accumulate Virtue. They do not hoard material wealth. Having Virtue, they teach simplicity. Having material wealth, they give to the poor.

既以為人己愈有，既以為人施設德化，己愈有德
"Having helped others, oneself gains more"
Having helped others to develop and reform their virtue, one's own virtue increases.

既以與人己愈多。既以財賄布施與人，而財益多，如日月之光，無有盡時。
"Having given to others, oneself continues to gain"
When valuables, money, and clothes, are freely given to others, their value and benefit

is increased. Like the light of the sun and moon, (this value) is never exhausted.

天之道，利而不害；天生萬物，愛育之，令長大，無所傷害也。
*"The Dao of Heaven is effective and does no harm"*
Heaven gives life to the myriad things. It lovingly rears them to become long lived and fully grown; it has no intention to injure or kill them.

聖人之道，為而不爭。聖人法天所施為，化成事就，不與下爭功名，故能全其聖功也。
*"The Dao of the Sage is to actuate and not oppose"*
Sages follow Heaven's principle of generosity by putting it into action. They transform and perfect things as situations present themselves. They do not follow lowly competitions for merit or fame, and as a result are able to retain their wisdom and merits.


## EIGHTY-ONE

Following chapter 80's description of autonomous villages, chapter 81's call for mutual aid reminds its readers that for communities and societies to thrive in Dao, a collective endeavour of mutual benefit must reach through to collective actions. As Peter Kropotkin explains in his *Mutual Aid: A Factor of Evolution*:

> [Darwin] pointed out how, in numberless animal societies, the struggle between separate individuals for the means of existence disappears, how *struggle* is replaced by *co-operation*, and how that substitution results in the development of intellectual and moral faculties which secure to the species the best conditions for survival. He intimated that in such cases the fittest are not the physically strongest, nor the cunningest, but those who learn to combine so as mutually to support each other, strong and weak alike, for the welfare of the community. "Those communities," he wrote, "which included the greatest number of the most sympathetic members would flourish best, and rear the greatest number of offspring" (2nd edit., p. 163) ... we may safely say that mutual aid is as much a law of animal life as mutual struggle, but that, as a factor of evolution, it most probably has a far greater importance ... together with the greatest amount of welfare and enjoyment of life for the individual, with the least waste of energy.[134]

In contrast to many traditions that base their teachings on the writings of a great teacher, there has never been any call for a Daoist fundamentalism – for an adherence to the strict letter of Lao Zi's teachings. Perhaps the simultaneously broad and terse nature of Lao Zi's teachings were a safeguard against the human susceptibility to complete reliance on authoritative validation. It would be difficult to form a

---

[134] Kropotkin, Petr A. *Mutual Aid: A Factor of Evolution*. London: Heinemann, 1908.

fundamentalist checklist out of the *Dao De Jing*, but this last chapter would, nonetheless, come as a disappointment to any who tried, finding that these words should never be taken as the final word.

> Those who (presume to) know do not remain open-minded
> The open-minded do not (presume to) know

Life is constantly moving and revealing itself. To even pay attention, one must open their mind and accept into their limited observational capacity the changes that have occurred since their previous blink. As we move, so does our correlation with the world. This is difficult enough to fully take in, let alone the endlessly diverse experiences of others.

As the saying goes, "every story sounds true until you hear the other side." Thus, it serves us to truly listen in an attempt to understand. At the very least, we can avoid causing others that most frustrating sense of not being heard, while finding out for ourselves how, as Lao Zi says, "Having given to others, oneself continues to gain." If we can suspend any sense that we are better than others, that we are something special, keeping an open mind and an open heart, the acceptance, respect, and support that we offer those around us can fill our environment, and reward us with a peaceful and supportive social ecosystem.

# *Appendix*

## Reading Classical Chinese

The following is a condensed lesson in Classical Chinese, which will help those who are interested to follow along with the Chinese text while reading the translation. This may help to reveal additional, or personal, interpretations of the original texts.

By recognizing the most commonly used words in these texts, it will be easier to navigate through each line and determine how each character relates to the translation. The definitions given below are only those which appear most often.

Please note that Classical Chinese is to modern Mandarin what Latin is to Italian, and that learning it will help one to recognize Chinese characters, but cannot be used to communicate in Mandarin. For this reason, and to simplify the learning process, pinyin spelling has not been included below. As is usually the case for Classical Chinese texts, traditional script will be used.

### *Beginning, ending, and transition words*

故 thus
是以 therefore
以 because of/by
則 transition word, similar to "thus"/then
使 transition word, similar to "thus"/then/send
乃 and then/brings about
而 and/yet/but
於 in/at/on/often indicates passive tense
夫 starts a new thought/"Now,.."
此 this/these
也 ends a thought
何 how/what/why/?
兮 exclamation! Oh!
言 words/(he or she) says/this is to say
謂 definition/(this) means/

### *Verbs, nouns, adjectives, etc.*

有 You: is/has/possesses/being
為 Wei: make/do/be/force/action

不 is not/do not
無 Wu: is not/is without/non-being
未 not yet

無為 Wu wei: without action/without force/effortless
事 duties, affairs, position
能 can/able
可 can/may
不能 cannot
不可 cannot
若 is similar to/as though
如 similar to/to like/to want
同 united

治 govern
行 walk/practice
守 guard
化 transform/become
知 know/knowledge
聖 wisdom
欲 desire
愛 love/affection
生 life/give birth to/give rise to
用 use/useful
得 obtain/attain to
失 lose
復 return to
止 stop

其 pronoun/the/their
之 pronoun/it/them
我 I/me/my/our
身 body/self
自 self/themselves
己 self/their
所 place/pronoun/may designate proceeding word as a noun
皆 all
多 many

少 few
貴 valuable/to value or honour
惡 dislike/hate
善 good/excellent
不善 bad
上 high/above
下 low/below
大 great/large
小 small
是 correct/this
非 incorrect/false
內 internal/inside
外 external/outside

道 Dao: Dao/path/principles of the universe / method /doctrine
德 De: De/mystical force of Virtue in nature/virtues /character/integrity

明 luminous/enlightened
心 heart and mind
虛 Emptiness
常 always/eternal
名 name/fame
神 Shen: spirit/gods
氣 Qi/Chi: energy/air/breath
精 Jing: essences/bodily fluid /vital/pure
精神 Jing-Shen: spiritual vitality
長 longevity/long
自然 Zi ran: naturally/spontaneously

天 Heaven
地 Earth
天下 the world/all under heaven
人 people/others/humanity
民 the people/the commoners/citizens
聖人 Sages
國 the state/country
物 thing
萬物 the myriad things
百姓 the hundred family names/all people/all types of people/Note: this excluded all but the ruling and aristocratic classes until around 500BC, as only these classes had clan names, 姓 xing, previous to this time.

*Common sentence structures*

Sentences are often created with an A=B structure, which can be accomplished by simply putting two thoughts or words next to each other. This is made more apparent when the end of a sentence is marked with 也.

Example 1:
作，生也
"Arise, here, means they are born"
("作 arise = 生 born")

A simple subject-verb-object sentence will use few if any articles, and will often appear in sequences of four words at a time:

Example 2:
多言害身
"Speaking too many words does harm to oneself."
(多 many 言 words/speak 害 harms 身 body/self)

A common fifth word might be 之, which is sometimes used to connect adjectives that follow the object or subject to which they pertain. It functions similar to the word "of," but with the adjective and object in the reverse order.

Example 3:
天地之間空虛
"The gate of Heaven and Earth is hollow and empty"
(天 Heaven 地 Earth 之 of 間 gate 空 hollow 虛 empty)
之 can also function as the pronoun "it":

Example 4:
壅之則止
"When obstructed it halts"
(壅 Obstruct 之 it 則 then 止 stop)

Example 5:
得之若驚
"Winning is startling"
(得 Winning/gaining 之 it 若 is like 驚 startle)
失之若驚
"Losing is also startling"
(失 Losing 之 it 若 is like 驚 startle)

Example 5 shows that, while pronouns common to English might be left out of

Classical Chinese phrases, Classical Chinese pronouns may occasionally be left out of English translations. Example 5 also shows the flexibility of certain words. Note that "若 similar" was used here (above) to say "also."

A common exception to the subject-verb-object structure, however, is when 者 appears after a description to say "those who/that which," or "as for."

Example 6:
治身者
"Those who govern the body"
治國者
"Those who govern the state"
(治 govern 國 state 者 those who)

Example 7:
自勝者強
"Those who overpower themselves are powerful"
自 self 勝 overpower 者 those who 強 powerful

When reading the commentary which follows a phrase, the reiteration of terms and ideas will usually make it easier to determine which characters correspond to the words in the translation.

Example 8a (from chapter 34):
大道氾兮，言道氾氾，若浮若沉，若有若無，視之不見，說之難殊。
*"Oh how the Great Dao is overflowing"*
The Dao is flooding, overflowing, covering, submerging. As though present, as though absent. It cannot be seen through observation. To describe it is unusually difficult.

The phrase *"Oh how the Great Dao is overflowing"* begins with two easily recognizable words – "大 great" and "道 Dao." From the list above, you will recognize "兮 exclamation!/oh!" so the remaining character of the sentence is revealed to mean "氾 *overflowing*" by following along with the translation.

The first character in the commentary is "言 this says" (see "beginning, ending, and transition words" above) which is implied, but omitted from the translation in this case. Then, as is common, some of Lao Zi's words are repeated. See how "氾 overflowing" is repeated twice to say "very overflowing." This device may also be used to turn a verb into an adjective. In this case, two definitions of 氾 fan were used to translate it.

There may be some confusion about the order of the remaining 16 characters;

however, by recognizing "若 *as though*," the words following this character can be ascertained. "有 *is/being*" and "無 *without/non-being*" can also be located in "*present and absent.*" Looking at the translation again, "*The Dao is flooding, overflowing, covering, submerging,*" it can be determined that 若 ruo was left out of the translation to avoid redundancy.

"*It cannot be seen through observation*" can be located in the line by finding "不 not" in "不見 *not seen.*" Then the rest of the sentence may begin to appear as "視 Observing 之 it 不 not 見 seen."

The characters for "*To describe it is unusually difficult*" can be determined by finding "之 it," and seeing that the verb (*describe*) before this object (*it*) was "說 describe" (see example 8, again).

Now, knowing which character means "*difficult*," and which means "*unusual*" might escape you (especially since they appear in the reverse order in English), but the objective at this point is to simply match the translation, phrase by phrase, and get a vague idea of how it was originally worded. As you do this, and your vocabulary expands, more characters will be recognized.

The next line reads:

Example 8b:
其可左右。道可左可右，無所不宜。
"It can go both left and right"
Dao can be on both the left and the right. It has no place that is out of place.

Recognizing the pronoun, 其, and the verb "可 can," it is understood that 左 and 右 mean "左 *left* and 右 *right*." Now these characters can be found in the commentary to determine how it says "*Dao can be on both the left and the right. It has no place that is out of place.*"

The first sentence should be easily discernable at this point. Now, knowing that 無 wu means "*without,*" it can be determined that 所 means "*place.*" The last word may be difficult to define, but there is enough information in the translation to determine that it means something along the lines of "宜 suitable."

While this is a very brief lesson in Classical Chinese, it should give those who are new to it a few tools with which to get started, eventually helping them to read the ancient masters' teachings in the same words through which they were transmitted.

# Brief Pinyin Prounciation Guide

Lao : sounds like loud without the D
Zi: sounds like the su in supper but with a DZ sound – dzu(pper)
Lao Zi: sounds like Louds-a / Loudz-uh
Dao: sounds like the beginning of tower with a D instead of T
De: sounds like the pronunciation of Zi described above, but with a D instead of Z
Xing: sounds like shing. The sound for X may be found by placing the tongue to make an S sound but then making a SH sound with the middle of the tongue closer to the roof of the mouth
Qi: sounds like chee
Zhuang: sounds like Jwong
Zhou: sounds like Jo, ending like show.
Liu: sounds like Leeyo
Lui: sounds like Lway
Di: sounds like Dee
Li: sounds like Lee
Yi: sounds like a Yee

# Straw-Dogs and Benevolence in Chapter Five of the Dao De Jing

For approximately 2000 years, scholars have been rather uncertain, and troubled, about the meaning of the opening lines in chapter five of the *Dao De Jing*. Following its most common understanding, these lines are translated:

> 天地不仁,以萬物為芻狗
> Heaven and Earth are not benevolent
> They treat the myriad things as grass-dogs
> 聖人不仁, 以百姓為芻狗
> The Sage is not benevolent
> He treats the hundred clans (all people) as grass-dogs

Given the phrase, "the Sage is not benevolent," it appears that the next statement, "he treats the hundred clans as grass(-)dogs," describes this inhumanity. What makes these lines difficult to accept, however, is that the way of the Daoist Sage, as described in any other chapter of the *Dao De Jing*, is quite to the contrary of this statement. Reading most any other chapter in this text, one sees that the Daoist Sage's role in the world is to bring harmony and fulfillment to all under Heaven.

Adding to the immediate impression of this phrase, are some apparently similar phrases in Confucian texts. In the *Book of History*'s "*Book of Zhou*" (Jun-Chen, in *Zhou Shu*, in *Shan Shu*), one finds:

> "[King Wu said] 'Formerly, the duke of Zhou acted as teacher and guardian of the myriads of the people, who cherish (the remembrance of) his virtue. Go and with sedulous care enter upon his charge; act in accordance with his regular ways, and exert yourself to illustrate his lessons; so shall the people be regulated. I have heard that he said, "Perfect government has a piercing fragrance, and influences the spiritual intelligences. It is not the millet which has the piercing fragrance; it is bright virtue." Do make this lesson of the duke of Zhou your rule, being diligent from day to day, and not presuming to indulge in luxurious ease. Ordinary men, while they have not yet seen a Sage, (are full of desire) as if they should never get a sight of him; and after they have seen him, they are still unable to follow him. Be cautioned by this! **You are the wind; the inferior people** (下民) **are the grass** (草). In revolving the plans of your government, never hesitate to acknowledge the difficulty of the subject. Some things have to be abolished, and some new things to be enacted going out and coming in, seek the judgment of your people about them, and, when there is a general agreement, exert your own powers of reflection." (trans. Legge)

In *Analects* 12:19, a somewhat milder use of this metaphor is found:

季康子問政於孔子曰：如殺無道，以就有道，何如？孔子對曰：子為政，焉用殺？子欲善，而民善矣。君子之德風，小人之德草。草上之風，必偃

"Ji Kang asked Confucius about government, saying, "What do you say to killing the unprincipled for the good of the principled?" Confucius replied, "Sir, in carrying on your government, why should you use killing at all? Let your evinced desires be for what is good, and the people will be good. The relation between superiors and inferiors is like that between the wind and the grass (草). [literally: "the superior man's virtue is the wind, and the inferior man's virtue is the grass"]. The grass must bend, when the wind blows across it." (trans. Legge)

The third and fourth lines of chapter five in the *Dao De Jing* are generally understood to say: "The Sage is not benevolent; he treats the hundred clans as (sacrificial) grass-dogs." This interpretation appears to be supported by a story from chapter 14 of the *Zhuang Zi*, in which music-master Jin is asked about Confucius' practices. Jin responds that they are akin to ceremonial straw-dogs, which are treated with utmost reverence, and then destroyed after they have been offered. Jin then continues to explain his meaning by saying: "If you take a boat which can move on water, and try to push it on land, it will never get you anywhere… To seek now to practice the ancient precepts of Zhou, in the state of Lu, will get you no further than a boat on land."

This shows that the purpose of Zhuang Zi's straw-dogs story was to say that things may be of use in some situations, but only a hindrance in others. Perhaps most revealing, is that the precepts from ancient Zhou, taught later by Confucius and considered by Zhuang Zi to be but fabricated, intentional, and willful enactments of benevolence and righteousness, are what Jin depicts as the worthless "straw-dogs."

Worthy of consideration, in understanding chapter five, is that Lao Zi specifies "百姓 the hundred clans" rather than simply "民 the common people." Until approximately 500BC, only people in the ruling and aristocratic classes held one of "the hundred family names." Thus, it should be noted that the statement in question was not advocating a tyrannical elitism, as it referred to all levels of society. Treating "the hundred clans" this way may, therefore, also suggest equality and justice throughout society, and that, like blades of grass, or dogs, all people simply have an equal place in the Oneness of all things.

Humanity is generally seen in Daoism to be above the rest of the myriad things, with the Emperor and sages bringing about their unification. However, Daoism also recognizes the interconnectivity of all things. While humans see themselves as most important, this self-mindedness is considered an illusion. Grass and straw grow on the earth, and mindlessly serve the biosphere, just as Dao and De nurture life without any intention or thought of doing so. Dao's actions are exemplified by De, Virtue, which can be seen throughout the text to be inalterably selfless and nurturing toward all of the myriad things. The Sage knows that he is a part of nature, and is not ostentatious, or resentful, for he knows that this is what it means to be alive. His intrinsic nature is not the same as that of grass and straw, but his function as part of the Dao is no different.

While the image of grass may seem to suggest lowliness, and unimportance, it should be noted that the perennial quality of many grasses has made it somewhat of a universal symbol of immortality. It was this quality that made wheat a symbol of the immortality of Osiris in ancient Egypt. The 4th c. BC Chinese book of mythology, the Shanghaijing, tells a story of the three legged "Sun Crows," also found on Neolithic pottery and imperial robes, feasting on grasses of immortality. Chapter 16 of the *Dao De Jing* also refers to perennials with similar imagery:

> Myriad creatures arise together
> I thereby observe them return
> So many things blossoming
> And each returns back to its roots
> Returning to the roots is called silence
> This means returning to one's destiny-life-force (ming)
> Returning to one's destiny-life-force is called eternality
> Understanding eternality is called enlightenment

What is generally evoked to explain the discrepancy between the statement "Sages are not benevolent," and the Sage's obvious concern for the wellbeing of others, exhibited throughout the *Dao De Jing*, is Lao Zi's treatment of "benevolence" elsewhere in the text. "Ren," translated here as "benevolence," carries with it a cumbersome degree of cultural context and influence, especially when linked to Confucian ideals of propriety, which are not associated with its English equivalent. Lao Zi explains that ren requires intention, even fabrication, and arises only when true harmony has been lost; thus, it was not the ideal but rather a sign that Dao had been strayed from. In chapter 18, this is illustrated as follows:

> When the Great Dao is abandoned
> Benevolence and righteousness appear
> When learnedness and intelligence are brought forth
> Great deceit appears
> When the six family relations are out of harmony
> Filial piety appears
> When the nation is on the eve of chaos
> Loyal ministers appear

According to Lao Zi's view of benevolence in chapter 38, even "highest benevolence" takes willful action, as opposed to "Highest Virtue" which takes no action:

> Highest Virtue is without action

> It does not exist by its actions
> Lower virtue takes action
> It exists because of its actions
> Highest benevolence takes action
> Yet does not exist by its actions

*Wu wei*, translated as non-action, effortlessness, or no wilful action, is held as the ultimate strategy, virtue, power, and necessity for bringing harmony to all under Heaven. Proof of this efficacy is found in the wu wei of Dao, De, and Heaven, all of which bring about positive transformations without taking action. Heaven, synonymous with nature, takes no wilful action, but spontaneously follows Dao; thus, Heaven cannot be benevolent, since even "highest benevolence" takes action. This purview of ren (benevolence) is reflected in Zhuang Zi's story of music-master Jin, and his relegation of ren to so many other limited forms, all to be transcended by those who walk the Great Path. To paraphrase the greatest masters of most every art: when the form is mastered, it is forgotten.

Heshang Gong explains the fourth line of chapter five with his comment:

> Sages see the hundred clans as they see grass and straw for dogs and farm animals. They do not value people with any expectation of reciprocal courtesy in their minds.

Straw ("for farm animals"), 草, is the character used to describe the grasses sought out by nomadic herdsmen. So, Heshang Gong appears to suggest that "grass-dogs" was meant as grass "for" dogs. Dogs are omnivorous and often eat various types of grasses as an abundantly available filler and source of fibre and nutrients. Enjoying it too much, some dogs eat grass too quickly and vomit it up, resulting in the common belief that they only eat grass to induce vomiting. This is not the case, however. Wild dogs will even eat the stomach contents of grass eating prey before anything else. The fact of the matter is that dogs have nearly the same affinity for eating grass as herbivorous animals. Given that few domesticated dogs now eat more than their owners give them, this formerly obvious connection between grass and dogs has been widely ignored.

So then, what does it mean that sages treat the hundred clans as grass *for* dogs?

If the preceding chapters are any indication, "grass for dogs" may suggest that the Sage does not act benevolently, but simply allows the hundred clans to roam and take care of themselves, knowing that they will find what they need, just as roaming dogs will find their own grass to fill up on. He lets the dogs be dogs, and the grass be grass. If so, this would create an image of the same idea, presented in chapters two and three:

2
When the whole world knows the pleasing to be pleasing
This ends in despising
When all know the good to be good
In the end there is "not good"
[…]
Therefore, sages handle affairs with non-action
They practice wordless instruction
And the myriad things all take their places
Without responding
Given life, but not possessed
Acted for, but not expected of
Perfection is cultivated, and not dwelled upon
Surely, what is not dwelled upon
Does not leave

3
Do not exalt the worthy
And the people will not fight
Do not praise goods which are difficult to obtain
And the people will not steal
[…]
Act by not acting
And everything will fall into place

Chapter four does not continue with this idea, but reflects the latter part of chapter five:

4
Dao is a container
Though used again and again
It is never full
[…]

5
[…]
The gate of Heaven and Earth
Is it not like a bagpipe?
Empty yet not finished.
It moves, and again more is pushed forth
[..]

These impressions of wu wei might carry into one's reading of chapter five, and likely informed Wang Bi's (226-249 AD) commentary on its opening lines. Wang Bi begins this commentary by saying:

> 天地不仁，以万物为刍狗：天地任自然，无为无造，万物自相治理，故不仁也。
>
> *"Heaven and Earth are not benevolent."*
>
> Heaven and Earth are zi ran (natural, not wilful). They are without action, and without endeavour. The myriad things are all governed together and managed in the same way. Thus, (Heaven and Earth) are not benevolent.
>
> 仁者必造立施化，有恩有为。造立施化，则物失其真；有恩有为，则物不具存。物不具存，则不足以备载矣。
>
> As for benevolence, it endeavours to establish reformation through kindness and wilful action. Endeavouring to establish reform, things lose their genuineness. Being obviously kind, and acting wilfully, these actions are not genuine. If things are not genuine, then there is no use in preparing them and carrying them about.
>
> 天地不为兽生刍，而兽食刍；不为人生狗，而人食狗。无为于万物而万物各适其所用，则莫不赡矣。若慧由己树，未足任也。
>
> Heaven and Earth do not make animals grow grass, yet they eat the grass. They do not make people grow dogs, yet they eat dogs. (Heaven and Earth) are without willful action toward the myriad things, yet the myriad things each develop their appropriate uses, and there is nothing which is not provided for. It seems self-evident from this that things will establish themselves, even if they have not yet reached self reliance.

Wang Bi shows that Heaven and Earth do not act willfully, yet the myriad things all find their places and are provided for. As Heshang Gong often notes, when the Sage's virtue is abundant, the people are naturally reformed without any interference from the Sage.

This recurring concept of non-interference, in fact, takes us back to Zhuang Zi's story of music-master Jin, and the sacrificial offering of grass-dogs. When these effigies are prepared, Jin relates,

> "Before the grass-dogs are set forth (at the sacrifice), they are deposited in a box or basket, and wrapt up with elegantly embroidered cloths, while the representative of the dead and the officer of prayer prepare themselves by fasting to present them"
>
> (trans. Legge).

Note that those who handle the grass-dogs purify themselves before touching them; they keep them in a box, wrapped in expensive cloth, and treat them with the utmost care and delicacy. This degree of delicacy, and the care taken not to pollute these vessels, is also represented in chapter 60 of the *Dao De Jing*, which is elucidated in Heshang Gong's commentary:

> "*Govern a large state as though boiling a small fish*"
> When boiling a fresh fish, the intestines are not removed, the scales are not removed, and you shouldn't dare touch it, for fear that it will become mashed (and thus contaminated). Governing the state with vexation brings chaos to those below. Governing the body with vexation causes the spiritual vitality to scatter.

Chapter 60 goes on to explain that a ruler must handle the state with such care, so that its people will not be polluted by noxious entities. This is reminiscent of officers of prayer, who must purify themselves before handling the grass-dogs to ensure that they do not contaminate these vessels with unwanted energies.

> Govern a large state as though boiling a small fish
> When Dao reaches all under Heaven
> Ghosts will not take over the spirit
> It is not that ghosts will not take over the spirit
> But that the spirit will not injure the person
> It is not that the spirit will not injure the person
> But that the Sage also will not injure people
> So both of them will not bring injury
> Thus, Virtue will intermingle and return

Was it this same care and delicacy, in the image of boiling a small fish, that was being suggested in the phrase "the Sage treats the hundred clans like grass-dogs?" If we are to understand this phrase in the context of the chapters leading up to it, and keep in mind the overall role of the Sage, which is to enable Virtue to enter and transform the myriad things so that they may be perfected and the world made harmonious, this would appear the most appropriate context in which to read this metaphor. Echoes of this delicate approach resound throughout the *Dao De Jing*, while the importance of purifying oneself to bring Virtue into the world, without disturbing, agitating, or interfering, is made abundantly clear throughout Heshang Gong's commentary.

Some of the most obvious examples of this are in the following excerpts, excluding those presented above:

> 29
> The wish to possess all under Heaven
> And control it
> I see this has no end
>
> The world is an instrument of the gods

It cannot be controlled
Those who try, spoil it
Those who grasp, lose

### 34
It accomplishes its work
Yet makes no name for itself
It loves and raises the myriad things
Yet does not act as their master
(note: Heshang Gong replaced "yi/cover" with "ai/love" in this stanza)

### 48
Conquering all under Heaven
Is best done without the endeavour to do so
Perpetually, this endeavour will continue
Without satisfaction
Even when all under Heaven is conquered

### 57
When taboos are abundant in the world
The people are extremely poor
When the people have an abundance of sharp weapons
The nation grows dark
When people have an abundance of skill and ingenuity
Irregular things flourish
When standards are increasingly publicized
Thieves and robbers abound

And from Heshang Gong's commentary:

### 37
*"When lords and kings can guard this within, the myriad things eventually transform themselves"*
When lords and kings can hold on to Dao, the myriad things progress and transform themselves by their own power.
*"Transforming yet desiring to do so intentionally, I pacify this desire with the simplicity of the nameless"*
"I," here, means within his body. Dao and Virtue are invisible in their unaltered simplicity. The myriad things transform themselves by their own power. When the desire to interfere through skillful artifice returns, lords and kings should pacify and soothe it with Dao and Virtue.
*"The simplicity of the nameless removes all desires. When the tranquility of desirelessness is established"*

> When lords and kings pacify and soothe (the desire to interfere) with Dao and Virtue, the people also stop desiring. Thus, clarity and tranquility must guide their transformation.
> *"The world stabilizes of itself"*
> Those who can be like this, help the world to align and stabilize itself.

By purifying themselves, officers of prayer allowed the grass-dogs to be purified, and not polluted, by those presenting them. These offerings would become worthy of gods, while being handled immaculately by those worthy of doing so. In the same way, the Sage helps people to return to their intrinsic nature (xing) by purifying themselves of desire, including any desires to control this transformation.

Heshang Gong also makes a clear statement in this regard, in chapter 74:

> It was troubling to Lao Zi that the kings of his day did not first reform themselves by Dao and Virtue, before they started punishing and penalizing others.

In the same way that the officers of prayer must treat the straw effigies immaculately, the Sage must avoid filling the people's minds with too many ideas about good and bad, or the need to be praiseworthy and not disgraceful (see chapter two). Thereby, the people may remain "empty" and become pure, just as the purity of straw offerings allows them to naturally accumulate pure energy, and be worthy of gods. As Heshang Gong explains in chapter 42:

> *"(The myriad things) are infused with energy-breath, and made to be harmonious"*
> Inside of all things is the original energy-breath (yuan qi), attainted to through harmony and softness. If it is concealed in the breast, it will also be within the bone marrow, just as it is in plants and trees, in the empty hollows where energy-breath circulates. Thereby, (all things) obtain long life.

Letting the people be allows them to revert to harmony and softness, and not become rigid and tense while trying to resist the force of willful manipulation. As Heshang Gong explains in chapter 67, "there is no way to resist what does not use any force." This softness and pliancy is crucial to the cultivation of life, according to Lao Zi, while the willful intentions of benevolence are not a true reflection of the Highest Virtue, for the Highest Virtue "unites Heaven and Earth. Its harmonious energy-breath flows and circulates, refining Virtue in the people" (Heshang Gong, chapter 38).

A similar treatment to that of the straw dogs can be found in practices of Daoist and folk herbalism, where prayers and intentions will be infused into the medicine. When the medicinal properties have been absorbed, the dregs will be thrown onto the road "thus symbolically casting the disease out of the house, there to be crushed by the wheels of passing buses and trucks."[135] The end treatment of the medicine is, of course, not the ultimate reflection of how these herbs are used. Prayers and intentions are infused into the medicine in hopes that they will bring peace and harmony to the patient, much as the prayers and intentions infused into the straw dogs were believed to foster peace and harmony in Heaven, and consequently on Earth and amongst Humanity. We may take from this that the Sage, therefore, does not simply tell people how to act and how to care for those closest to him, but puts his best attention and intention to all people, as though they were the mediums through which he would communicate his love and reverence for De and Dao.

---

[135] Bob Flaws and Honora Lee Wolfe. *The Successful Chinese Herbalist*. Boulder: Blue Poppy Press, 2005. p. 50

Dan G. Reid taught himself how to read Classical Chinese with the help of textbooks, online tools, and internet forums. His self-published work has been acclaimed by notable translators and scholars such as Red Pine, Dr. Michael Saso, Daniel P. Reid (no relation), Daoist Abbot Michael Rinaldini, and Wudang Daoist meditation teacher Hu Xuezhi. Dan practices traditional Chinese sports medicine as a Tuina massage therapist in Montreal, Quebec, including herbalism, and a variety of traditional Chinese therapeutic modalities. He also studies and practices sitting meditation, Qigong, internal martial arts (Xingyi, Baguazhang, Taji Chuan), and is a multi-instrumentalist including guqin, guitar, and percussion.

Bibliography:

Reid, Dan G., translation and commentary. *The Heshang Gong Commentary on Lao Z's Dao De Jing*. Montreal: Center Ring Publishing, 2015, 2019.

Reid, Dan G., translation and commentary. *The Thread of Dao: Unraveling Early Daoist Oral Traditions in Guan Zi's Purifying the Heart-Mind (Bai Xin), Art of the Heart-Mind (Xin Shu), and Internal Cultivation (Nei Ye)*. Montreal: Center Ring Publications, 2017, 2019.

(co-editor)
Hu Xuezhi, translation, annotation and commentary. *Discourse on Chuang Tzu: Expounding on the Dream of a Butterfly, Volumes I & II*. Calgary: ChuangChou Classics Press, 2016.


From the back-cover description for *The Thread of Dao*:

"… Modern scholars now believe that four texts, found in the ancient *Guan Zi* encyclopedia, are likely to have predated the completion of the *Dao De Jing*. These texts, *Purifying the Heart-Mind (Bai Xin)*, *Art of the Heart-Mind (Xin Shu I&II)*, and *Internal Cultivation (Nei Ye)*, provide exceptionally direct explanations of Daoist spiritual, mental, and energetic cultivation, making them invaluable keys to the teachings of early Daoist masters. *The Thread of Dao* translates and explores these texts alongside comparable teachings in the *Dao De Jing* and other Daoist, Buddhist, Confucian, and traditional Chinese medical sources, tracing their origins to a common thread of wisdom."

www.ingramcontent.com/pod-product-compliance
Lightning Source LLC
Chambersburg PA
CBHW060419010526
44118CB00017B/2274